WHY TRADERS LOSE HOW TRADERS WIN

Timing Futures Trades With Daily Market Sentiment

Jake Bernstein

PROBUS PUBLISHING COMPANY
Chicago, Illinois
Cambridge, England

ISBN 1-55738-252-2

Printed in the United States of America

EB

1 2 3 4 5 6 7 8 9 0

This book is dedicated to the thousands of traders who strive daily to succeed in the futures markets. We are all players in the same game and fighters in the same fight; we all attempt to defeat the invisible enemies—the foes which dwell in our archetypal selves. This book is dedicated to the profitable resolution of our struggle, a resolution which can begin and end only with self-understanding.

Jake Bernstein
Northbrook, IL
May, 1992

Contents

Introduction

My first venture into the futures market was in 1968. A broker promoting shell egg futures badgered me incessantly. I borrowed the money to open an account with him just to get him off my back. Before too long, I was making money. Within several months, my starting capital had been multiplied severalfold, none of it my doing. My attention had been captured. The futures bug had bitten me. I didn't realize then that my life had been changed, the course of my relationships altered, and my professional future dramatically influenced.

By the time I had decided to learn everything I could about futures trading, my investment had grown even more. A little knowledge proved to be a most dangerous thing indeed. My market studies were barely completed when I decided to expand into pork belly futures. Inspired by the success of my transactions in shell egg futures, transactions which were entirely the doing of my broker, I plunged headlong into bellies and, of course, very quickly lost all the money I had made in egg futures during the preceding six months.

After the initial shock and remorse of my painful lesson had been fully digested, I realized that there was much much more to futures trading than I had ever suspected. I understood that what I needed to learn was not to be found in books. I needed to develop my own style, method, technique or system, which would be based upon a rational theoretical analysis of futures trading. But my youth and inexperience would prove to be significant obstacles in developing these necessary skills. Little did I realize that in setting out to develop trading systems and theories, I was ignoring the single most important factor in futures trading—psychology. And this was especially ironic since my college training was in clinical psychology.

For several years my work on trading systems, methods and timing indicators continued at a feverish pitch. I acquired historical data. I read book upon book about timing signals. I studied numerous charting techniques and subscribed to many advisory services in order to complete my education. I discovered cyclical analysis, seasonal price tendencies, on-balance-volume and more. Eventually I was ready to apply my knowledge to the markets.

At first my success was limited. I found myself personally insulted by each loss. I was unwilling to admit to losses. When trading well, I was concerned about how long success would last. When extremely successful, I became overly confident. My reactions were not substantively different from those of almost every futures trader. It became very clear that trader psychology—indeed my own psychology—was at one and the same time the weakest link in the chain of success, and the strongest. It took me nearly a decade to finally believe this realization.

With the insight that trader psychology was the quintessential element for long-lasting success came the realization that my professional training in clinical psychology and behavior modification were tools which I had ignored for all too long, powerful tools which gave me the understanding I needed to achieve my goals as a futures trader.

On a summer day in August of 1984, Bob Tamarkin, at the time a writer for the *Chicago Sun Times,* called me. He was writing a book about futures traders and wanted to interview me. He claimed to have read about my work in the markets and wanted to include an interview with me in his book, *The New Gatsbys.* Flattered, I agreed to the interview and met him at his office in downtown Chicago. On my way to the interview I couldn't help but wonder what he would want to know and how he would use the information.

I spent the next several hours under a psychological microscope. How did I trade? What were my feelings about winning? About losing? What were my plans? How much did the opinions of others affect my conclusions? What was my lifestyle? How did my childhood affect my view of the markets? What were my parents like? I thought the questions would never stop. But they made me think.

I've come to realize that some of the greatest insights occur to me when I'm not looking for them. Sometimes I can look at the same three pieces of a puzzle in the same way I've seen them hundreds of times before. Suddenly a different perspective will fortuitously reveal a different arrangement and an entirely new point of view. And this is what my interview was all about. As I sat and squirmed in my chair under Tamarkin's probing eyes and bushy eyebrows, old pieces of the trading puzzle began to rearrange themselves. Exactly what he said, I'm no longer certain. All I can recall is leaving his office on Michigan Avenue with a new perspective, a new "Weltanschauung" (world perspective) which would mediate my understanding of the futures markets profoundly and persistently for years to come.

It was during the course of Bob's interrogation that I realized how much my attitudes and opinions in the futures markets were a function of my early childhood life in the slums of Montreal, Canada. My successes as well as my failures were intricately intertwined with these and other significant experiences. My parents' experiences in Auschwitz and Dachau; my very early childhood in the Bavarian Alps; and my sudden injection at the age of thirteen into Chicago's affluent North Shore from an impoverished existence in Montreal, were all formative factors in my life as a trader.

It became clear that the roles of attitude and opinion in futures trading were tremendously important. To ignore them was to ignore a wealth of information. To understand attitude and opinion in myself and in others was to befriend a great ally. And with this insight began my informal study of market sentiment; a study which would never be complete, but which would continually provide new understandings of market and trader behavior.

This book represents the culmination of many years' experience in the trenches of futures trading. It also represents the distillation of my years as an observer of trader behavior, a skill which I acquired during my years in the field of human psychology, behavior modification and projective psychological testing. While my observations and theories are not strictly scientific, my efforts in developing and understanding market sentiment are based upon scientific procedures. But futures trading is not a science. Futures trading is awash in emotion. And emotion is the raw material of market sentiment; it is the stuff of which trades are made. It is the enemy of profit—the accomplice of self-destruction. Yet, emotion harnessed and understood is the substance of success. Does this all sound paradoxical to you? Does it sound like I'm saying at least two different things at the same time? Yes, I am!

PART I

The Nature of Market Sentiment

Our study of market sentiment begins with an examination of several case studies in trader behavior. I've changed the names of the participants; I've deleted some irrelevant details and I've expanded on important aspects of each case in order to illustrate my points. After presenting the case studies, I will analyze them in terms of market sentiment. As you read them, I urge you to put yourself into the position of each main character. Attempt to identify feelings and behaviors you have observed in your own trading behavior, attitudes and opinions.

In Part 2, I will present several different methods for applying daily market sentiment (DSI). Part 3 provides a day-by-day and weekly history of the daily sentiment index readings back to the first day of their collection in April of 1987.

Part 4 provides a collection of historical charts with daily market sentiment data which may be used for your further study of the principles you will learn. These charts are currently unavailable from any other source and will prove extremely valuable in your research with market sentiment.

CHAPTER 1

The Secret Life of Traders

The three tales which follow will serve as real life examples of how trader sentiment and psychology are hard at work every day in the futures markets; how they influence the markets; and how they are influenced by the markets. While the names of the players have been changed, and details have been reconstructed, all situations are based on real events.

Jerry's Bellies

At 6 A.M. the traffic south on I-94 isn't too bad. And when Jerry makes his return trip, usually at about three in the afternoon, he'll beat the traffic back to his large suburban home. There's that Chicago skyline again; Sears Tower, the Hancock, the early morning summer haze, probably pollution, he thinks, but it's still not as bad as L.A. He reviews briefly the upcoming day: another day in the pits; some yelling, too much pushing, considerable strategy, possibly several minor errors, and at least a few thousand bucks. It's all in a day's work. And then it's back home again. He's done it so many times now, it seems mechanical, even easy, like watching a champion diver or gymnast. The moves seem to come almost naturally; they flow and blend into winning ways that appear to be inborn.

Behind the seemingly automatic performance are years and years of intense practice. And everyone watching knows that it's not nearly as effortless as it appears to be. It's the mark of a professional to make things seem easy. But for Jerry, as for a vast majority of futures traders both on the trading floor and off, things were not always so predictable.

When pork belly futures began trading in the 1960s, Jerry was one of the first traders in the pit. He's learned many lessons since then, perhaps the most important being that successfully trading pork belly futures is difficult. Of course he knew that making money consistently in any futures market was among the most challenging tasks possible. When he first came to the pit at the Chicago Mercantile Exchange he was just as "green" as many of the other traders. He came to the trading floor with a host of preconceived notions similar to the excess intellectual and emotional baggage that accompanies many traders when they make their first venture into the futures markets.

Having come from a wealthy family on Chicago's affluent North Shore, Jerry attended some of the best schools in the United States, and he did well. He learned his history, political science, his mathematics and physics, and, to be sure, his economics, a subject which he found truly fascinating. Like many other "North Shorite" offspring, Jerry was sitting in the catbird seat: he was an only son, his older sister had married into money, his father owned a successful meat processing business, and he was the heir apparent. To this end, the persual of business and economics were logical. After all, his father reasoned, Jerry would need to know about the family business in order to run the company successfully. Nowadays economics was so important, that a good background in theory couldn't hurt!

His car parked, Jerry takes the short walk over to the "Merc" building. The cloak room clerk recognizes him immediately and has his gold-colored trading jacket waiting on the counter. They exchange a few perfunctory words about the Chicago Cubs, but Jerry can't hear them. Assuming an intentionally diminutive posture, he strides on to the trading floor as he's done nearly five thousand times since the 1960s.

You'd think it would be boring by now. You'd imagine that Jerry must be tired of it all after so many years. But he's not. Is it just the money? Is it the thrill of the battle? Or is it the challenge that keeps him going?

Slowly strolling past the banks of telephones and row upon row of order desks, he sees the flashing telephone lights, hears a few telephones ringing desperately, and attempts to overhear some bits and pieces of conversation. Now at his desk, he scans the news wire with the eyes of a surgeon.

As a belly trader, Jerry is most assuredly tuned into the fundamentals of the market. He is aware of the latest storage figures, cash prices, and retail bacon movement. Tucked in the back of his mind are myriad facts and figures; the last Pig Crop statistics, hog price trends, open interest, the trend of corn prices, beef steer price trends, interest rates and the overall condition of the U.S. economy. He wonders about the situation in Iraq. Would a war be bullish or bearish for the meat markets? Do troops in combat eat more meat? Would the government freeze commodity prices in the event of a war? If so, what effect would it have on the futures markets? Jerry glances over the latest membership transactions and seat prices. He notices that some familiar names have left the floor, selling their memberships; some were veteran traders and a few others had only been there several years. He remembers the countless traders who have come and gone through the years.

Random thoughts emerge, are examined briefly, assigned their relative importance and dismissed as Jerry checks his positions. He is long approximately 130 July pork belly contracts from an average price of 65.45. Yesterday's closing price was 67.70; a tidy little profit in only three days! He reformulates his main concerns in order of importance: first, he will not allow this profit to turn into a loss; second, he must determine if today is the day to exit his position; third, he must develop a plan for liquidating his position in a fashion which does not affect the market. While 130 bellies is not an especially large position to dispose of, Jerry must consider the size of his position in light of several more important factors. First and possibly most significant is the fact that Jerry is well-known and respected (possibly feared) by the pit. Other traders watch him closely, some attempting to learn his winning style and others wishing to coattail his trades. A second important fact is that the size of a position is only important in relation to the overall trading volume and open interest in a market.

In a market which trades perhaps 10,000 contracts in one day, a 130 lot position is minor and will not affect prices appreciably. However, in a market which trades 1,000 contracts a day, a 130 lot is 13 percent of the day's trading volume.

Jerry now begins one of his most important activities of the day, the goal of which is to determine when and how to liquidate his position and whether, in fact, to reverse his position from long to short. He knows that he is being watched. He knows that other traders are aware of his every move and that they are in constant communication with their order clerks who in turn are in touch with "upstairs" traders and brokers. He knows that he can barely make a move without the news being flashed to traders throughout the country. And the importance of the news about Jerry will be very much a function of the position size he is trading. However, Jerry learned long ago, after many years of tremendous effort and mediocre performance, how to use trader psychology and mob behavior to his advantage.

What Jerry must do in order to maintain his success is to carefully monitor the consensus of opinion among his fellow floor traders in order that he may use it to his advantage. He must use what he has learned about mass psychology in order to win at this difficult and risky game. In order to do this, Jerry must not only know what "the floor" is thinking at any given point in time, but he must also know how to prompt them to action in order to "play" the market like a finely tuned instrument, something he has been doing for many years. Jerry has derived from his understanding of trader psychology a variety of strategies which he uses regularly in his trading. While his methods don't always work for him, they work often enough to allow consistent success.

After examining the trading data and assimilating the latest news, he calls a few retail brokers (i.e., brokers that deal primarily with the public). He's most interested in their opinions and they're even more interested in his, given his reputation as a successful trader. What exactly is it that Jerry can learn from his daily (and on occasion more frequent) talks with retail brokers? The nature of his questions will give us a clue. "Are your customers bullish or bearish on bellies?" he asks. "Bullish . . . uh-huh . . . how bullish? Are they primarily long or short? And how about your own work, is it bullish or bearish? I see, bullish. How bullish? How high do you think they're going on this move? How about your in-house research department? What's their conclusion? I see, bullish. OK. What do I think? It seems as if there are too many bulls around. We might be putting in a small top. Sounds like the public's too bullish." He hangs up the telephone. His suspicions are confirmed.

It doesn't take too much to turn the public bullish, he muses. He ponders again one of the market facts he has learned time and time again; the public is almost always wrong at important market turns. It's sad, it's unfortunate, it's true and, praise the Lord, it can't be helped. For Jerry and a handful of other market professionals, both on and off the trading floor, market psychology is an ally and a primary reason for their success. While it is not their intention to take advantage of the public, their goal is to succeed using whatever means they can, so long as they are moral, legal and ethical.

Jerry watches the crowd swell. Traders are taking their favorite places in the pit. He scans the crowd. There's Miles wearing his lucky tie, and Lee, sporting his lucky trading pants. A few other traders he knows well are anxiously pouring over charts; some studying trading-card-size point-and-figure charts in their order decks, and still several others off in a corner studying charts on a computer screen. Now he makes his move. Leaving his trading desk he walks toward the pit, at times pushing his way through the elbow-deep crowd. The public address system drones on, calling traders to the telephone endlessly. Anonymous runners with order tickets scurry to and from the pit like homing pigeons. It all seems very unreal to Jerry, even now, after so many years of playing the game. Jerry has his ears riveted to the growing roar. He is very interested in what other traders are saying; what they're doing; what they're expecting. He exchanges greetings with several traders, stopping here and there to gather more information about their expectations. Jerry knows from his years of experience that even the trading pit can be wrong. He has observed repeatedly an uncanny correlation between the degree of bullishness or bearishness in the trading pit and important market turning points. Even some of his most successful peers have been very wrong at significant market junctures, both long-term and short-term. And it has been a constant struggle for Jerry himself to avoid the emotion of the moment, going contrary not only to the crowd but to his own expectations as well. Like many a trader, Jerry has taken some of his worst losses when he enjoyed the greatest self-confidence, and when he held the strongest opinions about the expected direction of the market.

Now Jerry is in the pit. He knows what he must do. He has done his homework. Does he care about the fundamentals? Not a bit! Does he care about the opinions of other traders? Absolutely! So much so that he knows he must exit his position. He is uncomfortably aware of the fact that many eyes are upon him. Since he has accumulated a fairly large position during the last few days, the pit knows that Jerry is long the market. Should he raise his hands and gesture to indicate that he is selling, the news will spread like a brush fire, creating panic and undermining his own position. Even if he begins by selling just five bellies, the pit will fear that he is beginning to liquidate his entire position unless, of course, his five lot is gobbled up by yet another respected trader. Jerry can't afford to take the chance of "spooking" the pit. The opening bell rings, prompting a surge of activity. Hands reach skyward in virtually all areas of the crowded pit. "Five at 60 . . . five at 60," shouts Jerry, his hands moving toward him. Within an instant his bid has been hit. Jerry has just bought five more bellies at 65.60, ten points below the previous day's close. Is he making a mistake? Why is he buying when his plan clearly calls for liquidation of his position? And he's not through yet. As trading continues, bellies begin to drop sharply, declining ten to twenty points at a tick as only bellies can do. Soon the market is 120 points lower on the day. Jerry has been standing silently since buying his original five lot. Without warning, he throws his arms up bellowing "fifty at 40," bidding 64.40 on a 50 lot. Two traders rush in to fill his bid. One trader offers fifteen at 45. "You got it," responds Jerry, and turns quickly to accept another offer of twenty at 55 from a trader on his right. With great haste, he marks his trading card. He now owns a total of 170 bellies.

Some traders are now seen signalling from the pit to their runners. One in a multicolored jacket steps to the side: "Tell 'em Jerry's buying again . . . he's bought at least fifty-five so far this morning." The word goes out to the trading desk. The desk calls upstairs to inform the brokerage house. Brokers, upon hearing the news, push buttons to call their best clients. "Jerry's buying more July bellies today." "What are they doing now?" inquires the client. "Well, they were down over 100 until he started buying, now they're only down 25 on the day." "Let's add to the position" responds the client. "How many?" asks the broker. "Let's buy three more at the market."

The orders go in. Soon bellies have recovered their opening losses. And within fifteen minutes they're 30 points up on the day as the news of Jerry's buying spreads. Soon the market is helped by news that retail demand for bacon is up. Bellies are over 100 points higher on the day and Jerry, who came into the pit this morning with 130 bellies, bound and determined to close out his position because there was too much bullishness, is now long 185 bellies, and he's afraid to start closing out his position, since he may panic the market into a selling frenzy that could put bellies limit down, erasing much of his paper profit. Why did he buy? Because of market psychology. He knew that he was being watched. He knew that he couldn't sell. Using market psychology, he added to his position. This was a statement to the rest of the pit and to the public watching him that he was still bullish. Its purpose was not only to prompt more buying by playing on the psychology of the pit and the public, but to support his own position as well. For him to have stood idly by and not support the market when it was falling would have indicated to the rest of the pit that he was concerned; but as long as he was willing to support his position, the rest of the pit was satisfied that all was still well.

After the first half-hour of trading the market has slowed down considerably, with prices up 45 points from the previous close. Jerry can take a break now without arousing too much attention. He leaves the pit unobtrusively, seemingly with no particular direction in mind. He retires to a seat at the order desk and ponders his strategy. He must never forget his goal. Although it can be altered, he must do so only under very special circumstances. Is there some bullish news that might send the market up sharply, possibly to the limit which will allow him to sell 185 bellies without trouble? Nothing appears imminent. Impatience sets in. Quickly he figures his approximate profit, taking care not to spend too much time on the calculation. He has become superstitious over the years. He remembers the veteran grain trader who said to him many years ago, "Jerry, the time to close out your position is when you take pencil to paper to figure your profit." And Jerry has always taken this advice seriously—perhaps too seriously. He shies away from knowing exactly how much of a profit he has at any given point in time. Yet he watches his losing positions like a hawk.

His quick mental calculations have produced the expected result: a mixture of pleasure and pain—the pleasure of anticipated profits and the pain of knowing that he must close out his position in order to realize the profit. And this may be difficult to do. Time passes. Jerry holds his position close to his vest, as does an expressionless poker player not wanting to scare off the bets. He'll have to resort to another strategy if the market won't accommodate him. What to do? Quickly, Jerry reaches for an order ticket. He jots down his account number, and on the buy side he writes, "55 market." Again, Jerry resorts to his bag of market psychology tricks. It's noon now, just another hour to the close. He refuses to carry his position overnight. Anxiously, Jerry writes five more order tickets; all market orders which would bring his position to a total of 240 July bellies. He's anxious but confident. He's used this strategy many times over the years. He now writes a series of other orders, all to sell. He calls another runner over. "Do something for me. I'm going into the pit. I'll be buying fifty-five at the market. When I'm done, time-stamp these orders, run them into the pit and give them to the guys whose badges I've marked on the back of the tickets, but don't do it until I'm done with my 55 lot—O.K.?" The runner understands the directions very clearly. They've played this game before. It's a simple strategy indeed. Jerry will be buying more in hopes of running the market higher. At the same time he'll have orders with other pit traders to sell out as the market rises.

Jerry makes his move. He walks confidently into the pit. The market has backed off to 68.25. There's a 5 lot being offered at 25. He hits the offer, buying five at 25. The market pushes to 40 offer. He buys two at 40. The next offer is at 55, Jerry buys three at 55 for a total of ten. Suddenly the pit pushes toward Jerry. He needn't raise his hands because offers are being shouted at him from virtually everywhere in the pit—not a good sign, he reasons. But things may change by the time he's done. He takes a 5 lot at 65 and another 5 at 70. His buying appears to be having the desired effect. He slows down a bit to give the market some time to digest his buying. News travels fast. The news mill is active today and the calls are going out. The offer is 80 and Jerry intentionally bids 60 on a 5 lot, but now there are no offers at his price. He stops bidding and waits a few more minutes. The market continues to trade between 70 and 90. He glances secretively over at his runner. "Still here and waiting," the runner implies with a glance.

Now the orders are beginning to come in from outside the pit. The market pushes to 6900, then to 05, 07, 17 and 20. Only a few trades take place at 20. Jerry anticipates the arrival of his big moment. He has thirty-five more bellies to buy before his sell orders are distributed to the traders he has selected. He bids for thirty-five at 20.

No offers. He bids 25. Still no offers. The market has become tight. Sellers have backed away. He bids 30, then 35. The market is now limit bid, 200 points higher on the day. At limit several traders raise their hands to sell Jerry his thirty-five bellies. Now the runner, earning his title, speeds back to the order desk to time-stamp the tickets. He races back to the pit, and recruiting the help of several other runners, distributes order tickets to the designated traders.

Back in the pit, bellies are 190 points higher to limit bid with good activity. There are buyers at limit bid. Jerry holds back and waits for the onslaught. Without warning, one of his designated sellers throws up his hands to hit several bids at 195 points higher on the day. Within seconds, 45 bellies have been consumed by the contract-hungry mob. Two other large sellers emerge, hitting bids right, left and center. Ninety more bellies are gone, but not as easily. The bids are marked down on heavy selling. Soon the market is only 40 higher on the day. Two more large sellers emerge, this time pushing the market down to 30 points lower on the day, all within three minutes.

Jerry's quick mental math tells him his position has been liquidated. The job done, he steps from the pit. To some it appears that Jerry has had a bad day, and they're secretly pleased to see him suffer. Others are confused, but a vast majority of the floor is oblivious since they have not had a personal stake in the events. They are merely order-takers, paper-fillers, and they were glad to have the paper to fill since their livelihood comes from commissions and not from speculation. By the time the dust clears only a few savvy traders have realized what has transpired during the last few emotional minutes. It was all mass psychology.

Upstairs, brokers realizing the quick price break, call their clients, who sell in an emotional response. The decline is exacerbated. By the close of trading, bellies have touched limit down in a frenzy of selling and in an environment which was, until now, very bullish. It's 1:17 P.M., Jerry has checked his positions. There are no errors. He's had a good day. Although he could easily leave the pit and head for home, his work isn't done. He's back on the telephone again talking to retail brokers. "What do you make of today's activity?" he asks. "I think we've made a small top," he responds. His calls continue as he accumulates information. On his way from the trading floor he stops to talk to a few other pit brokers. No, there's not enough bearishness around yet. And the bullishness has subsided for awhile. He must await another opportunity.

At 2:19 P.M., Jerry's back in his car heading north. Reviewing the day, he wonders how long the game can continue to be played this way. He remembers other good trades he's made, almost all of them based on the same psychology he had used today or on variations of the same theme. To calm his frayed nerves he has taken the long way home today via Lake Shore Drive. The view of Lake Michigan quiets him. He thinks about the human condition and wonders again how long the game can be played this way. He decides that as long as there are markets which are traded by people, there will be fear, greed and emotion. He drives on confidently, assured that the market will be the same tomorrow as it was today and yesterday.

They Love to Hate Silver

"They can't possibly mine silver for $3.50 an ounce," shouts Al, slamming the telephone down in disgust. Yet another potential customer has been immune to his sales pitch. "For three years the price of silver has been going down and I can't sell a single customer on the idea of beginning to buy. It makes no sense to me whatsoever. What are they waiting for? Do they think they'll be able to buy it at zero?" he demands rhetorically. "They don't want it at $3.50, Al," comes a voice from the back of the office. "They'd rather pay $5.50 on the way up because only then they'll be convinced that it's going higher." "Makes sense," mutters Al after a few moments of sullen thought.

Al gets back on the telephone. This time he calls some of his current customers, thinking that they might be more responsive to his ideas. Six calls and six refusals later, Al's ready to call it quits. As an experienced broker he's become accustomed to rejection, but he's never quite understood human nature. Why is it that customers are so negative about markets at the bottom and so bullish at the top? Why is it that customers always seem to want a bargain, except when they can really get one? Why is it that so many customers are afraid to buy into markets when prices are so very low, but so willing to be bold when prices are very high? It's the nature of the beast, he reasons. He pulls yet more leads from the stack on his desk, and he's back on the telephone again. "Yes, Dr. Bryan, this is Al Fortune calling from New Age Futures in Chicago. We've received your request for more information on our long-term silver accumulation program. Do you have a few moments now so that I may explain how our program works? Good. I'll explain it to you and please interrupt me if you have any questions. Have you traded futures before? Good. Then you're familiar with the way the markets work and so forth. Here's how our program works. I'll send you a complete brochure for review."

Al continues, "As you know, the price of silver has been moving lower for the last three years. The fundamentals now are so terrible that many silver mines are shutting down. They can't possibly mine silver and make money at these prices. Eventually the current oversupply of silver will be absorbed because of the limited production and then the market will reverse. There will be a shortage of supply and prices will probably move up sharply. We think that silver has excellent long-term potential from these levels and we propose to buy silver futures that expire eighteen months from now, putting up approximately 50 percent of the usual margin. This means that silver would need to go down to $1.75 an ounce for you to lose 50 percent of your money and that hasn't happened in many, many years. But, if silver goes up to $5.00 an ounce, you'll make $1.50 an ounce, or about $7,500 per contract. And if silver stands still, all you'll lose is commission. How does that sound to you, Doctor? No sex appeal? What do you mean? Oh. I see, you think that silver is too boring. You don't want to wait eighteen months. Well, you won't have to. It might explode to the upside next week. We just don't know. Yes. Yes, I know that the economy is not inflating right now and that silver is primarily an industrial metal. I know all that. Yes. I know that, too. It's true that India has an oversupply. Yes. I know the fundamentals, but you don't understand—we recommend buying because the history of silver shows that whenever prices get this low, they eventually turn much higher. Well, of course you can do it by buying Sunshine mining and your contract won't expire in eighteen months. But you can put up less margin. Why not put up 25 percent instead of 50 percent for our futures program? Then you'll have more leverage than you will in buying silver mining shares. What if Sunshine goes broke? Then you lose all of your money. You want to trade Treasury Bond futures? O.K., that's fine, I'll put you in touch with our T-Bond analyst. Please hold on and I'll transfer your call. If you change your mind about silver, please call me back. I'll send you our program brochure anyway. Please hold and I'll transfer you to Jim Bateman. He'll be glad to help you."

Al transfers the call and marks Dr. Bryan's lead sheet accordingly. Then it's back to the telephone again. Another five rejections and he leaves the office for home. He has made over sixty-three calls today, without a single positive response to the silver program. After his many years of experience in the futures brokerage business, Al knows what's happening. He knows for certain that the market is making an important bottom. He knows that it's very close because the reactions he's getting to his program are nearly 100 percent negative. Al knows that when negative opinions are pervasive, lows can't be too far off.

The next day Al is back at his job, dialing for dollars, but again with limited success. He's running into the same objections: silver may be cheap, but it's not exciting; the fundamentals are still bad and they'll get worse before the market bottoms; the charts don't look good and the technical indicators don't show any promise right now; the experts are all bearish and seem to agree that it will probably be several years before the market has cleaned up its excess supplies; there are more profitable markets to trade in right now. And so it goes for Al, day after day. He doesn't mind too much, though, because there are other markets people will trade and he's doing what a broker should do—he's opening new accounts. Naturally, however, he's dismayed because his good advice is falling on deaf or disinterested ears.

Several months pass and the slowly-but-surely declining silver market continues to languish in a sideways-to-lower trend without any new bullish news. In fact, the market remains bogged down in a quagmire of heavy fundamentals and negative expectations. Then one day the Indian government announces that it plans to sell over one half of its silver stockpile, even at the current low prices. Silver futures respond by dropping the daily limit and are now at $3.11 per ounce. Al analyzes the situation and concludes that this is the "wash-out," the final piece of bad news that virtually insures a low. Again, he gets on the telephone only to soon realize that the objections he encountered before have turned into hostility. "You were dead wrong, Al! If I'd listened to you three months ago I'd already be 15 percent behind," chides his first caller. And when his next three callers each hang up on him, he knows that there is even less chance of selling them on the idea now than there was when silver prices were higher. Yet everyone wants a bargain! Perhaps the other broker in his office was right; maybe they won't want to get in until silver prices are $2.00 higher.

Al reflects upon the rejection of his program. Pearls before swine, he concludes—the program is just too good for the general public. Meanwhile, silver prices stop their decline. Perhaps Al was right. Perhaps the last bit of bearish news was the washout. Slowly at first, the market begins to move higher. There are no great fireworks, no tremendously bullish announcements and no bullish surprises. In fact, the fundamentals are still as negative as they have been for the last few months. From time to time, Al attempts to promote his silver program. Well over 80 percent of those he contacts have no interest. He finds it hard to believe that of the several hundred people he had called during the last six months, only three had actually opened accounts, and of these three, two were hounding him every day. But Al is well-acquainted enough with customers and the public to know that this is part of the business. While he doesn't like it, he knows that it "goes with the territory."

Several weeks pass. One day after market closings, General Motors announces development of a new, low-priced catalytic converter that uses silver instead of platinum or palladium as its key ingredient. Each converter will require about thirty ounces of silver; however, even at $10 per ounce, the $300 cost would be well below the cost of using platinum or palladium. Silver prices jump nearly 45 cents per ounce in London and the New York market takes off, up the daily limit, except for the nearby contract, which has no daily limit. It rises nearly 67 cents per ounce. The next day the deferred contract months remain locked limit-up all day, and the spot month rises several cents. Suddenly, silver bulls emerge like ants at a picnic.

Newsletter writers who were bearish and disinterested just a few days ago are suddenly claiming that their clients were advised to go long many months ago. Brokers are busily calling clients and there's a sudden rash of calls to Al's office from people he had contacted during the last few months. The account papers go out by overnight mail. The customers are in a big hurry. They don't want to miss the big move. After all, when silver was nearly 70 cents cheaper it was no good, but now that there's some news to make it move up, they're ready to buy.

Al has his doubts. He's seen it all before. He knows that when customers are beating the doors down to buy it's probably time to sell. Yes, ultimately they may be right. In the long run, silver prices will probably make the big move Al has been forecasting, but in the short run the public is much too bullish. In fact, it seems to Al that the public is just as bullish now as it was bearish just a few weeks ago. Nearly 100 percent of those who call him are convinced that the road to $10 silver is a fait accompli. But, as a good broker must do, he warns them that they may be able to get in a little cheaper in the next few weeks. Al's just a dumb broker—what does he know?

The rumor mill begins to do its job. General Motors announces that it was misquoted in its silver catalytic converter announcement. For one thing, the converter is still experimental. It won't be ready for market until it's approved by the EPA, and this will take at least eighteen months. Moreover, they're not certain that the process will use thirty ounces of silver. Smaller cars may require only eleven ounces and some cars with extremely large engines will not be able to use the silver converters due to their large volume of exhaust gasses. Furthermore, the California Environmental Protection Agency has examined the process and disapproved of it. Silver prices drop the daily limit.

Another announcement comes out the same day. Three European countries reject the silver converter idea after examining initial lab results. It's another blow for the market, which drops yet another 18 cents on the news. Prices have now settled back nearly 40 cents from their recent peak. Those who opened accounts with Al, contrary to his advice to wait, are very upset. "We didn't know that this program was so volatile," some claim. A few others decide to close out their accounts quickly so as to avoid a further loss. And a few others give Al stop losses to get them out if the market drops any further. However, as is the case with many new bull markets, the first rally from the lows is quickly erased as lows are "tested." And silver follows the usual model, dropping even more and falling to within 3 cents of its pre-converter bottom. Of the forty-three accounts Al has opened for his silver program, seventeen closed out as soon as the GM correction news was released. Another nine accounts were stopped out near the contract lows on the test of the bottom, and six others closed out on the rally from the test of lows, thankful they were out before new contract lows were made.

But new contract lows are not made. The market begins a slow and steady move to the upside, and soon there's a new rush of activity on the upside as the converter story is resurrected. Now the subject has become a favorite in the financial press. Brokerage houses and market analysts that hated silver at $3.25 now love it at $4.00. Al's not running into too much resistance anymore. He's mastered the rhythm of marketing his program: solicit for business only on up days and stay off the telephones on down days. The public won't buy a market that's down, but they love to get in when prices are rallying.

As experienced as Al was, he learned a few things from his experiences with the silver program. He summarized them as follows:

- The trading public hates bear markets and it is difficult to convince them that a market may have upside potential unless they can see a reason for it, aside from the mere cheapness of prices. Yes, there are some who will accept the logic and take the appropriate action; however, the vast majority is unwilling to buy when the situation seems very bearish, and they are unwilling to sell or sell short when a situation appears to be very bullish.
- The more bearish the public consensus of opinion, the more likely prices are near or at a bottom.
- The more bullish the public consensus of opinion, the more likely prices are near or at a top.
- The stronger the opinions, the more likely they are to be wrong.
- The general public is not always wrong; however, they are usually wrong at important turning points.

Victim of the "Whipsaw"

Glancing through the current issue of a popular futures market magazine, Bill is attracted to an advertisement offering what appears to be one of the most incredible trading systems he has ever seen. The ad promises well over 100 percent annual return on average, and claims back-tested results through 1972, supporting its claims with several powerful testimonials and a real-time trading account which has been in effect for six months. At a cost of well over $2,000, the system is not a bargain, but if the claims are right, it could pay for itself in just one average month. The system is fully computerized. As one of its key features it offers the user mechanical and objective application of its trading rules; in other words it does not require any interpretation or judgment on the part of the user.

Clearly impressed, Bill calls the toll-free number and requests the demonstration disk. Several days later it arrives. Eager to see the demo, Bill leaves work early upon learning from his wife that the disk has finally arrived. Now seated before his computer, the disk in place, Bill launches the demo and sits transfixed as it takes him on a guided tour of its principles, features and operating procedures. He is impressed not only with its ease of use, but with the theory and research behind its trading methodology. Visions of sugar plums are dancing in his head.

There's no time to use the U.S. mail—this program must be ordered immediately, before the 200 program limit is reached! Telephone in hand, he searches through his small stack of plastic, looking for a credit card that will be accepted. It's the fourth ring and still no answer. They must be there! Finally, an answer. Within five minutes the deal is made. Bill is poorer by more than $2,000, but he has just acquired the key to vast wealth and success in futures trading. Now an anxious vigil begins. Of course, he has selected overnight delivery for his software at only $17 additional. The package will arrive the next day, Friday, and he'll have the entire weekend to install, learn and orient himself in the program's operations. It's all so very exciting!

Friday, Bill rushes home. His computer humming and his disk drive clicking, the software begins to install itself with only one command. After answering just a few questions about the configuration of his system, Bill is ready to generate his trading signals for Monday's markets. Within minutes the printer makes its impression upon paper. No hesitation. Bill hovers over the paper, curious to see what he'll be trading on Monday. The report is done. Not only does Bill get a list of trades for Monday, but he also gets a listing of current open positions, open profits and losses and stop loss points for all trades. The list is truly impressive. There are nine open positions, of which six are profitable and only three show open losses. Of the three open losses, the largest is slightly over $1,500, but the largest open profit is well over $4,000. While Bill has only been trading futures for three years, he is experienced enough to recognize immediately that this system is long several markets which have been in well-established uptrends and short several markets which have been in well-established downtrends. He is pleased. This is a wonderful trend-following system. From everything Bill has learned, the big money is made in the big pull, and this system is definitely in on the big pull!

For Monday there are three trades: buying gold with an approximate risk of $2,300; selling short Treasury Bond futures with a risk of about $1,800; and buying soybean futures with a $1,200 risk. Reflexively, Bill finds himself adding up the potential losses and he's not pleased with the result. If all three positions are closed out at losses, nearly half his account equity will be gone. What good is a trading system without an account? On the other hand, Bill reasons that unless he follows the trading system explicitly, he will not be able to reproduce its results. This is truly a troubling dilemma. On the one hand, the system is clear in its performance history and rules; on the other hand, Bill has limited capital and must make choices. He knows from past experience with trading systems that if confronted with several choices in the futures market, he will almost invariably make the wrong choice—and he is bound and determined that this will never happen again. He has examined his behavior, knows his limitations, has adjusted his thinking and will not make emotional decisions. The commitment to buy this trading system was just one expression of Bill's newfound self-discipline and he will not err on the first step. The problem, however, is clearly difficult to resolve. Bill recognizes the fact that, like many futures traders, he is undercapitalized, but he is also a realist and accepts the limits on his speculative capital. What to do now?

Fortunately, the weekend gives Bill the luxury of time to consider his problem. He reviews the trades time and time again. He examines the performance history of his trading system in each of the three markets, concluding that there is no significant difference in results. This adds to his indecision. Bill, of course, is well aware of the fact that what he should do is to follow all of the trades. However, it is very clear that the fear of loss has caused him to second-guess the system. Although he has not yet made his first trade, he is already uncomfortable with his new trading system. He takes refuge, however, in the fact that he recognizes the problem and feels that he can control it.

He decides to enter orders for all three trades, and retires very late Friday evening, well content with his decision. By mid-day Saturday, however, Bill is haunted by the nagging thought that he will lose money. He realizes that his emotions are beginning to interfere with his trading decisions, and this upsets him. In an effort to gain emotional support, he turns to a close friend who also trades futures, soliciting his opinion as to the best course of action. Before long, the friend offers his opinion as to which of the trades should be implemented, an opinion derived from an entirely different understanding of the futures markets. But, because it is in fairly close agreement with his own analysis of the situation, Bill finds solace in his friend's opinion.

At this juncture Bill has started to forfeit his objectivity—one of the most serious errors a futures trader can commit. He is, however, not fully aware of what he is doing. Seeking even more justification for his actions, Bill calls his broker on Sunday evening. He is not hesitant to call his broker at home because he feels it is part of the personalized service to which he is entitled as a full-service customer. Bill's broker doesn't mind the call. After all, he perceives his job as that of serving the client. He listens intently to Bill's dilemma and offers several suggestions, the most intelligent and rational of which is that Bill enter all three trades, but in smaller contract sizes. This is certainly a possibility, but Bill rejects it. Although he does not verbalize his objections, he feels that it is not masculine to trade in smaller contracts and, furthermore, since his broker will charge him the same commission for the smaller size contracts, he has a vested interest in recommending all three positions. Bill pushes for another opinion from his broker. He indicates that he'd rather trade one full-size contract in one of the recommended positions than a one-half-size position in all three markets. The broker slowly but surely comes around to Bill's way of thinking, and soon there's a consensus. Bill rests peacefully on Sunday night.

On Monday morning the time comes to enter the orders. Now, to validate his decision further, Bill asks his broker to consult the several advisory newsletters received by the brokerage house as well as the in-house market analysis. Yes, they all agree: the gold trade is the one to make. After all, the market has been in an uptrend, inflation seems to be picking up again, tensions in the Middle East are escalating and with them the price of crude oil. Furthermore, the market has moved up strongly for the last three days and it's very clear that this market is destined for higher levels. It all makes good sense, and the little survey that Bill has taken certainly favors the gold trade. With confidence, Bill enters his buy order as well as his stop loss exactly as dictated by the system. This trade is certain to work!

Gold opens several dollars higher, triggering the buy stop that Bill has placed above the market. Within several minutes the market backs away from Bill's entry price. It seems as if the market has a mind of its own, reaching for the buy stops, moving through them by several ticks and then falling. But this is of no concern to Bill—after all, he's following a trading system and if this trade turns into a loss, so be it. There's always the next trade. Meanwhile, Bill takes a break at work and calls his broker. He finds out that his gold is against him by about $2 per contract (i.e., $200 in open loss) and that the two trades he did not take would now be slightly profitable. The "story of his life" he tells himself sarcastically. He's not concerned, though; he's following a trading system.

His work done for the day, Bill heads home. He turns on the business report while driving. "In financial futures today, Treasury Bonds closed twenty-three points higher on news that the Fed was intent on keeping long-term interest rates from rising appreciably and short term rates also fell, leading to a fourteen-point rise in nearby Treasury Bill futures. Gold prices fell four dollars on news of the Fed action. Meat and livestock futures closed about unchanged from Friday's levels and grains moved higher, lead by soybeans which reacted favorably to positive export news." Of course, Bill is disappointed. He had three trades to choose from and he chose wrong. But he isn't worried; a little upset, perhaps, but worried—no. He's following a trading system which will eventually work for him.

Naturally, Bill didn't realize that he wasn't following his trading system at all. He had never even started to follow it since he broke the rules on his very first trade. It is quite clear that Bill was destined to lose money from the very start. Not only did he violate the rules by picking and choosing among trades, but he also solicited the opinion of other traders and used the consensus of his opinion and theirs to violate the rules of his system.

I'm certain that you can predict the outcome of Bill's story. The gold trade was eventually closed out at a loss, while the Treasury Bill trade was closed out at a small profit. The soybean trade was still showing a large profit when Bill stopped trading the system. Disenchanted with the trading system and unable to accept full responsibility for his failure to act appropriately, Bill calls the trading system vendor to ask for a refund. His request is politely refused. Bill displaces his anger and threatens to take legal action, claiming that he did not have sufficient capital to trade the system.

This phase of Bill's story is over. However, he'll be back again and he'll probably lose again. It is truly a sad story, yet, Bill is not the only one to have been in this position. By the time you have finished this book—in fact, by the time you are less than halfway through this book—you will have considerable insight into the dynamics of Bill's actions and into the underlying meaning of all three situations I have depicted. Before proceeding, though, I'll review all three scenarios and present some preliminary ideas about the relationship between markets, traders, their opinions and their actions in response to their perceptions.

An Analysis of the Case Studies

The three tales I have told are reconstructed from actual events. The names have been changed to protect the participants. While all of the details are not exactly as I have presented them, they are all basically accurate. I am certain that you either know of similar events or that you have actually experienced them. I've presented them to illustrate how attitudes, perceptions and opinions affect trader behavior and how traders can use these characteristics to their advantage. Let's begin by looking at Jerry and his belly trade.

Jerry's Understanding of Traders and Markets

How did Jerry use his knowledge of human behavior to his advantage? First, he knew from years of experience on the trading floor that when most traders share the same opinion about a market, the market has most likely reached a turning point. This, he found, was true of both professional traders and the general public. Because all traders both on and off the trading floor are slaves to emotions such as fear, hope and greed, they are apt to respond in the same way at approximately the same time. When an overwhelming majority of traders are bullish, for example, it is a reasonable assumption that they are either supporting a position they have already taken or that they are responding to the emotion that accompanies a very bullish market. In other words, they may either be long, wish that they were long or are afraid or ashamed to tell anyone that they are not long. If they are already long, it is reasonable to assume that they have committed the funds they plan to commit to the long side and that their potential buying power is no longer a force in the market. Those who are not long are likely to be unwilling to go long now, given the fact that they have missed yet another move. They are, therefore, not a potentially supporting factor for prices. In effect, then, the market has reached a point at which *it can no longer be sustained by new buying.*

Having learned this from years of hard experience, Jerry found it very important to monitor the consensus of trader opinion daily, but he was especially interested in the consensus of opinion *once it reached an extreme level,* both at tops and at bottoms. This was, in fact, one of the most important and consistent things that Jerry had learned about the futures markets since he started trading, and he was able to use it to his advantage almost every day.

Jerry knew that traders are influenced by three factors: expectation, emotion and perception. And he knew that of these three, perception was the most important. If traders perceive a situation to be bullish, they will respond to this perception of the situation. This will cause them to have certain expectations which will be accompanied by particular emotions. For example, he knew that if traders perceived him to be successful, they would be inclined to perceive his actions in a given way. Therefore, if he was buying, it must mean that he was bullish; and if he was bullish then they were bullish. If they expect profits, then their emotions are prompted primarily by greed. Jerry knew that if he wanted to sell, he had better buy first. The insecurity of the traders both on and off the trading floor who coat-tailed his trading eventually led the majority of them to take losses.

Jerry did not feel that he was using or abusing other traders. On the trading floor every trader competes against all other traders to a given extent. Jerry was there for one reason—to make profits. If other traders were so insecure that they had to play Jerry's game, then they would lose by playing by his rules. It was that simple. Moreover, every trader had to be cognizant of the fact that when bullish or bearish opinions were pervasive, the existing trend was often, but not always, apt to change very soon. Jerry had learned that while excessive bullish opinion was closely correlated with market tops and excessive bearish opinion with market bottoms, the relationship between these two events was not perfect. But it was reliable enough to use as a trading tool.

The lessons of history were also quite clear regarding the consensus of opinion and market turning points. Many important market peaks have come on the heels of very positive news and bullish fundamentals, and many important market bottoms have been born of negative fundamentals, bearishness and despair. The underlying cause of this market truism is the fact that traders and investors together form the underlying force which makes prices move. Jerry reasoned that if he could understand traders and their emotions as well as he understood himself and his own emotions, he could significantly improve his market performance—and he was right.

Al and the Brick Wall of Bearish Sentiment

The second scenario relates an essentially similar situation with slightly different results and development. Al, a broker for many years, has come to realize that the trading public has very poor judgment at important market turning points. His efforts to sell a silver futures investment program met with failure because the price of silver was moving down. While there were a few astute investors, the overwhelming majority was opposed to putting money into silver because it was going lower, professional opinions were bearish, the fundamentals were bearish and the market just wasn't exciting enough. Although his program had merit, it was not accepted by a skeptical public. In other words, the majority was still bearish on silver; they expected that prices would go lower and that there was still time to get aboard the program when the bottom finally came.

This made the silver program very difficult to sell. Again, the majority opinion was bearish at the bottom and the prospects Al called refused to consider the program—a reflection of the fact that a majority of investors was bearish. This, paradoxically but not surprisingly, convinced Al that he was correct. He knew that when prices turned around to the upside, investors would flock into the program, and that they would probably abandon it at the very first sign of a possible loss. He was right: the majority was bearish at the bottom, turned bullish near a short-term top, and turned bearish again, bailing out of the program when the market fell to its recent lows.

As you can see, the situation is not that much different than in Jerry's story. In this case, however, the majority was bearish at the bottom of the market. Unfortunately, Al was not able to use the knowledge to his advantage other than, perhaps, to buy silver for his own account.

Bill's Blunder

The final story in my trilogy reflects the same principles on a smaller scale. Bill was intent on success. He bought a good program, one with proven historical potential. However, lacking funds, he was insecure and turned to other traders to help him cope with his insecurity. By taking his own little opinion poll and by doing what the majority thought was right, Bill felt he would succeed. He failed to realize the fact that the majority is often wrong and that his best bet was to trade strictly by the rules of his program. As you can see, insecurity proved to be Bill's undoing. In soliciting the opinions of other traders and in doing what they suggested, Bill was using trader opinion in an opposite way from what Jerry was doing and from what Al knew to be true. In other words, the best thing Bill could have done would have been to follow his system mechanically without asking the opinions of others, or to do the opposite of majority opinion—which, in this case, would have been to follow his system. Actually, his broker's first suggestion—to trade smaller size contracts—was the single best alternative, since it did not substantively alter the intent of the program.

What It's All About

The purpose of the three preceding stories is to introduce the idea of market sentiment on a personal level. Anyone who has traded futures for even a short period of time soon realizes that "we have met the enemy and it is us." The enemy within has many disguises. At times it appears as the excitement generated by a very profitable trade; at other times, it appears as the despair or negativity of a bad position. As I have pointed out previously, trader behavior consists of three elements: perception, expectation and emotion. Each (or all) of these forces acts upon different traders in different ways affecting their behavior differently. On occasion many traders will be affected in the same way; in other words, they will be moved emotionally to have certain expectations.

This book explores my theory and application of market sentiment principles. While this is not the only book ever written on market sentiment, it is certainly one of only a few. My insights into market sentiment may not be entirely correct from a psychological point of view; however, I can assure you that they are very valid from a behavioral point of view. Those of you who have been traders for many years can certainly appreciate the value of market sentiment. You have probably had the nagging feeling that there is more to market opinion than meets the eye.

There have been a number of books on contrary opinion, the art of contrary investing, the art of contrary thinking and bullish consensus, but I am not aware of any other book that has probed the topic of daily market sentiment, providing several operational ways in which it can be used as a valuable market tool. In the chapters which follow you will find valuable information, presented in the hope that you will come to better understand, appreciate and apply the fantastic power of daily market sentiment:

- The social and psychological aspects of attitudes and opinions.
- Group and mob psychology.
- The development of attitudes and opinions through perceptions and expectations.
- How market sentiment is measured.
- How market sentiment can be interpreted.
- How market sentiment can be applied objectively.
- A complete history of daily market sentiment dating back to the first day of my data collection, in April of 1987.
- Specific suggestions on how you can employ daily market sentiment in your own trading and market analysis, both as a trading system on its own and as an adjunct to your own trading systems and methods.

Markets and Systems Come and Go; Emotions Stay

Traders often complain that the markets of today are different than the markets of yesterday. Traders nowadays are concerned about program trading, the influence of large, managed fund programs, unscrupulous floor traders, trading systems, thin volume, heavy volume and a host of other variables which they claim have changed the character of the markets. Yet it is clear from a study of history that there is one thing which has never changed—human emotion. It is also clear to me that human emotion will never change. It has been argued that as the markets become more complex and as worldwide trading occurs virtually twenty-four hours a day, trading will become more mechanical and will be managed primarily by computer. This may be true. Ultimately, however, it will be human beings who will either carry out the transactions or override the decisions spewed forth by computers.

Let's assume that I am wrong. Let's assume that eventually computers take over trading. Let's assume that computers are programmed to take advantage of market swings in an efficient way which attempts to capitalize on minor and major market moves. What will eventually develop is a system which is so highly efficient that the incentive to speculate will disappear. The speculator will disappear from the market and will no longer be there to buffer the transactions between large buyers and large sellers. I predict that in such a situation the markets will eventually return to human interaction as the basis of most transactions.

Traders Respond in Their Unique Patterns

The study of human behavior and emotion has revealed that each individual responds to stress in a particular way. Some of us have a gastric response and are prone to ulcers under stress; others suffer elevated blood pressure. Studies on newborn children have clearly demonstrated this fact. Furthermore, not all individuals perceive situations in the same way. Following a further discussion of market sentiment and its pragmatic aspects, I will revisit the philosophical aspects of attitudes, perceptions and opinions.

We must understand that, in reality, what appears to be constructive, positive and bullish to one trader will not necessarily affect other traders in the same way. What appears to be negative to one trader will be understood as a positive development by yet another. From time to time, however, there are certain developments which virtually all traders agree are either positive and bullish or negative and bearish. These are the situations which market sentiment attempts to isolate. In studying and applying market sentiment to futures trading, it is very important to remember that we are not attempting to isolate major market peaks and troughs through the assessment and analysis of sentiment. Rather, we are attempting to isolate periods of market excess, both positive and negative. In other words, market sentiment, from time to time, will be closely correlated with major price highs and lows; however, on a short-term basis, market sentiment will only allow us to determine when prices have moved temporarily too high or temporarily too low. These extreme levels are a reflection of strong market sentiment, which I have found to be closely correlated with temporary reversals in market trend. In other words, it is very possible for the majority to be right about the trend of a market. It is possible for all traders who see things in unique ways to be correct about their expectations on an intermediate-term or on a longer-term basis. However, when traders become emotionally attached to a given point of view to the extent that an overwhelming majority have the same expectations, they will usually be incorrect about their expectations in the short run.

Figure 1-1 illustrates how market sentiment relates to accuracy of expectations. As you can see, I theorize that the stronger or more certain the expectations, the less likely the accuracy of the expectations on a short-term basis. I reiterate my point: *in the long run, the majority may very well be right; however, in the short run, excesses in bullish or bearish opinions tend to correlate inversely with accuracy of expectations.*

I may be guilty of overstating my case. However, you must understand that I am presenting a subject which is not based on a mechanical model of the futures markets. Rather, it is based on an interpretation of trader psychology and behavior which flies in the face of apparent logic, and which contradicts what many traders and investors believe. In fact, the concepts I have discussed place responsibility directly on each and every one of us—and this may be a difficult thing to accept. We all like to think that we are rational,

Figure 1-1 Theoretical Relationship between Market Sentiment and Accuracy of Expectations

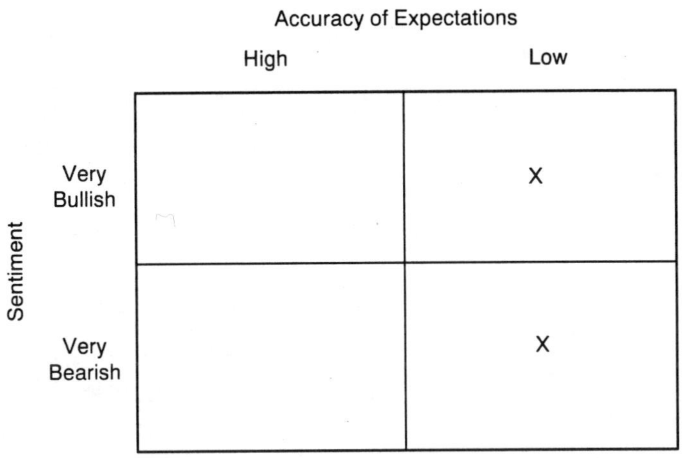

understanding, perceptive, fair, logical and self-disciplined human beings. None of us likes to acknowledge the fact that, at times, we are irrational, illogical, animalistic or ruled by impulse. But in our hearts we know this to be true. In short, I would rather overstate my point of view and have it understood than understate it and have you miss out on the valuable information which this book contains.

Now let's move on to a more detailed examination of trader sentiment so that we can observe and understand the mechanics of sentiment assessment, application and performance.

CHAPTER 2

How Market Sentiment Works

One of the books I have cherished most during my more than twenty years as a futures trader is the classic, *Reminiscences of a Stock Market Operator,* by Edwin LeFevbre. I have read and reread it so many times that the pages of my original edition are frayed with use and fading with age. During times of need I have turned to *Reminiscences* as a source of inspiration and refuge, and during times of success I have consulted it for sage advice on the virtues of having realistic expectations.

Often I have wondered what it is about this gem which has so captivated not only my attention but the respect of several generations of traders as well. While I can't speak for other traders, I know that my attraction to this book stems from the fact that it concentrates more upon the psychological, personal and interpersonal aspects of the stock and futures market and the speculator than it does upon the mechanics of the markets. It views the markets from an internal perspective rather than from the external, mechanical or technical perspective that is so common nowadays.

In these days of system trading and innumerable market theories, it is rare to find a source of information which concentrates upon the psychological aspects and considerations in stock and futures trading. Yet we all know from personal experience that market psychology provides the quintessential structure of all trading systems, even those which are purported to be totally mechanical. Even tyros learn very early in their exposure to the markets that positive psychological adjustment and virtually flawless trading discipline are their two greatest allies, as well as their two most difficult tasks. Traders and investors are ever waging a battle against three formidable foes. These enemies are not floor traders, speculators, large mutual funds, "the market" or arbitrageurs. They are, rather, invisible enemies who are constantly attacking from within: inconsistency, emotion and indecision. All of these are variations on one theme: trader psychology.

In spite of the fact that our real struggle is an internal one, many of us perceive the "market" as our chief enemy—we mistakenly consider the market to be the entity which we must overcome; the enemy which we must defeat; the obstacle which stands in our way. Effete market colloquialisms such as "beat the market," "make a killing," "fight the trend," "outperform the market," "took a beating in the market," are clearly symptomatic of how traders visualize their relationship with the market. And the struggle has been going on for hundreds of years.

Once traders and investors realize that the market is not a living organism, and as soon as they realize that they must find their own systematic and mechanical approach to trading, the market is no longer seen as an adversary; rather, it is seen as a vehicle at the very least, or as a friend at best (from whence the expression "the trend is your friend" was likely derived). Yet a trading system alone, no matter how mechanical, is always at the mercy of the trader who is, without a doubt, the weakest link in the chain. It is the trader who can transform a promising mechanical system into a debt machine; and it is the trader who can hone a marginal system into a winning vehicle. Skill and experience are important tools for which there are absolutely no substitutes. Self-control, self-knowledge and rational behavior are the fruits of experience.

Though the market is not our adversary, the three foes I have cited are real indeed. They are not foes which dwell in the external world—they are not physical entities. Rather, they are deeply rooted in the unconscious of every human being, whether trader, engineer, street person or cleric. To paraphrase Edwin LeFevbre: "the chief enemies of the speculator are always boring from within." Inconsistency is expressed in the inability to follow a trading system with discipline. Emotion shows itself when traders act on tips, rumors, fear of loss, greed or desperation. Indecision goes hand in hand with both of the above.

In recent years there has been a trend toward computerization in virtually every industry. The computer has been seen by many as a space-age miracle. Many traders are reveling under the sadly mistaken impression that bigger, better and faster computers will solve their problems. I have found that the opposite is most often true! A computer can only be used effectively by an individual who has the discipline and positive mental health which will facilitate its use. In the hands of an individual who is emotionally unhealthy, a computer can only make matters worse. It is simply another tool that can be used for self-destruction. I'm reminded of the admonition often given to young people wishing to marry—"marriage will create problems, not solve them"—or the old adage that "having money creates more problems than it solves." I find that both are true if the individuals involved are not prepared to use their new relationship(s) in an effective and healthy fashion. The best trading system in the world becomes a self-destructive weapon in the hands of an inadequate trader, while the toss of a coin can be used effectively by an accomplished trader. As with virtually everything in life, it's a question of *mind* over *matter* and *motion* over *emotion.*

When traders act on their emotions they are often wrong. It is usually but not always true that decisions which are prompted by emotional reactions are bad decisions. Since this is not always true though, the trader or speculator does not know in advance whether his panic, greed or fear will be the correct response on a given occasion. In other words, the speculator is the subject of inconsistent learning. In one situation, panic selling or buying may prove profitable, yet in another, panic will lead to a loss. This type of inconsistent learning, or differential and unpredictable reward versus punishment consequence, has been termed by B. F. Skinner as *intermittent* or *random reinforcement.* It tends to result in the kind of learning which is the most difficult to change, the most difficult to forget and the most likely to return after it has seemingly been forgotten. This kind of learning causes experimental animals to exhibit behaviors which are termed "superstitious," and it is probably the type of learning which is at the root of myriad deviant behaviors. An emotional response to the market—a response often based on unexpected news—can, at times, yield positive results. If a trader has experienced a positive result to an emotional reaction in the markets, then he or she will be more likely to respond emotionally in the future. If every emotional response has a negative result, or no result, then sooner or later the frequency of emotional responses would most likely diminish. If, however, the positive result was not predictable, then the result would be a behavior which is often very difficult to change. It is a fact of market life that traders tend to react emotionally to the markets, particularly when they respond to news as opposed to objective factors such as timing signals, charts and such. Since emotional responses are characteristic of a vast majority of traders, it might be valuable to know when a majority of traders are responding in the same way. In all probability the majority will, in such cases, be wrong because their responses are based upon emotions which, more often than not, are based upon nothing more than fear, greed, panic and/or unrealistic expectations.

The Majority Is Usually Wrong . . . So What!

The chapters which follow explore the theory, dynamics and history of sentiment in great detail, so that you may understand its importance, basis and applications more fully. In addition, I will also explain some of the problems associated with assessing market sentiment. First, however, I'd like you to humor me for awhile. Assume that there is indeed a relationship between attitudes, opinions, sentiment, emotion and market behavior. Assume that the following general statements are essentially correct:

1. Most futures traders lose money most of the time.
2. Most futures traders make incorrect decisions at major and minor market turning points.
3. When futures traders are in general agreement that a given market is bullish or bearish, they will usually be incorrect.

4. The larger the degree of agreement, the more likely it is that the strongly held opinion will be incorrect.

5. Since most futures traders are buyers rather than sellers, they are most likely to be wrong when they are in strong agreement that a market will move up.

6. It is more important to determine the opinions of average traders as opposed to professional traders, since professional traders are professionals by virtue of their skills.

The reasons behind these six assumptions will be examined in considerable detail as we continue. For now, however, if we accept that these assumptions are valid, then we can readily see their potential value and appreciate their importance in the markets. How? Let's say that we assess the daily opinions of a group of everyday futures traders and convert these opinions, or raw data, into a percentage of traders who are bullish or bearish on each of the markets. If our theory is correct, we would find that opinions as expressed in percentage of bullish responses would track the markets closely. As prices rise, the consensus of opinion would rise also. The higher prices rise, the higher the percentage of bullish opinion would rise. When a vast majority of responses are bullish and have been bullish for several days, prices are likely to be near their peak and likely to begin a decline. As prices decline opinions would become slowly but surely negative as the percentage of bullish responses decreases. Eventually the percentage of bullish opinion would become very small and as it does the market would bottom and the "cycle" would repeat. Figure 2-1 illustrates the ideal relationship between market sentiment and price.

I realize that the situation I've just presented is an ideal one. If market indicators always worked in practice as they do in theory, there would probably be no markets because they would be totally predictable. On the other hand, some market indicators are more reliable than others. Compare the ideal situation illustrated in Figure 2-1 with the chart of an actual situation as presented in Figure 2-2. Do you see the "uncanny" similarity? Now turn back to my six hypothetical assumptions. Read them again, and as you do, compare them to the actual results of Figure 2-2.

Figure 2-1 Ideal Relationship between Market Sentiment and Price

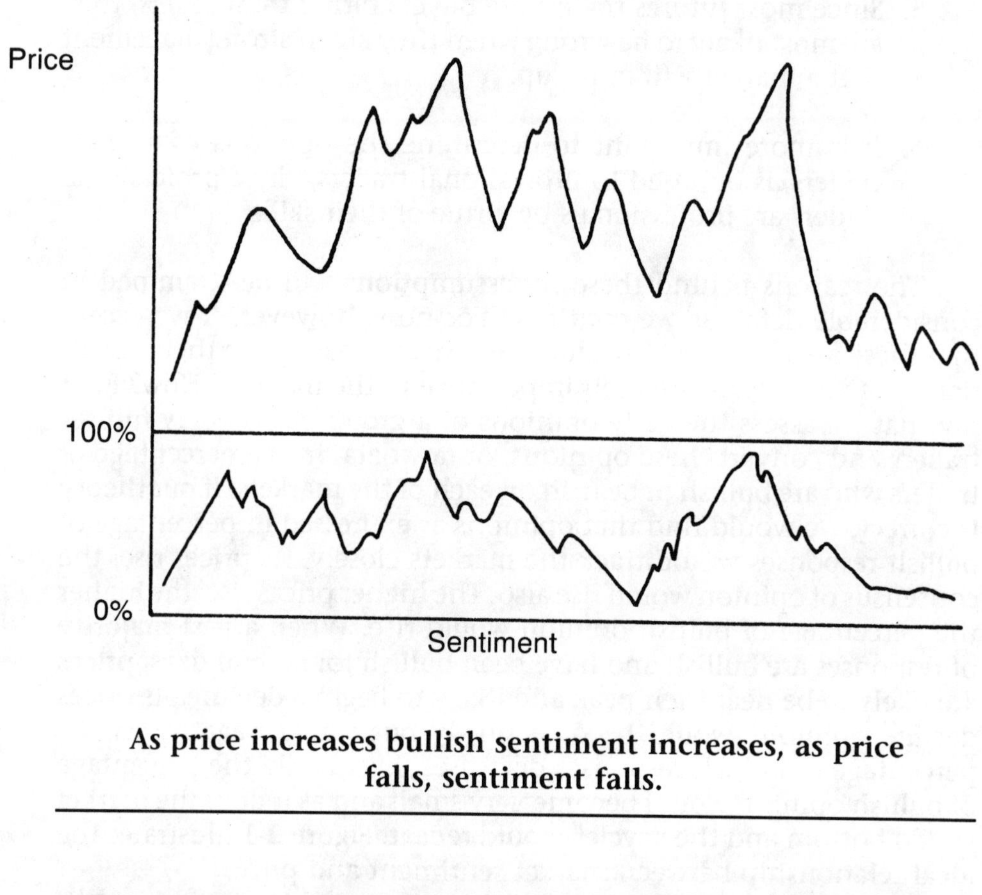

As price increases bullish sentiment increases, as price falls, sentiment falls.

You may now be thinking that I've searched long and hard to find an example (i.e., Figure 2-2) which agrees with my assumptions. There are in fact numerous examples, one as good as the other. In actuality there are many more examples which conform to the six assumptions stated earlier than there are which do not. Still, the question remains as to how one might best employ this type of information. While a theory may have both actual validity and face validity, it is the pragmatic application of that theory which ultimately validates it. In futures trading, theories and beliefs abound; but few translate into useful indicators, systems or methods. I feel very strongly

Figure 2-2 Actual Daily Market Sentiment and Closing Prices

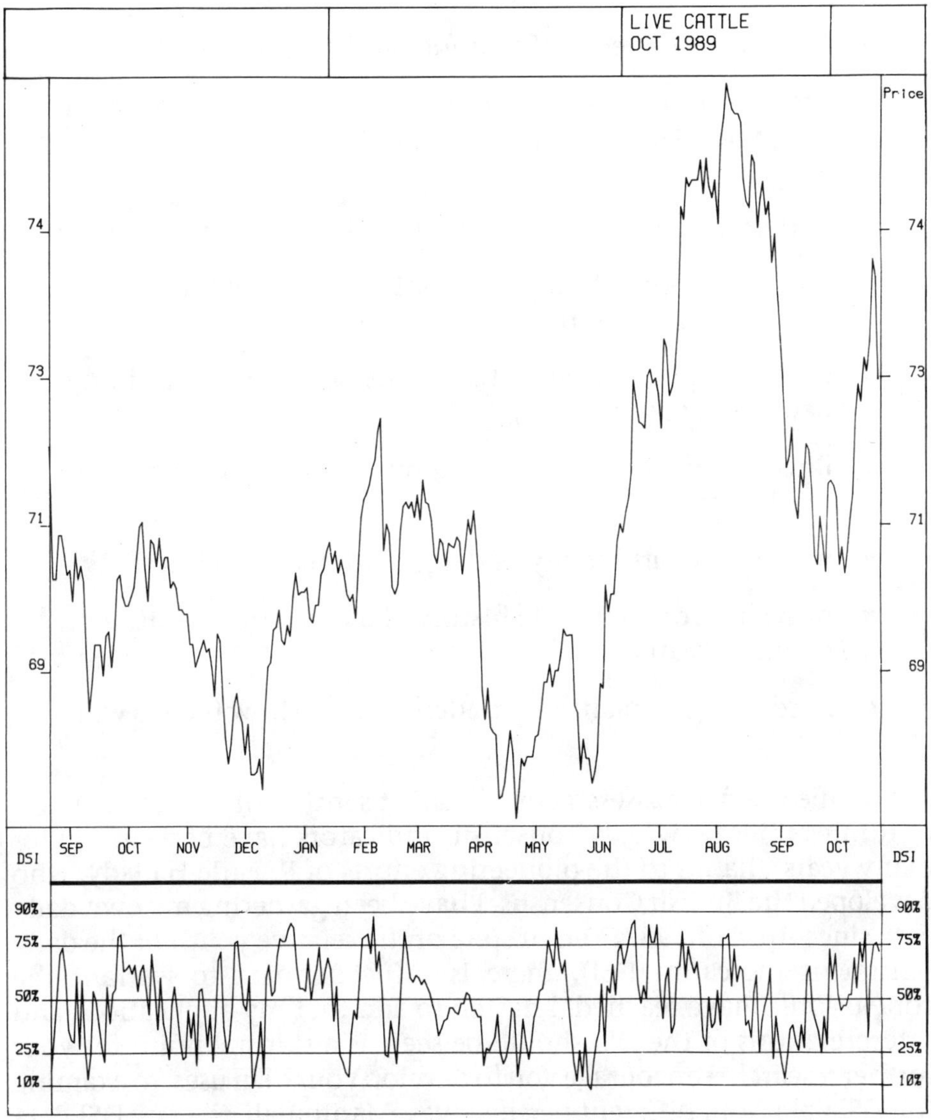

Note the close correlation of sentiment with price trend. Sentiment peaks closely correlate with price peaks and vice versa.

that the appropriate interpretation and application of market sentiment indicators can dramatically improve market timing and, as a result, profits. The balance of this book will:

- examine the theory of attitudes and opinions;
- provide some classic historical examples of how human emotion relates to important events and market turns;
- discuss theories of contrary opinion in the stock market and how they are applied to the decision-making process;
- discuss theories of contrary opinion in futures trading and how they have been used;
- explain the assessment technique used in determining daily market sentiment;
- illustrate various technical applications of daily market sentiment;
- provide a chart history of daily sentiment and prices;
- provide a complete data history of daily market sentiment by market, and
- in so doing, explain why traders lose and how traders win.

While the daily assessment of market sentiment is relatively new in futures trading, weekly consensus indicators have been in use for many years, thanks to the pioneering efforts of R. Earle Hadady, who developed the Bullish Consensus. I have been gathering my own daily data since April of 1987. Yet, in spite of the relative youth of the daily sentiment indicator (DSI), there is sufficient data to warrant the conclusions I have reached. I hasten to add that my applications and interpretations of the DSI should be seen as a starting point for your further research. I encourage you to develop your own uses, to examine the DSI data from different perspectives. Manipulate the raw DSI data in various ways and observe the results. Employ the DSI data as a filter with your own particular trading systems or methods and see if the DSI improves them. But whatever you do, please take the time to observe daily sentiment on your own. I am most confident that when you do you will find, as I have, that there is indeed an important and predictable relationship between market sentiment and price. The higher the bullish sentiment, the closer we are to a top, and vice versa. As I have stated before and as I will tell you repeatedly throughout this book, the DSI is not considered a trading system or a "Holy Grail" indicator. It is, however, considered an important adjunct or confirming indicator, and it is an indicator which, at the very least, deserves considerably more study.

Once you understand the whys and wherefores of market sentiment you will also understand the emotional components which cause many traders to make losing decisions, and you will also understand why traders who win have mastered the art and science of using market sentiment to their advantage. In some cases their ability to use market sentiment effectively is not conscious; it has been internalized; it is automatic. And in other cases the ability to effectively use market sentiment is deliberate and conscious. In either case it is clear that one very important distinguishing characteristic between winners and losers is their ability to understand and use market sentiment to their advantage. Finally, winners are also well acquainted with their own emotions and know how to keep them in balance.

CHAPTER 3

The Psychology of Attitudes and Opinions: A Brief Overview

In 1908, British psychologist William McDougall published his *Introduction to Social Psychology,* in which he gathered and discussed numerous concepts, theories and observations about human behavior. Previous to McDougall's unifying work, psychologists Stout, Stand, Spencer, Bain and Shand were all responsible in part for introducing various concepts about human group behavior. In fact, the early work on attitudes, opinions and social psychology was derived from what has been termed "sentiment" by Shaftesbury and others. According to Eysenck in his classic study, *The Psychology of Politics* (1954), Shand defined sentiment as "denoting systems of character which organize and direct the various primary emotions and impulses." As Eysenck pointed out, these are not feelings per se, but rather predisposing factors. They dispose an individual to have certain feelings when presented with an object or objects around which the sentiment has grown. Sentiment is an acquired quality, one which has been learned by association.

Although Eysenck and other psychologists were specifically interested in studying political behavior, attitudes and opinions, their work can be used to understand the various aspects of market sentiment which are the focus of this book. If we can first understand how sentiment develops, why it develops, how it is maintained and how it is expressed, we can then have a better understanding of how to employ it as a trading tool. More importantly, we can understand the meaning of especially high and low market sentiment.

While political attitudes and opinions are closely related to social class, market sentiment is more directly a function of market behavior and individual psychological make-up. Investors and traders who watch the markets daily are easily influenced by price, a plethora of external and internal forces such as news, the size of their positions, their open profits or losses, chart patterns, technical indicators, weather, government reports and so on. These forces—whether external, internal or both—do not always influence all traders to respond in a similar fashion at the same time. On occasion, however, a majority of traders and investors will be affected in a similar fashion. As a result, their collective sentiment will become either highly positive (bullish or optimistic) or highly negative (bearish or pessimistic). Trader sentiment is defined for our purposes as:

The opinion of an investor or group of investors regarding the future direction of a given market or markets.

While this definition is somewhat general, I feel that we must allow for a broad definition inasmuch as the market perception and time orientation of every trader is slightly different. (My reasons for such a general definition as well as my open-ended assessment technique for evaluating sentiment will be explained more fully later.)

Another aspect of market sentiment is based on the collective opinion of a group of traders. While the opinions and sentiment of one investor are not significant in terms of their ability to affect a market or markets, the collective sentiment of a group of traders can be and often is significant enough to affect prices. We know that sentiment seems to forecast market direction at times, yet it does not seem to do so at other times. And while we know that the development of trader attitudes, opinions and sentiment is a function of various inputs, the precise ways in which sentiment develops are not readily discernible. I do, however, have some observations to share with you;

yet I hasten to add that they are merely observations which are not supported by hard experimental facts. Nevertheless, I think that most experienced traders will agree that they have face validity (i.e., appear to be reasonable and logical although not scientifically tested). Due to the inherent difficulties in testing theories with human subjects, some psychological theories cannot be conclusively validated. Furthermore, results from animal studies cannot be completely generalized to humans. Hence, some degree of conjecture and observation must enter into virtually any approach to the study of human behavior, unless operational and quantifiable observations can be formulated. In short, my observations are merely observations, and while some readers may choose to take issue with my conclusions (as I am sure they will), I urge you to consider them in the light of your own practical experiences. If you find my explanations familiar, perhaps even very similar to your own experiences, then accept them as highly probable or even factual.

Psychological Correlates of Sentiment in Bull Markets

Bull markets are exciting, attention-getting, emotional and seemingly without upper boundaries. It is the fantasy of "unlimited" upside potential which attracts the average trader to bull markets; it is the promise or expectation of new historic highs and multiple percentage price increases which causes investors and speculators to seek out potentially bullish opportunities. It is the lure of bull markets which eventually traps longs at the top, as professionals liquidate their holdings to a recklessly bullish and blindsided public. This is how it has always been. We can certainly seek to understand the whys and the wherefores of mass bullish hysteria, but it is unlikely that we will ever be able to change it.

Perhaps the most well-known of all bull market-induced buying frenzies dates back to the Dutch tulip mania of the 1600s. Charles MacKay, in his *Extraordinary Popular Delusions and the Madness of Crowds* (1841), discusses the tulip mania in great detail. The mania swept across Holland, bringing with it ever-higher prices for bulbs whose only value aside from their aesthetics was their resale value—their speculative value. He traces the mania from its beginnings to its cataclysmic end, pointing out repeatedly that it was human emotion in its most base forms which fueled the entire insanity. Here is a brief synopsis of the tulip market at its peak. In reading what follows, observe the similarities between the tulip market and the stock and futures markets of today:

> The demand for tulips of a rare species increased so much in the year 1636 that regular marts for their sale were established on the Stock Exchange of Amsterdam, in Rotterdam, Harlaem, Leyden, Alkmar, Hoorn . . . Symptoms of gambling now became, for the first time, apparent. The stock-jobbers, ever on the alert for a new speculation, dealt largely in tulips, making use of all the means they so well knew how to employ to cause fluctuations in prices. At first, as in all these gambling mania, confidence was at its height, and everybody gained. The tulip jobbers speculated in the rise and fall of tulip stocks, and made large profits by buying when prices fell and selling out when they rose. Many individuals grew suddenly rich. A golden bait hung temptingly out before the people, and one after the other, they rushed to the tulip marts, like flies around a honey pot . . . (*Extraordinary Popular Delusions and the Madness of Crowds*, 93-94)

As you can see, speculation in bull markets is not new to civilization. Greed is an integral aspect of the human condition. The tulip mania is merely one example of the type of hysteria which accompanies bull market tops. A more recent tulip mania was, of course, the 1980s precious metals blowoff which ended with silver prices increasing in value nearly 1,000 percent as they moved from under $5 per ounce to over $50 per ounce while the general public was fed a steady diet of one bullish fact after another. The most outrageous of these was the expectation that silver prices would eventually find their way to $100 per ounce, stimulated by the Hunt brothers' market corner.

I remember a hot summer day in Dallas at the Real Money II conference in 1980. I had just finished my presentation to a very large group of extremely bullish attendees. Attendance was the largest I'd ever seen at a money conference—a sure sign, I thought, that the market top in precious metals was not too far off. As I entered the adjoining large auditorium which was reserved for the next speaker, Bunker Hunt, I saw many familiar faces: faces of fellow speakers, "recognized experts" in their fields and the faces of hopeful followers whom I had seen at "hard money" conferences for the last several years. I, too, was anxious to hear the forecasts.

Gold and silver were magic words to the hoarde . . . platinum and palladium were sure to be rocketing skyward as well . . . and let's not forget the most promising of all metals groups, the strategic metals! I felt very strongly at that time that it was a very sad group; nothing but sheep, lemmings, I thought. But the reality of the markets did not agree with me. Prices were clearly in bullish trends, consistent not only with the prognostications of virtually every visible gold analyst the world over, but also with my own cyclical interpretations. Clearly, the entire capitalist world was in serious financial trouble. The economic ship, without a captain, was immobilized by the threat of unbridled inflation as it sank slowly in an ocean of immeasurable debt. The attempt to reach dry land by finding and clinging to a golden life preserver proved futile; the buoy eventually proved too heavy to support even its own weight, carrying its desperate cargo to a watery demise.

Another sign of those times was the fact that a majority of precious metals analysts agreed that gold, silver and platinum prices were destined to move higher, possibly for quite a few years. The consensus of opinion was very clear; however, the one major disagreement among "gold bugs" was how high prices would go. There were forecasts of $1,000 gold or higher by the end of the 1980s; and with gold in the $600 range, these forecasts held much promise. But gold had already climbed substantially, and the forecasters should have been suspicious of their own emotions. Yet, the optimistic prognostications were readily accepted by many investors and traders. Clearly it was no longer a question of whether gold prices would rise; it was only a question of how much. This, by the way, is one of the warning signs of a bull market in its final stages—the majority is asking how high; the top is likely to be very close at hand. The possibility of a downside move is usually not considered other than by a very small minority of traders or investors.

Of course this is only one of literally thousands of examples of how market sentiment is very bullish at or near market peaks. A more recent and classic example is the petroleum price rally of 1990 which came on the heels of Iraq's invasion of Kuwait. You will probably recall this event very clearly. It is most interesting to note that the price of crude oil actually began to move up sharply well before the invasion. Figure 3-1 shows a chart of December 1990 crude oil futures.

Observe my notations. There is no question whatsoever that the crude oil market appeared to anticipate a bullish move well before the news actually broke. It is also interesting to note that on or about the day of the contract high, the news backdrop and the consensus of opinion was extremely bullish. As in the case of the silver bull market, there were forecasts of $100 per barrel of crude oil. These forecasts correlated closely with the market top. And the forecasts were dead wrong!

I'll take this example just one step farther. Figure 3-2 shows the same crude oil futures chart as Figure 3-1; however, I've added several other notations. Note the percentage readings on the chart. What is the relationship between these percentages and the various tops and bottoms in crude oil futures? Clearly the relationship appears to be a very close one. At various price lows on the chart the percentage readings are also low, and at several price highs the percentage readings are also high. As you may have gathered by now, these numbers represent the percentage of respondents to my Daily Sentiment Index survey who were bullish on the indicated dates. As can be seen, the majority was very bullish at market tops and not bullish (that is, bearish) at market bottoms.

Strong bullish sentiment as determined by an assessment of opinions is closely correlated with changes in market trend and with market turning points. The examples just cited are real-time illustrations of this situation. Although the process by which bullish sentiment becomes high is not always the same, it does tend to follow similar developmental patterns which are generally as follows:

1. Prices have been in a declining trend and most analysts are bearish. The fundamental situation is also negative. There usually seems to be no apparent reason to buy since there is no apparent reason to expect higher prices. Sentiment is negative.

2. An upmove begins seemingly for no reason whatsoever and generally unrelated to any specific event or events. The upmove is usually not accompanied by any significant degree of increase in bullish sentiment.

3. The move tends to continue with reasonable and normal corrections, perhaps even with a test or temporary penetration of the recent low. Bullish sentiment does not grow appreciably

Figure 3-1 Crude Oil Futures Before and After Iraqi Invasion of Kuwait

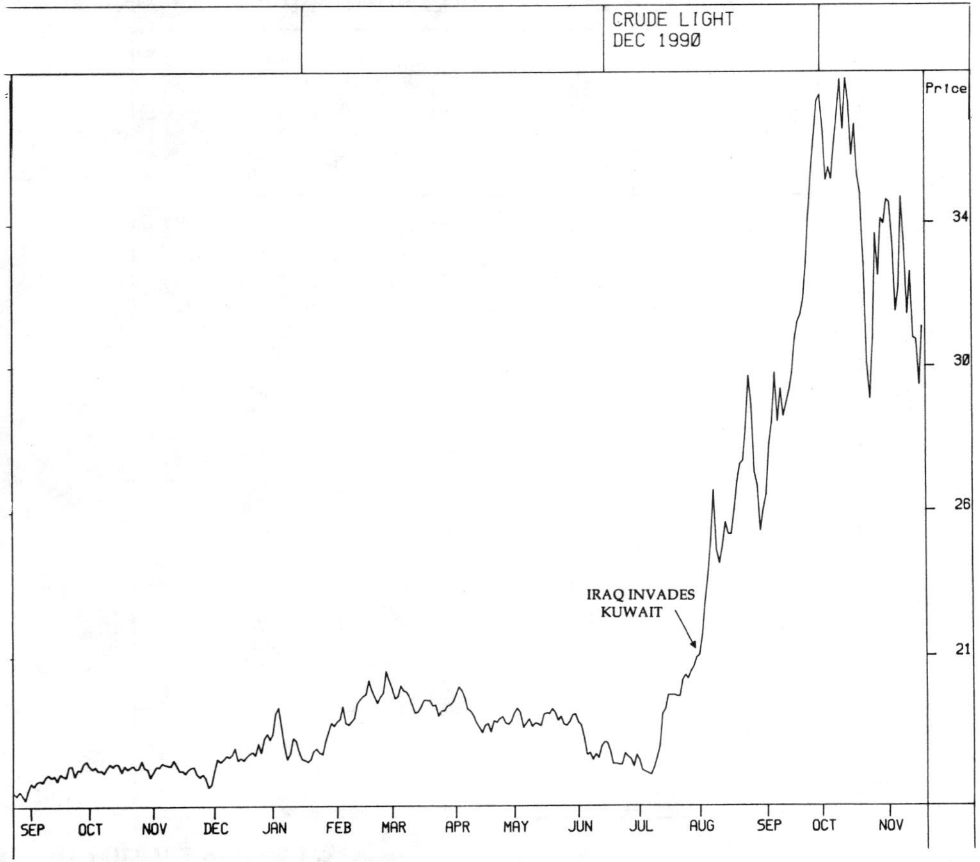

Figure 3-2 Crude Oil Futures versus DSI

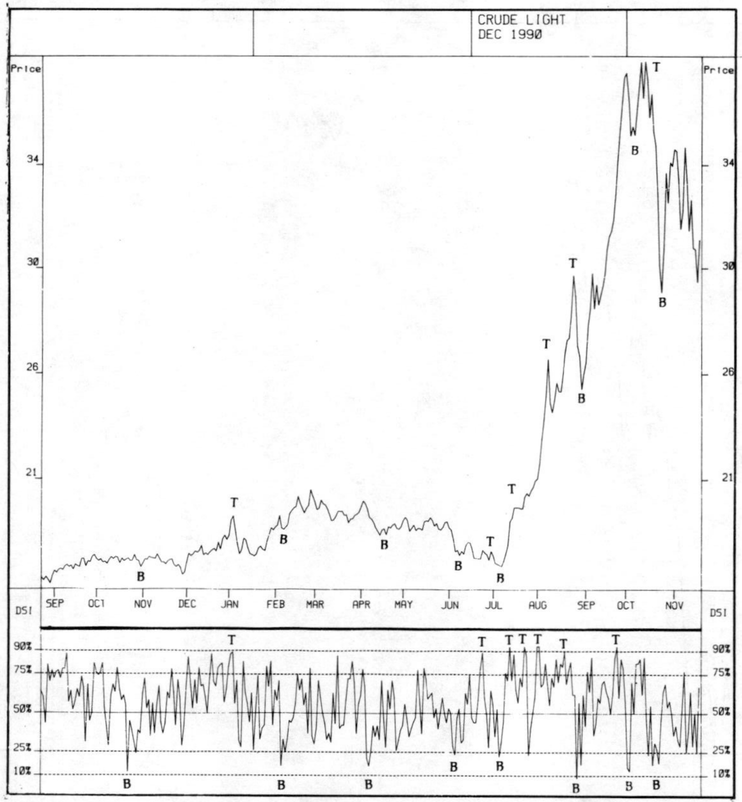

Note Top and Bottom Correlation; T = Top, B = Bottom

as long as price movement is slow and volatility and trading volume are relatively low.

4. Naturally, there will be peaks in bullish sentiment when prices move sharply higher for a given day or series of days. Sentiment will become low when prices again move lower.

5. As the fundamental factors supporting a given move begin to develop, so will public interest, and bullishness will increase. While the day-to-day changes in bullish sentiment may vary considerably, a weekly or even monthly average of sentiment will show more trending behavior and will correlate well with price movement, rising in an uptrend and falling in a downtrend.

6. As the price move gains momentum, as bullish fundamentals become more widely known, as buyers begin to control prices and as the feeling that prices can move even higher begins to grow, so does bullish sentiment.

7. The news backdrop eventually becomes very bullish. All roads lead to higher prices, and it is difficult to envision a scenario which will reverse the trend. The more bullish the market sentiment, the more likely the current bullish move is apt to be near its end.

8. Finally, the market surges higher and bullish sentiment increases to its highest levels in many days or weeks, perhaps even months. This is often a tell-tale sign that the top is being made. The greater your inclination to buy, and the closer your inclination is in agreement with the consensus of opinion, the greater the probability that you are incorrect.

9. Then, as if for no reason, and often in response to very bullish news, the market peaks and longs are caught with large positions at an important price peak.

While not all bull markets develop this way in relation to news and bullish sentiment, the general trend and characteristics are frequently similar to those I've just described. Clearly the psychological correlates of bull markets are hope, anticipation, wish fulfillment and greed. These emotions are counterproductive and cloud judgment; all the bulls can see is higher prices. Their opinions reflect their greatest hopes, wishes, expectations and ambitions.

Psychological Correlates of Sentiment in Bear Markets

Strong bearish sentiment as determined by an assessment of opinions is closely correlated with changes in market trend. The process by which bearish sentiment becomes high is not always the same. *Remember that high bearish sentiment is, for our purposes, defined as low bullish sentiment.* Sentiment in most bear markets tends to follow similar developmental patterns which are generally as follows:

1. Prices have been in a rising trend and most analysts are very bullish. The fundamental situation is also positive and there usually seems to be no apparent reason to sell since there is no apparent reason to expect lower prices.

2. A downmove begins seemingly for no reason whatsoever and generally unrelated to any specific event or events. The downmove is usually not accompanied by any significant degree of increase in bearish sentiment.

3. The move tends to continue with reasonable and normal corrections, perhaps even with a test or temporary penetration of the recent high. Bearish sentiment does not grow appreciably as long as price movement is slow and volatility and trading volume are relatively low.

4. Naturally, there will be peaks in bearish sentiment when prices move sharply lower for a given day or series of days, and bearish sentiment will become higher when prices move lower.

5. Even as the fundamental factors supporting a decline begin to develop, public interest will frequently not increase appreciably since bear markets attract little public attention. While the

day-to-day changes in bearish sentiment may vary considerably, a weekly or even monthly average of sentiment will show more trending behavior and will correlate well with price movement, falling in an uptrend and rising in a downtrend.

6. As the price move gains downside momentum, as bearish fundamentals become more widely known, as sellers begin to control prices and as the feeling that prices can move even lower begins to grow, so does bearish sentiment.

7. Eventually the news backdrop becomes very bearish. All roads lead to lower prices and it is difficult to envision a scenario which will reverse the trend. The more likely the move to lower levels and the more bearish the market sentiment, the more likely the current bearish move is apt to be near its end.

8. Finally, the market drops precipitously and bearish sentiment increases to its highest levels in many days or weeks, perhaps even months. This is often a tell-tale sign that the bottom is being made. The lesser your inclination to buy, and the closer your inclination is in agreement with the consensus of opinion, the greater the probability that you are incorrect.

9. Then, as if for no reason, and often in response to very bearish news, the market bottoms and short sellers are caught with large positions at an important price low.

While not all bear trends develop exactly this way in relation to market sentiment, the general trend and characteristics are similar to those just described. Clearly the psychological correlates of bear markets are hope, anticipation, wish fulfillment, and fear of loss. These emotions are counterproductive and cloud judgment; all the bears can see is lower prices. Their opinions reflect their hopes, wishes, expectations and ambitions.

Several examples of market bottoms and daily market sentiment will help illustrate how negative sentiment correlates with prices. See Figures 3-3 through 3-6. *Again, remember that low bullish sentiment is considered high bearish sentiment for our purposes.*

Figure 3-3 Daily Sentiment versus Price

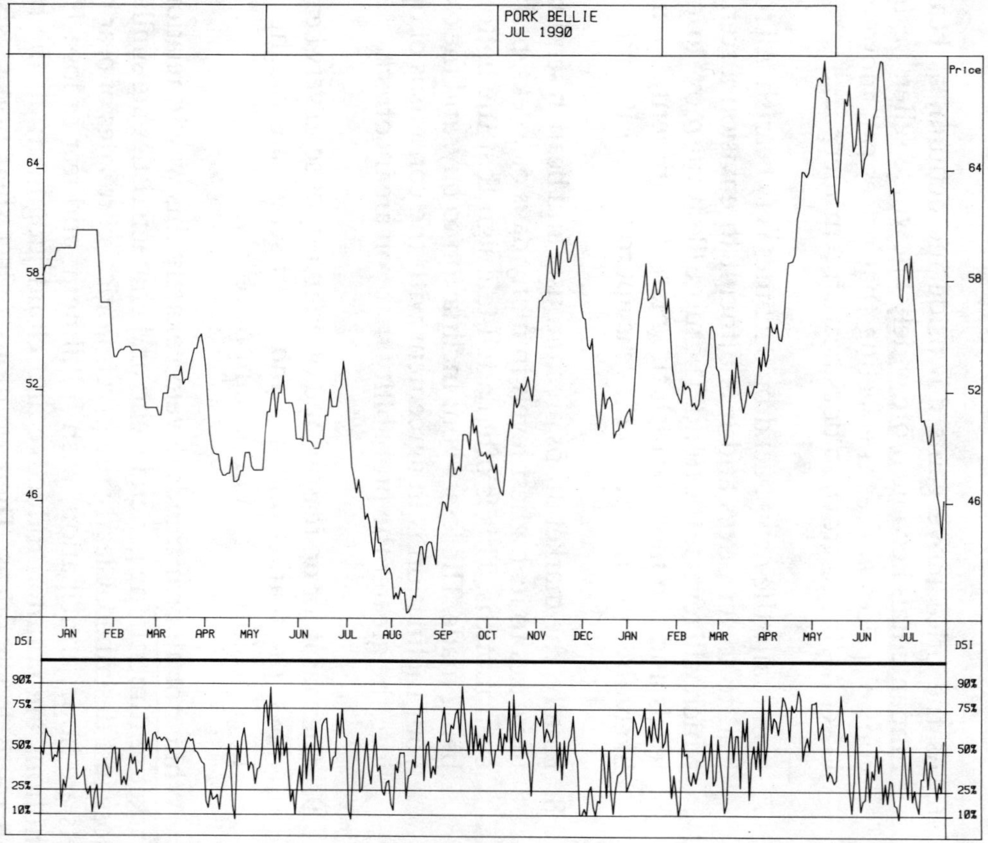

Note the relationship between price laws and sentiment laws at 10% or less.

Figure 3-4 Daily Sentiment versus Price

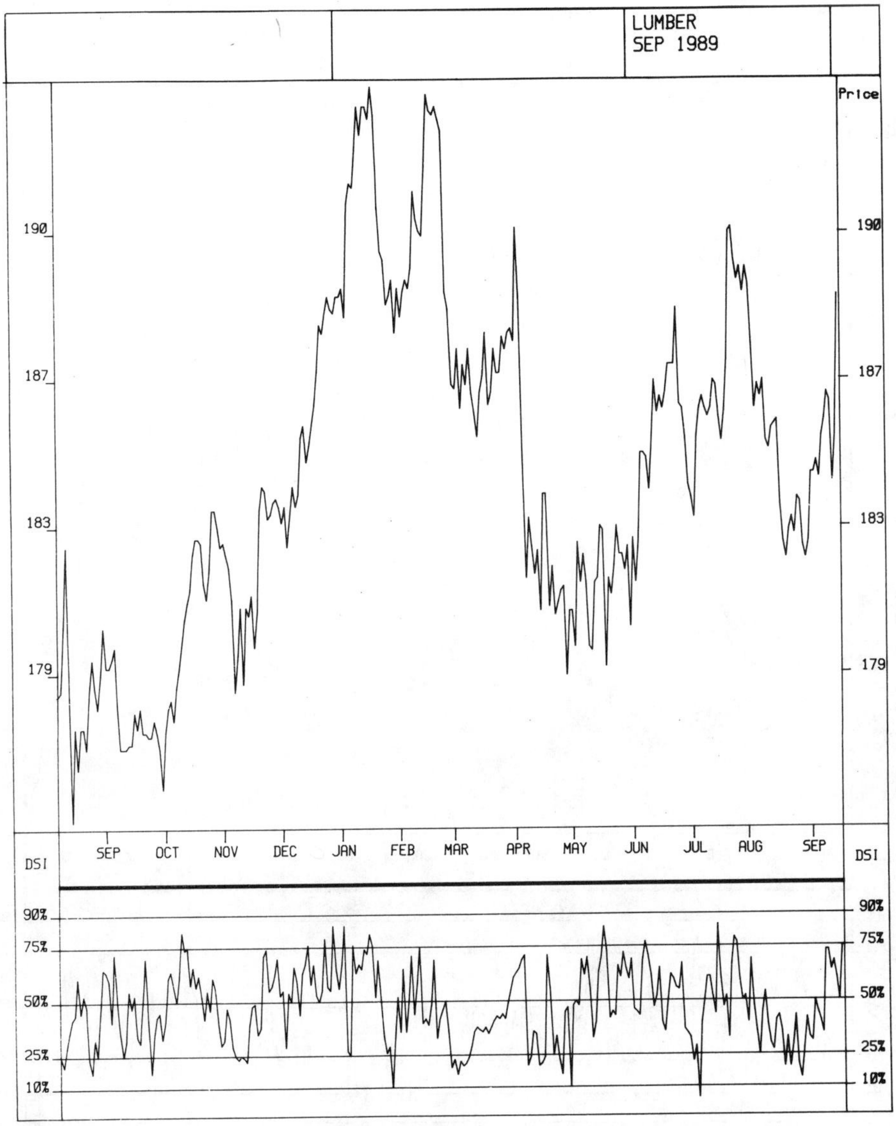

Note the correlation between sentiment of 25% or less and significant bottoms.

Figure 3-5 Daily Sentiment versus Price

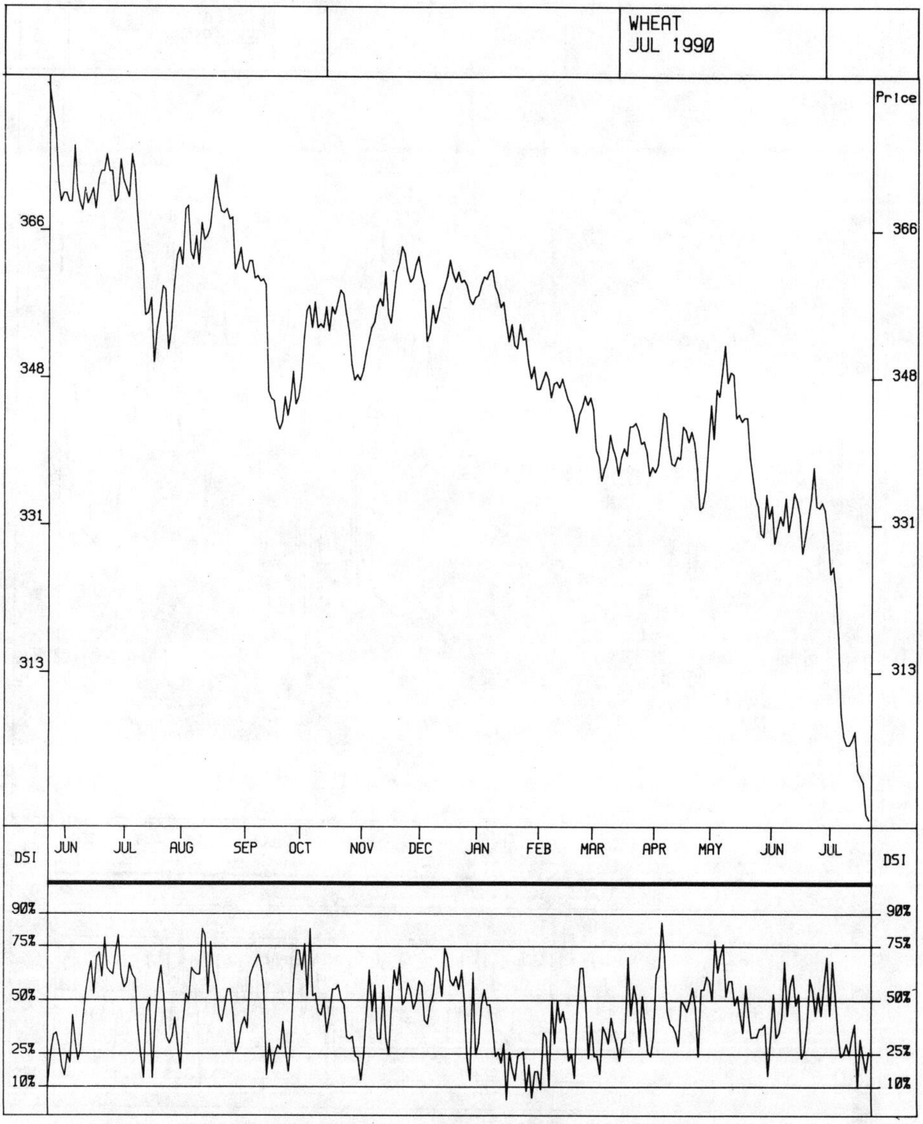

Note the bear market rallies which correlate closely with sentiment readings of 25% or less. Note also that there *are exceptions* to this relationship. It is *not* perfect!

Figure 3-6 Daily Sentiment versus Price

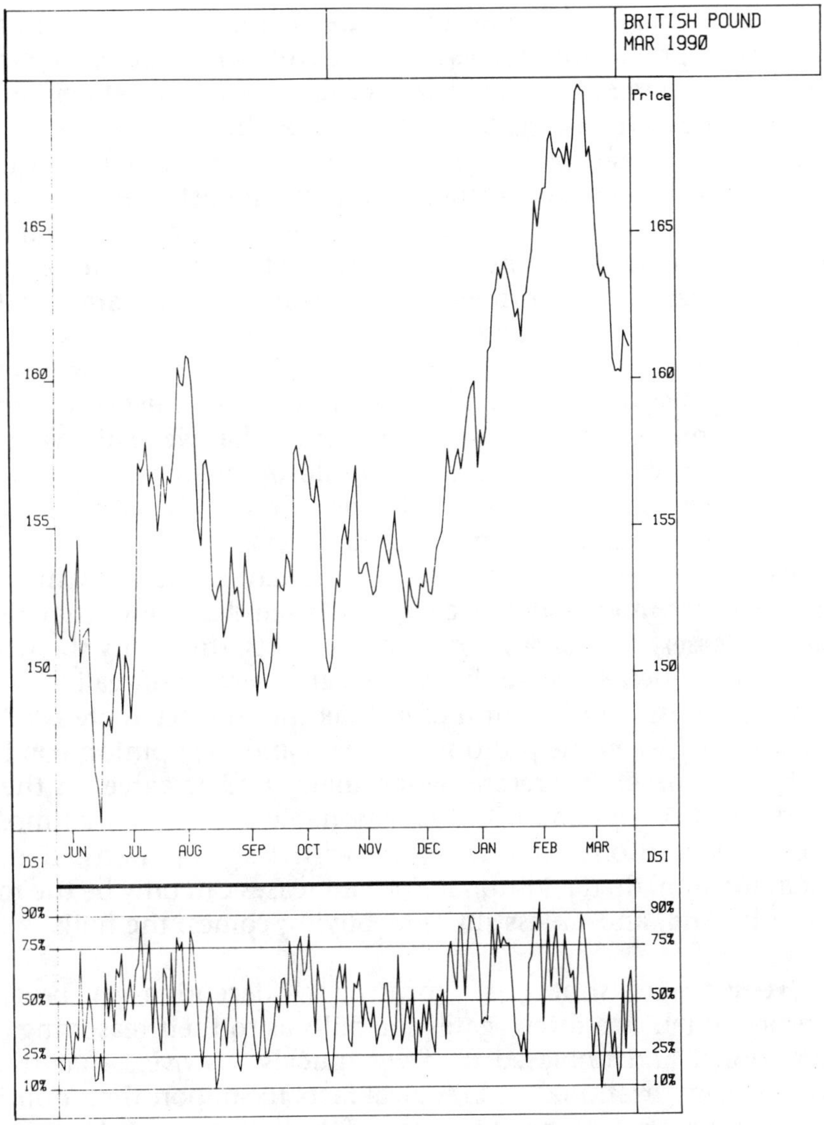

Note the near perfect correlation between major price lows and sentiment of 25% or larger. It's *not perfect,* but well worth further study.

Self-Deception

Life as many of us know it is an adventure in disguises. We use clothing to cover and protect our bodies from the environment and to prevent others from seeing our nakedness. We use psychological defenses to avoid dealing with reality. Some men color their hair when it turns gray; others get transplants or hairpieces. Many women wear make up. Men and women get cosmetic surgery. The list goes on.

Virtually every aspect of human life is either directly or indirectly affected by the need to either deceive the self from the pain of reality or by the need to keep others from knowing who we are, what we believe, why we are as we are, or what our true feelings may be. Yet, try as we might, we cannot always keep our guard up; we cannot always keep a strong front; and sooner or later we must come face to face with who we are, what we really think, what we really want and why we really want it. Religion and philosophy are only two of the tools that we use to combat the learned need to be consciously or unconsciously untrue to ourselves and others.

Self-deception is an important component of market sentiment. It is a fact that most traders are experts at self-deception; they refuse to accept losses, they misinterpret market facts, they deny the worthlessness of an ineffective trading system and they set unrealistic goals. Excessive bullishness is a form of self-deception since there is a high correlation between the position you own and the opinion you have about that market. Therefore, when many traders agree on the expected direction of a market, it is reasonable to assume that most of them hold positions commensurate with their opinions. If many traders are long, then additional price increases can only be the result of new buying, and unless the new buying comes, the bulls will be wrong.

Excessive bullishness as a form of self-deception can be easily discerned when one interrogates the bulls as to their reasoning. The unemotional and unbiased observer quickly discovers that traders advance many irrational and illogical facts to support their opinions and positions, often citing opinions as if they were facts. Self deception is yet another variable which distinguishes winners from losers. To be honest with yourself puts you in the company of winners.

Here are the important points I've raised in this chapter:

1. Extreme behavior is usually wrong behavior. When individuals react too strongly in unison, it suggests that they view a situation in the same way. At times they are correct, but most often they are wrong because they act on impulse and emotion. The fact that over 90 percent of all traders lose money is the single most telling piece of evidence in support of this statement.

2. Mob psychology influences faulty perception. Consider a theater fire. Someone yells "fire," and three hundred people rush to the same exit door. Only a handful of people will go to the other doors because they are not influenced by the behavior of the mob. Consider the highway "gaper's block." You're driving your car in rush-hour traffic, and suddenly it slows to a crawl. You drive three miles in twenty-five minutes only to discover that all drivers are slowing down to look at a disabled car or accident on the shoulder.

3. Emotions and trader psychology are different at tops than they are at bottoms. At market peaks traders are greedy, hopeful and stubborn. They envision primarily higher prices with only minor corrections, and they find bullish facts and opinions to support their anticipation. At market bottoms traders are fearful, pessimistic and dejected. They are often depressed and continue to cling to their losing positions.

4. Self-deception is a primary aspect of market sentiment. Traders fool themselves; they talk themselves into positions and they scare themselves out of positions. They create pet reasons for buying and selling, reasons which all too often have no basis in fact.

Perhaps the single most important thing I can tell you about trader psychology and market sentiment is that traders, being human, are imperfect. The fight-or-flight response, the need to possess and the desire to control date back to our prehistoric ancestors. As long as people are influenced by their environments, they will be slaves to emotion.

CHAPTER 4

Compiling Daily Market Sentiment

In gathering my daily market sentiment data, I have made some assumptions which are based on my understanding of and experiences with market sentiment. I am certain that there will be some points of contention and disagreement. However, daily market sentiment—in fact, market sentiment as a whole—is an area of market analysis which has not received much study or attention; there has not been much research and there have not been many solid studies. Given the uncharted nature of daily market sentiment studies, I have taken *carte blanche* in formulating concepts and methodologies. Those who have their own ideas are encouraged to pursue them. What follows is a detailed examination of my methods, assumptions, definitions and procedures.

History

I began gathering daily market sentiment in April 1987 with the assistance of my good friends and associates, Mark and Deb Lively.

The Lively's enlisted a group of respondents for participation in their daily survey in exchange for which the participants would have access to the daily sentiment readings, as well as a monthly newsletter containing a summary of the percentages and ideas regarding their application in the futures markets. We agreed to call our survey The Daily Sentiment Index (DSI).

Initially the sample size was rather small; however, as interest in the DSI grew, the number of traders who were polled daily increased. As an interesting sidelight, we observed early on in our daily data gathering that our number of respondents tended to fluctuate with bull and bear market trends. In bull trends participation was high; in bear trends participation was low. This is not surprising at all given what we know about trader and market psychology.

The daily polling procedure was very simple. Each respondent provided his or her opinions by way of telephone. The opinions were either bullish (designated by a "+" on our tally sheet), bearish (designated by a "-" on our tally sheet) or neutral (designated by a "0" on our tally sheet). Some respondents regularly gave opinions on all markets; others expressed opinions on certain markets only—markets in which they felt particularly knowledgeable or in which they were especially interested.

Characteristics of Respondent Base

Careful consideration and discussion preceded the selection of a respondent base. We were careful to avoid the use of a biased sample. If we were to assess only brokers and newsletter writers, as do virtually all other sentiment services, we would have a clearly biased sample. While it is not necessarily true that brokers and newsletter writers are more often right than is the general public, restricting our daily poll to this group was clearly a form of bias in sample selection. This is a most important point, one which I feel makes our method of data collection more valid than that used by other sentiment services.

We thought long and hard about the theoretical basis of market sentiment. If brokers and newsletter writers were the only people who actually traded, then we would be right to restrict our choice to these groups only. However, we know that many brokers do not trade for a variety of reasons. In some cases brokers are prohibited by their brokerage firms from trading. In other cases brokers decide on their own not to trade for fear that trading may be a conflict of interest with what their clients are doing and with what they are advising their clients to do. In yet other cases brokers refuse to trade because they feel their judgement may be clouded by what their clients are doing.

The same may be true of newsletter writers. Some refuse to trade claiming that it diminishes their objectivity; others feel that it is a conflict of interest; still others are prevented from trading by their employer. Given this situation, we felt that we would not want our sample to be weighted by brokers and advisors.

Furthermore, we decided that we were most interested in assessing the opinions of average traders—in other words, we were most interested in the general trading public. However, we also wanted to include other traders as well, and consequently we arrived at a base of respondents which consisted of various market participants including several hedgers and producers, brokers, Commodity Trading Advisors, a relatively large number of independent traders (i.e., the general public) and a few professional traders. Our sample consisted of traders with very limited capital at one extreme and on the other a firm headed by one of the most successful and well-known money managers in the futures markets. (Naturally, the identities of our respondents must remain strictly confidential.) Over 90% of our respondents were "average everyday traders."

The exact composition of our respondent base was not constant. Some respondents have stayed with us since the first day. Others have come and gone, only to return. I have observed that the comings and goings of some DSI respondents is very much a function of their success or failure in the markets and, as I have noted earlier, of the market trends themselves. Our base is therefore constantly and unavoidably changing. We seek to maintain as stable a respondent base as possible; however, this is not always possible. We do not aggressively solicit for participants, nor do we attempt to keep participants from leaving. They are free to participate as they wish, to respond or not respond, to take vacations, days off, and so on. We have intentionally left various aspects of the data selection open-ended in order to avoid bias.

Daily Procedures

Daily procedures for gathering DSI are also designed to avoid influencing responses. Instructions to our respondents have therefore been general. They are as follows: "You will be called every day at the time you specify, or if you prefer you can call us any time you wish during the day. You will be asked to express an opinion on every market. Your opinions must be either bullish (or plus), bearish (or minus), or neutral. You need not express an opinion on every market every day. We prefer that you respond as either bullish or bearish." These instructions are intentionally general and avoid any interpretations of the markets. In response to questions such as, "Bullish for how long?" or, "I'm bullish for the next three days and then bearish, what should I say?," our response is, "We need your opinion as of this moment."

In gathering the daily sentiment, we do not discuss markets with the respondents. Data collection is performed by clerical staff who are not acquainted with markets or market terminology, in order to avoid any undesired verbal interactions which might influence responses. We take every possible measure to avoid contaminating responses in the collection procedure. Furthermore, we make no effort whatsoever to coerce respondents to express an opinion or to continue as part of the daily survey if they do not wish to do so. All individual responses are kept confidential.

The data, once collected, is calculated by computer and the daily report is printed. The printout consists of market, percentage bullish or bearish, the three-day moving average of DSI, the five-day moving average of DSI, and the nine-day moving average of DSI (the suggested applications of which will be discussed later). The reports are checked for accuracy and then disseminated to DSI respondents and subscribers via recorded hotline, computer bulletin board and through one of the futures quote systems vendors as part of their news service. We release DSI data to all sources simultaneously.

Daily Recording Sheet

Figure 4-1 shows the daily recording sheet used by subscribers. As you can see, it is a fairly simple recordkeeping device from which the various derivations of DSI can be computed. The next section describes

Figure 4-1 Daily Sentiment Index Tally Sheet

1991

	01/04	01/07	01/08	01/09	01/10	01/11	01/14	01/15	01/16	01/17	01/18	01/21	01/22	01/23	01/24	01/25	01/28	01/29	
T-Bond																			T-Bond
Euro Dollar																			Euro Dollar
S&P Index																			S&P Index
Swiss Franc																			Swiss Franc
Deutsche Mark																			Deutsche Mark
Japanese Yen																			Japanese Yen
British Pound																			British Pound
Canadian Dollar																			Canadian Dollar
Dollar Index																			Dollar Index
Crude Light																			Crude Light
Heating Oil																			Heating Oil
Unleaded Gas																			Unleaded Gas
Gold																			Gold
Silver																			Silver
Platinum																			Platinum
Copper																			Copper
Corn																			Corn
Wheat																			Wheat
Oat																			Oat
Soybean																			Soybean
Soybean Oil																			Soybean Oil
Soybean Meal																			Soybean Meal
Orange Juice																			Orange Juice
Coffee																			Coffee
Cocoa																			Cocoa
Sugar																			Sugar
Lumber																			Lumber
Cotton																			Cotton
Live Cattle																			Live Cattle
Live Hog																			Live Hog
Pork Bellie																			Pork Bellie
CRB Index																			CRB Index

MBH Commodity Advisors, Inc. (708) 291-1870

some general procedures for developing your own daily sentiment collection program. I suggest that you incorporate a form such as this one into your program if you decide to collect sentiment on your own.

How to Develop Your Own Sentiment Program

Although I am the developer of the DSI, I do not hold a monopoly on trader sentiment. If we assume that a relatively random sample of trader opinion will show extremes in sentiment at market tops and bottoms—which is a function of perception and emotion—then we must also assume that different samples, so long as they are relatively randomly selected, will show essentially similar percentages at the same time. Therefore, you could develop your own network of DSI respondents if you wish to do so. My firm, MBH Commodities, offers my DSI service to subscribers who wish to avoid the time and effort of developing their own DSI networks. Here are some suggestions if you would like to strike out on your own. Please be forewarned, however, that the names DSI and Daily Sentiment Index are the author's trademarks and cannot, therefore, be legally duplicated.

SELECT YOUR RESPONDENT BASE This is the single most important part of your program. I suggest that you attempt to make your selections relatively randomly. In other words, avoid choosing several individuals from the same firm, or several traders who share market opinions during the trading day. Although you can probably achieve reasonable results with as few as fifteen respondents, I recommend you attempt to recruit as many as seventy-five. Naturally, your base will vary from day to day; however, the size of the base, as long as it is not too low, is not as important as is the distribution of the base.

ATTEMPT TO SELECT FROM DIFFERENT GEOGRAPHIC AREAS This will help avoid a built-in sample bias, and therefore help assure the relatively random nature of your respondent base. Attempt to avoid duplication of sentiment by including respondents who are close friends, partners or office associates. It will be best to gather opinions from as many diverse sources as possible in order to achieve valid readings.

DO NOT INFLUENCE YOUR RESPONDENTS' OPINIONS To do so would be to defeat the purpose of your daily survey. Each respondent must be as free as possible to express his or her opinions without any influence from the individual who is gathering the data. If you are personally acquainted with the respondents, do not gather the data yourself; have it done by a neutral party. Your respondents, particularly if they are friends of clients, may not want you to know their opinions. Anonymity of response is important if you wish to obtain responses that reflect actual opinions. In order to further insure anonymity, assign each respondent a number code so that you will not have a permanent record of their responses by name.

YOU MUST OFFER RESPONDENTS SOMETHING IN RETURN The most obvious thing you can offer them is the daily report. And this is a very reasonable reward since it will save your respondents both time and money.

AVOID THE TEMPTATION TO USE OR RELEASE DAILY READINGS EARLY You may find some respondents wish to know sentiment readings during the day, before the markets are closed. Since I suggest you allow your respondents the liberty of calling in (or being called for) their opinions at any time during the trading day, there are some who will want to know the status of readings during the day. I urge you to avoid releasing them early and I urge you not to use the figures for your own trading before the end of the trading day. To release data before data collection is complete would be inaccurate and may influence opinions, therefore contaminating the sample.

These are the general guidelines you can follow in developing your own program for daily market sentiment collection. Your major concerns and difficulties will be as follows:

1. *Maintaining sufficient sample size.* You will find that the markets themselves can influence your sample size. During bull markets participation in the survey will be high; however, during bear markets or periods of low trading volume participation will be low. You will need to plan ahead in order to maintain adequate sample size.

2. *Avoiding bias.* This will be a problem both in selecting your respondent base and in avoiding release of the data prior to the completion of daily collection procedures.

3. *Organization and recordkeeping.* These will be very important. It is not difficult to be organized in collecting daily market sentiment, and it is important to be so both for your own benefit and for the good of your respondents. You must be consistent, professional and meticulous in your collection and recordkeeping procedures. I strongly suggest the use of a computerized recordkeeping system, such as any of the popular spreadsheet programs. You might also consider a computer bulletin-board system for gathering, calculating and disseminating your daily statistics.

Naturally, there will be situations which must be dealt with on a case-by-case basis. While I cannot address myself to each and every situation you may encounter in developing your own daily market sentiment program, the above guidelines will prove very helpful.

Self-Fulfilling Prophecy

One of the most frequently asked questions is whether the DSI sample itself could be contaminated by the respondents' awareness of daily DSI readings. In other words, assume that the DSI for gold was 93 percent on a given day. The DSI respondents, after market closings, will be aware of the very high reading and might therefore temper their bullish responses the next day since they may feel individually that they are too bullish. Or they might reason as follows: "It seems that everyone is bullish; perhaps I'd better not be bullish tomorrow." In fact this may happen, but tomorrow is a long way off. The market itself will probably exert a strong influence on today's opinion, and additional thought may also alter the predisposition to be bearish because yesterday's reading was too high. Furthermore, the emotional need to be bullish when things look best, or to be bearish when things seem to be the worst, overrides intellectual processes.

PART II

Practical Applications of Daily Sentiment

CHAPTER 5

Application of Daily Market Sentiment

This chapter provides a number of methods for the application of the DSI or other daily sentiment indicators to the futures markets. These are methods which I have developed and tested myself; however, there are other techniques which you may develop on your own. There has been very little research on the application of DSI statistics to precise trading systems and methods. The field is still ripe for research. Where possible I have provided the results of statistical analyses which validate my opinions and theories. However, due to the still limited historical database of DSI, more intensive testing and analyses are still pending.

The application of DSI to futures market trading is based upon the following principles.

1) **The DSI is measured in percentage of bullish response based on an exact calculation of the raw daily response data.** If 50 of 100 respondents are bullish (as represented by a "+" or "bullish" response), then the corresponding DSI percentage is 50 percent. If 20 of 100 respondents are bullish, then the

corresponding DSI percentage is 20 percent. By definition, this means that 80 percent of respondents are bearish. Figure 5-1 shows a typical daily DSI report.

2) **The DSI tends to move up as prices move up, and the DSI tends to move down as prices move down.** In other words, there is a close correlation between DSI trend and price trend. Although the correlation is not one-to-one, the relationship in terms of trend is a fairly close one. Figure 5-2 shows the ideal relationship between daily closing prices (top) plotted against the raw (unaltered) daily DSI readings for the same time period. I have marked the corresponding up and down trends.

   Figures 5-3 and 5-4 show two actual price versus DSI charts as well as their related up and down trends. As you can clearly see, there is a close relationship between DSI trend and price trend.

3) **Peaks in DSI correspond closely with peaks in price, and troughs in DSI tend to correspond closely with tops in price.** Figure 5-5 shows the ideal relationship between DSI and price peaks and DSI and price troughs. As you can see, the theory proposes a very close relationship between the two. Figures 5-6 and 5-7 show actual price versus DSI charts and the relationship between peaks and troughs in both. As you can see, extreme DSI readings relate to short-term tops and bottoms in prices. As you can also see, the DSI is not always correct. It's tops and bottoms are, however, often very close to actual price tops and bottoms.

These are the general principles of DSI application. There are, however, additional methods and principles which are variations on the above themes. These will be discussed in greater detail in the chapters which follow.

Figure 5-1 Daily DSI Report Showing Date, Raw %, 3- and 5-Day Moving Averages of Raw % DSI

	12/27	*3MA*	*5MA*	*12/28*	*3MA*	*5MA*	*1/02*	*3MA*	*5MA*	*1/03*	*3MA*	*5MA*	*1/04*	*3MA*	*5MA*
T-Bonds	69	54	47	40	51	49	93	67	59	71	68	64	67	77	68
Euro Dollar	69	59	56	60	66	57	79	69	63	88	76	73	43	70	68
S&P Index	42	61	58	40	53	57	57	46	56	25	41	48	50	44	43
Swiss Franc	27	22	26	70	39	32	71	56	41	63	68	50	64	66	59
Deutsche Mark	25	22	29	70	39	31	79	58	43	56	68	50	43	59	55
Japanese Yen	9	14	14	78	33	29	77	55	39	80	78	51	46	68	58
British Pound	33	31	27	90	54	39	86	70	54	75	84	65	64	75	70
Canadian Dollar	31	39	40	45	40	41	79	52	48	87	70	57	92	86	67
Dollar Index	64	74	72	44	65	70	25	44	58	23	31	49	33	27	38
Crude Light	55	48	47	78	61	51	15	49	48	13	35	42	23	17	37
Heating Oil	45	47	49	67	54	48	17	43	45	20	35	40	17	18	33
Unleaded Gas	55	46	47	67	57	47	17	46	44	13	32	40	17	16	34
Gold	38	48	55	60	51	52	40	46	49	47	49	48	47	45	46
Silver	29	33	51	55	40	50	38	41	39	67	53	45	44	50	47
Platinum	17	32	50	60	37	48	36	38	39	53	50	40	50	46	43
Copper	42	57	61	90	63	67	86	73	69	60	79	67	58	68	67
Corn	29	35	29	27	37	28	18	25	30	33	26	32	35	29	28
Wheat	36	39	30	18	36	28	47	34	36	17	27	35	35	33	31
Oats	23	27	22	36	33	25	19	26	27	18	24	27	38	25	27
Soybeans	21	27	21	9	27	19	6	12	19	22	12	22	59	29	23
Soybean Oil	21	27	22	18	28	23	6	15	21	17	14	21	47	23	22
Soybean Meal	14	27	23	18	27	21	6	13	21	28	17	23	63	32	26
Orange Juice	78	62	59	75	68	63	42	65	60	36	51	56	27	35	52
Coffee	55	30	28	22	30	25	17	31	26	50	30	31	62	43	41
Cocoa	36	34	34	30	26	34	31	32	33	27	29	27	21	26	29
Sugar	54	55	50	10	45	45	13	26	38	18	14	33	27	19	24
Lumber	82	55	53	90	72	59	46	73	60	38	58	60	50	45	61
Cotton	82	72	77	70	73	76	31	61	63	73	58	65	67	57	65
Live Cattle	69	67	64	45	65	61	47	54	59	71	54	62	88	69	64
Live Hogs	15	28	33	36	30	31	33	28	31	41	37	33	50	41	35
Pork Bellies	8	30	34	30	27	30	14	17	27	44	29	28	57	38	31
CRB Index	18	32	43	56	37	41	31	35	37	36	41	36	46	38	37

Figure 5-2 Ideal Relationship: Price versus DSI Trends

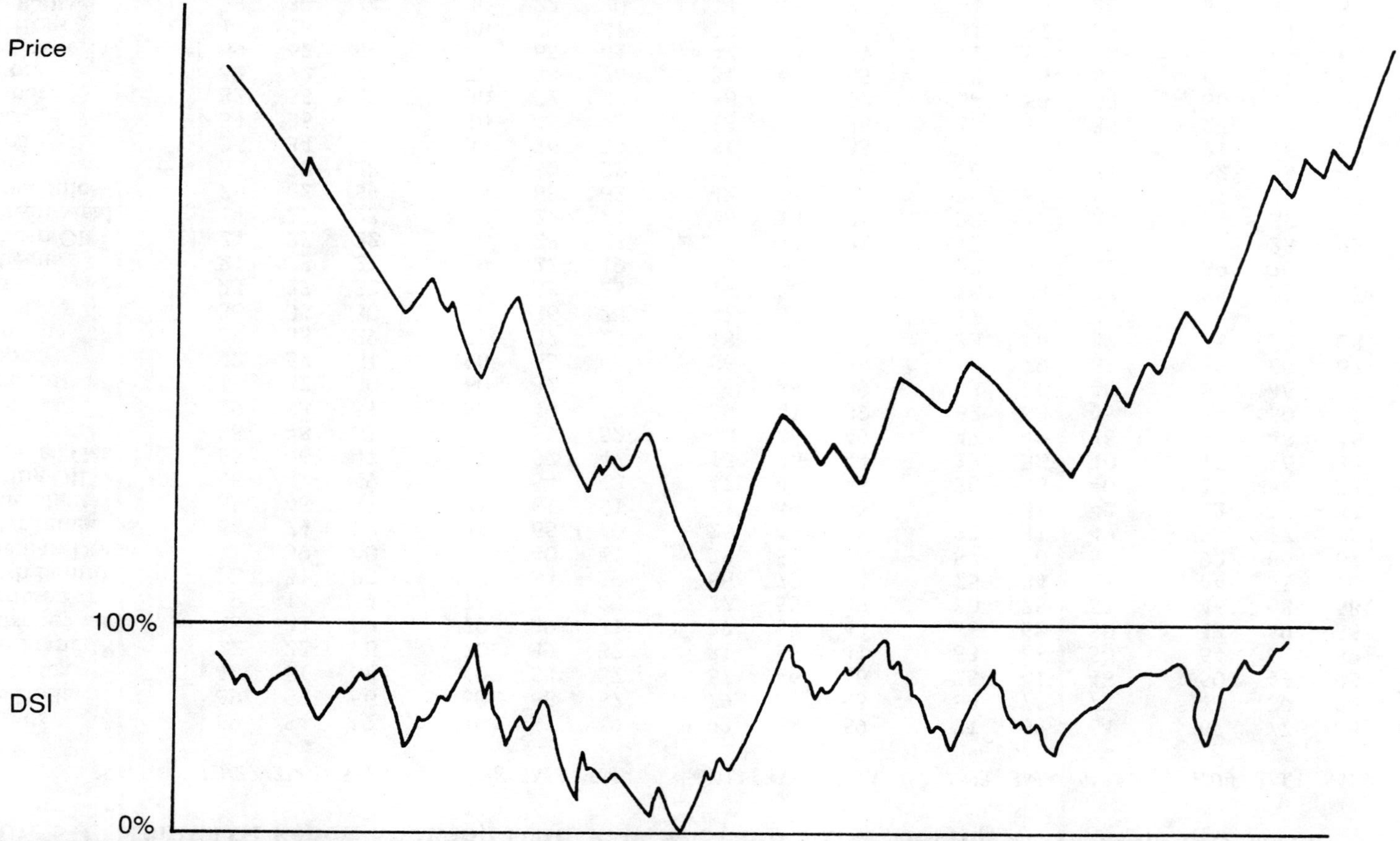

Figure 5-3 Actual DSI and Price Trends

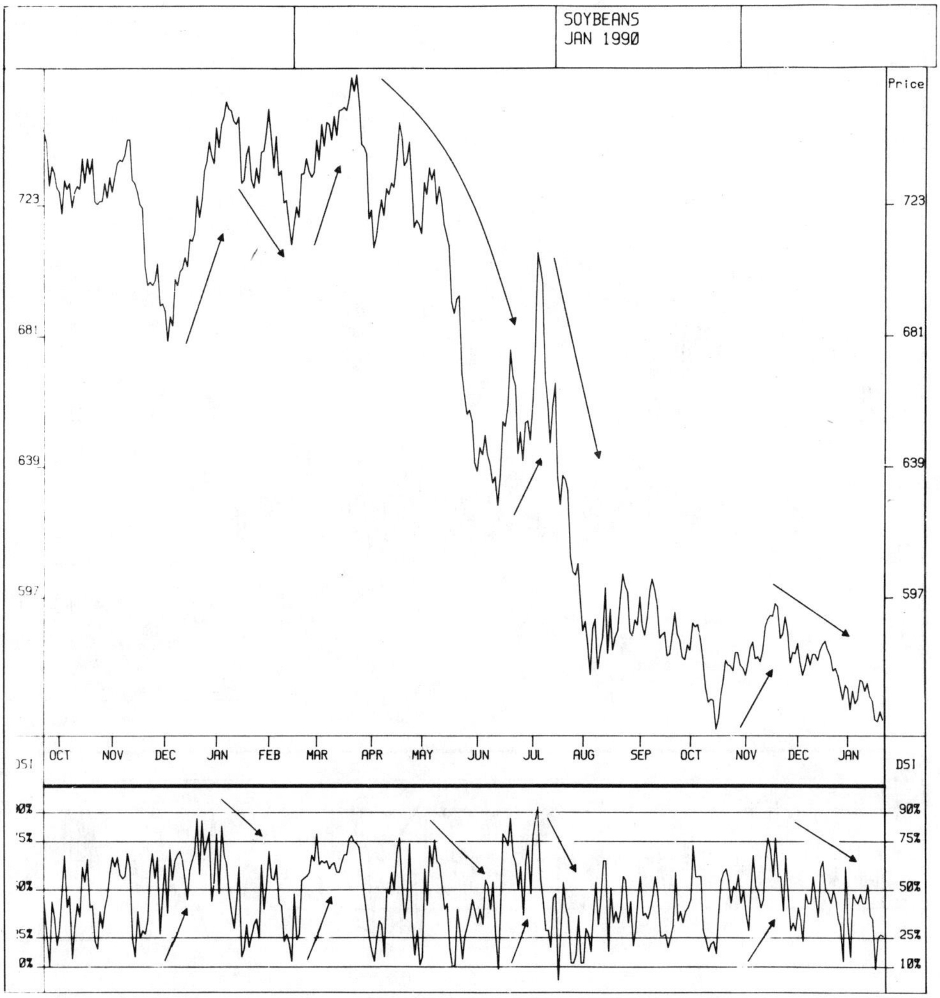

Figure 5-4 Actual DSI and Price Trends

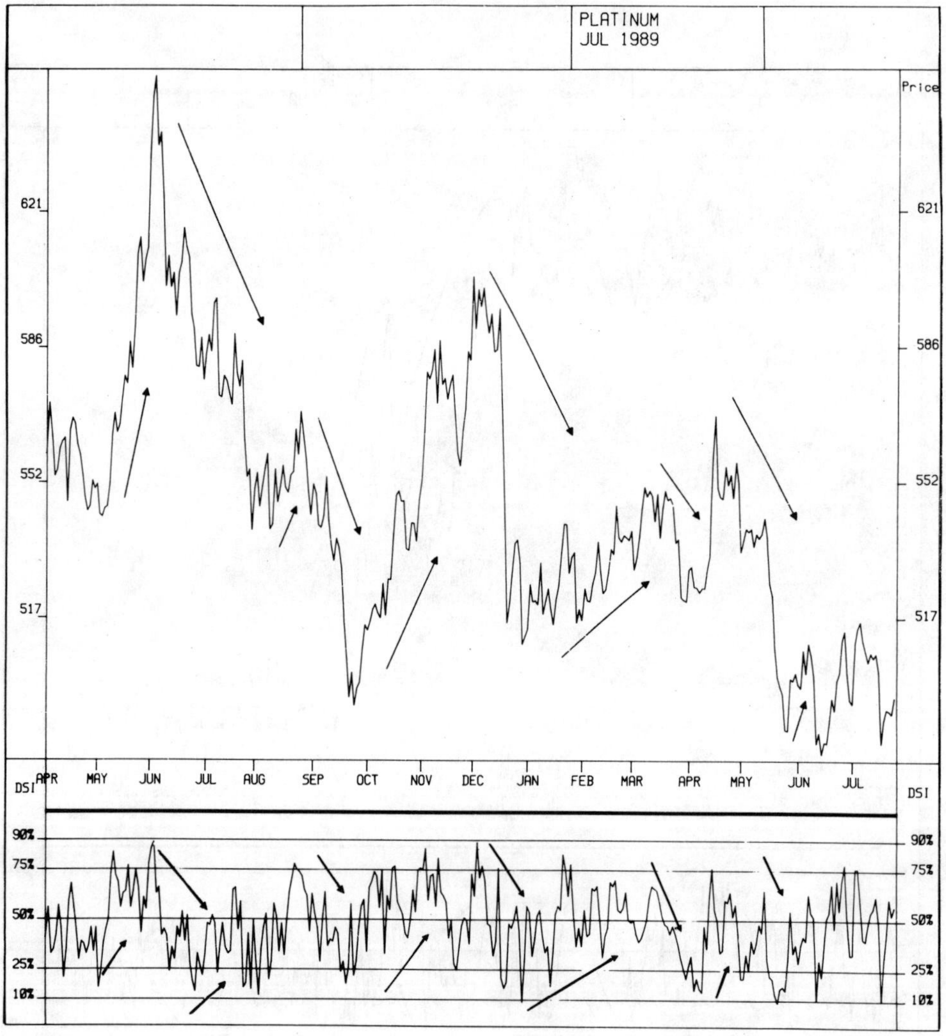

Figure 5-5 DSI and Price Top/Bottom Relationships

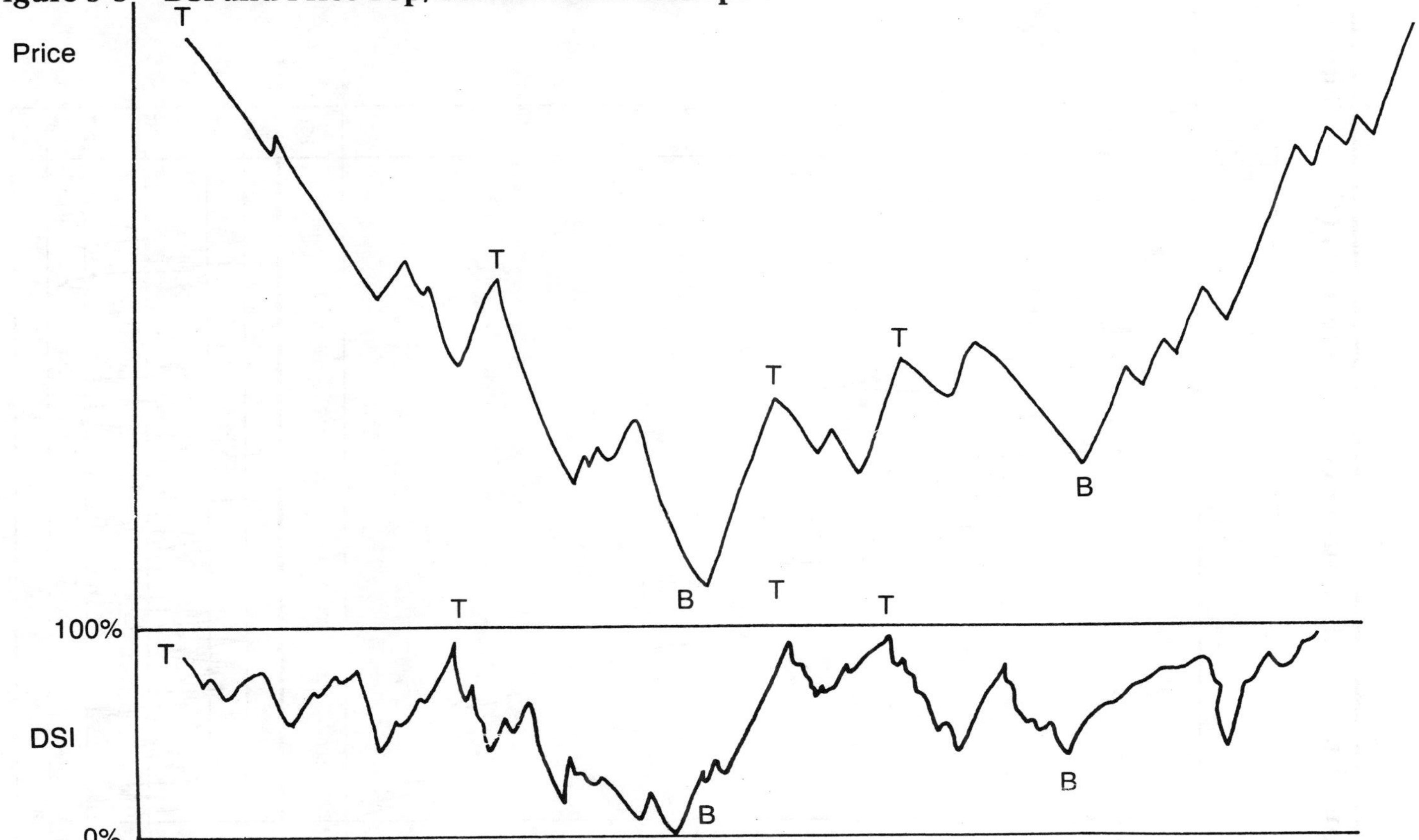

T = Top, B = Bottom

Figure 5-6 DSI versus Price Showing Tops (T) and Bottoms (B)

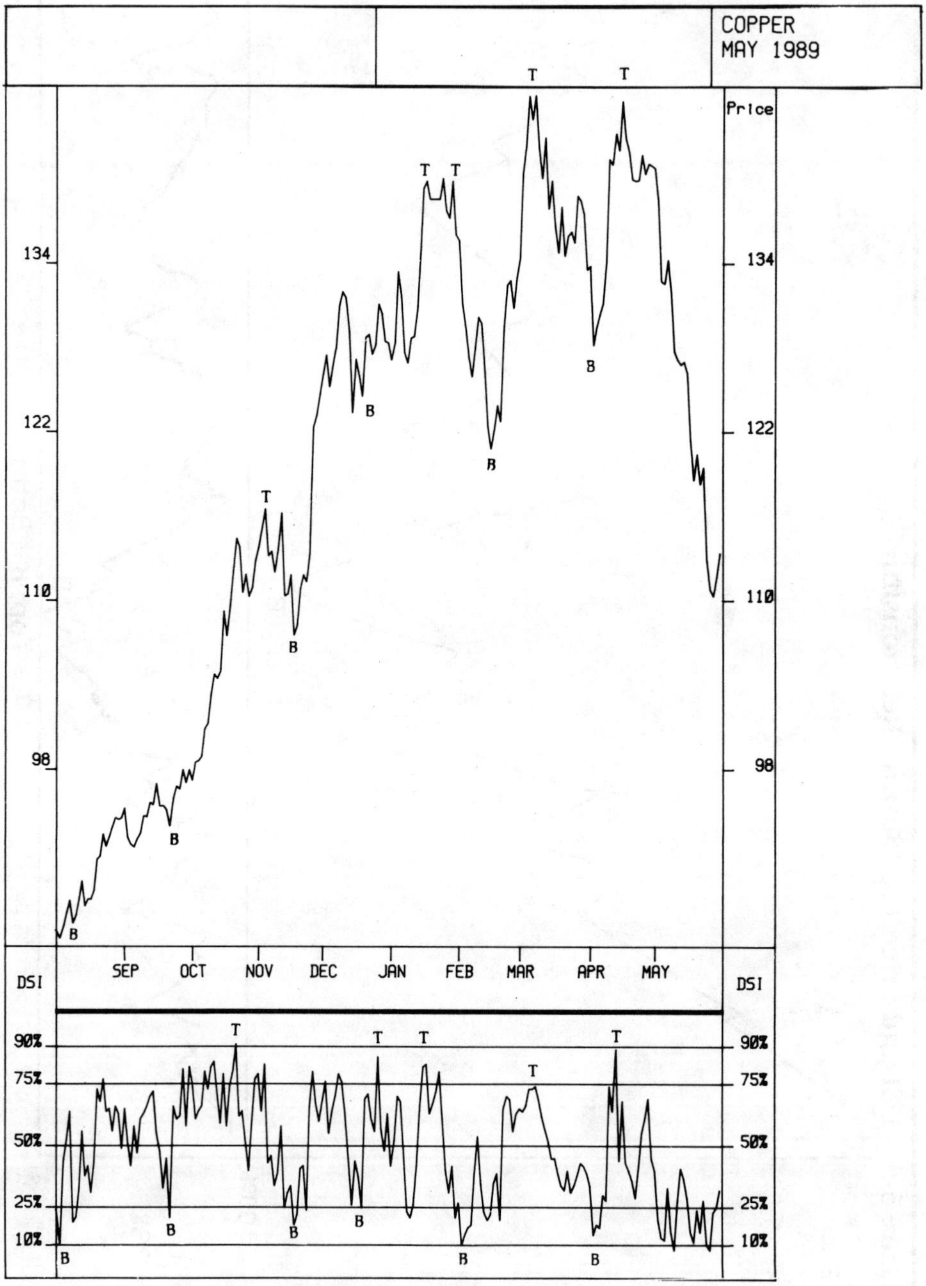

Figure 5-7 DSI versus Price Showing Tops (T) and Bottoms (B)

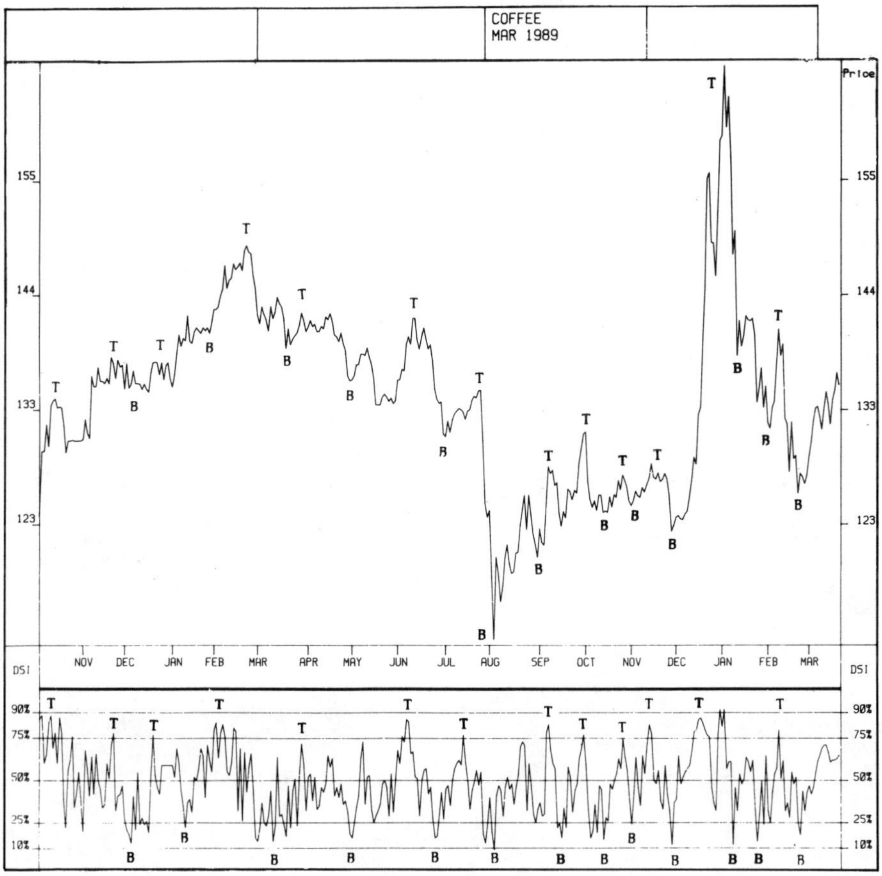

CHAPTER 6

Using DSI at Extremes

Before discussing the application of DSI derivations, let's look at the behavior of raw DSI at extremely high and extremely low readings. First, though, let's define what I mean by "extreme." It is difficult to provide a definition of "extreme" DSI readings a priori; rather, a posteriori definitions are possible based on the actual behavior of DSI. For example, to arbitrarily state that a DSI reading of 90 percent or higher is more significant than a DSI reading of 87 percent is clearly insufficient. We can, however, arrive at reasonable cut-off levels based on observations of actual market behavior. And even such definitions may prove insufficient in the long run. Given the relative youth of the DSI, we must do the best with the tools and data we currently have.

Therefore, I will provide the following general definitions, which will be altered slightly as we examine some historical price versus DSI charts:

1. EXTREMELY HIGH DSI is defined as a raw DSI reading of 90 percent or higher.

2. HIGH DSI is defined as a raw DSI reading of 75 through 89 percent.

3. MODERATE DSI is defined as a raw DSI reading of 26 through 74 percent.

4. LOW DSI is defined as a raw DSI reading of 25 through 11 percent.

5. EXTREMELY LOW DSI is defined as a raw DSI reading of 10 percent or less.

Again, please realize that to a certain extent these categories are arbitrary; however, levels 1 and 5 are based on considerable observation and study of the relationship between price and DSI.

Let's examine a few historical price charts and raw DSI within the parameters listed above. Figure 6-1 shows June 1989 Live Cattle futures daily closing price (top of chart) versus raw DSI (bottom of chart). I have marked a number of points with letters which correspond to a raw DSI reading of either HIGH or EXTREMELY HIGH. Note how well the highs in price correspond with the highs in DSI readings. As you can see from examining points A through L on price and on DSI, the correlation between extreme readings on raw DSI and price highs is very high. Clearly, the prices and DSI points do not correspond 100 percent of the time; however, the correlation is very high, possibly even uncanny. While this is a real example it is, to be sure, one of the better examples of price and DSI relationship.

Now examine the same figure for low DSI and price lows. These are represented by letters M through X on price and DSI. As you can see, the correlation here is not as precise if we use the 25 percent or less cut-off level. Note that at points S on price and DSI there was a succession of low DSI readings as prices continued to decline. The second lowest DSI on this chart at point T, however, corresponded almost perfectly with a major price low. Points W were not too significant, but the very low readings at X preceded a very large price rally. As you can see from this single observation, it may be that a lower level of DSI at market bottoms will be necessary as a cut-off point. Sentiment does not seem to be uniform at the extremes. It appears that a more negative level of sentiment is necessary at lows and that the preliminary definitions offered above will not suffice. Let's redefine as follows:

MODERATE DSI is now redefined as a raw DSI reading of 16 percent through 74 percent.

Figure 6-1 Raw DSI versus Tops and Bottoms in Price

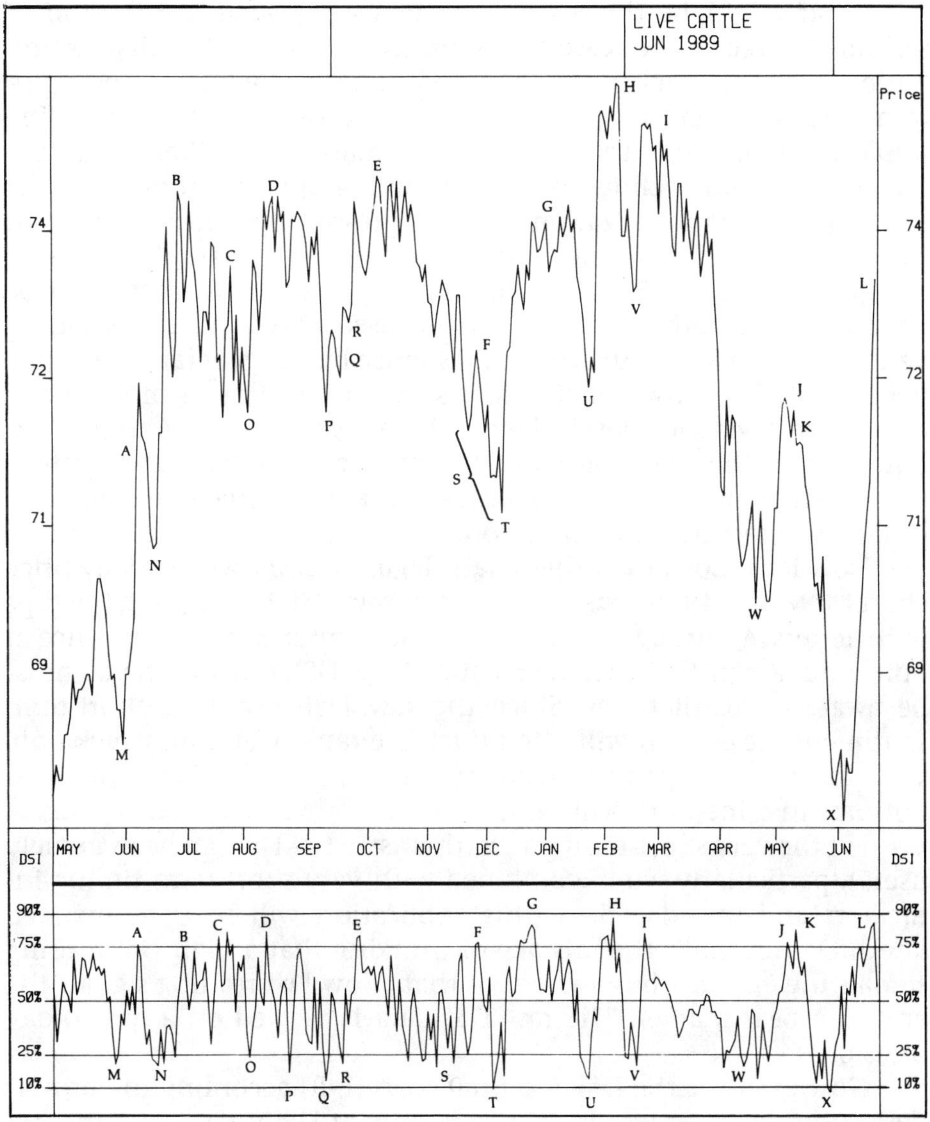

LOW DSI is now redefined as a raw DSI reading of 15 through 11 percent.

EXTREMELY LOW DSI is now redefined as a raw DSI reading of 10 percent or less.

What might be the reason for such a lopsided distribution of sentiment? While the reason may not seem apparent at first examination, a little thought shows this to be a perfectly logical finding in terms of market sentiment theory. We know for a fact that the trading public is enamored of the bullish side of markets. In other words, the public often sees declines in price as buying opportunities. Consider the following rationalization often expressed by bulls: "I thought cattle were cheap at 63 and so I bought the market. And if they were cheap at 63 then at 57, which is where they are now, they must be an even better buy." You may have used this kind of reasoning yourself. However, a truly bearish response by the general public may need to reach "gut-wrenching levels" or, to put this in more operational terms, very low levels, before the bulls can be convinced to sell out. This is the level we want to achieve in order to generate a meaningful barometer of market lows. It appears that the data does, in fact, support this interpretation.

Now let's look at another chart. Figure 6-2 shows the daily price chart for March 1990 Swiss Franc versus raw DSI. I've marked the tops with letters A through K. This is a most interesting chart since it points out a significant characteristic of raw DSI, one which you must be aware of at all times. Since the raw DSI is only a short-term sentiment measure, it will often fluctuate rapidly and may pick only very short-term tops in a major uptrend and only very short-term bottoms in a major downtrend.

For the very short-term trader, this aspect of DSI can be extremely useful, particularly when combined with very short-term timing indicators and intraday data (this application will be demonstrated later). Do not make the mistake of thinking that a high DSI reading signals the end of a bull market or that a low DSI reading signals the end of a bear market. The raw DSI data is viewed on a day-to-day basis only.

Now examine the DSI and price lows (L-R) according to our new definition. In other words, let's look only at DSI's of 15 percent and lower as indicators of possible short-term lows. With our new definition as the guideline, you can see a strong correlation between DSI lows and price lows. Again, I urge you to remember that raw DSI is

Figure 6-2 Raw DSI versus Tops and Bottoms in March 1990 Swiss Franc

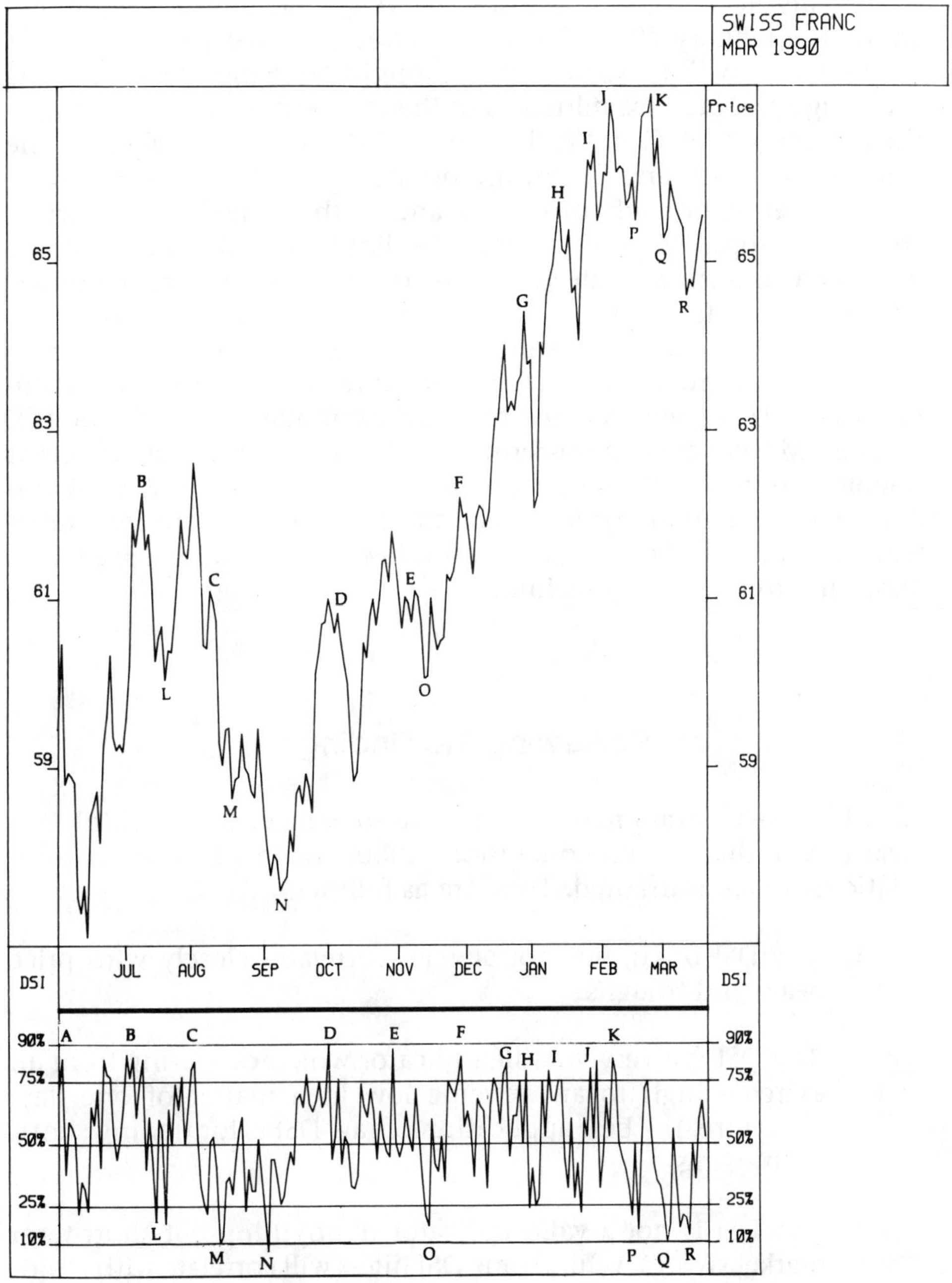

a highly sensitive and variable indicator which cannot be used as a guide to the end of bear markets.

Finally, let's examine a third DSI versus price chart. Figure 6-3 shows the January 1989 platinum futures chart daily closing prices versus daily raw DSI. I've marked the tops in price and DSI with letters A through J. A brief examination of the tops will show you that with the exception of B, C and F, the tops in DSI correlate closely with the tops in price. The single most important aspect of this chart is that, with the exception of tops A, D and I, the majority are merely short-term tops. As you can see, the limitation of using raw DSI without a confirming indicator tends to generate some false signals. The issue is to find a way which filters out a majority of the false signals while retaining the valid signals. This will be discussed later.

Now, examine the bottoms in the same figure. I've marked them K through U. As you can see from an examination of the lows, K through M were good short-term lows, N and O formed an excellent double bottom which preceded a major upswing, as did P. Q, R and S through U were minor lows. The major bottom in late September was missed by a DSI reading which was low, but not quite low enough according to our new guidelines.

Reviewing the Findings

Now that we've examined a few DSI versus price charts, I think it is clear to you that certain conclusions about the raw DSI versus price relationship are warranted. They are as follows:

1. Raw DSI often, but not always, correlates closely with price peaks and troughs.

2. Raw DSI is a very volatile indicator which can swing from an extreme high to an extreme low in a matter of one day. Therefore, the best application of raw DSI is for trading short-term swings.

3. Raw DSI is not a valid indicator of anything but short-term market swings. While some DSI highs will correlate with major

Figure 6-3 January 1989 Platinum versus Raw DSI at Tops and Bottoms

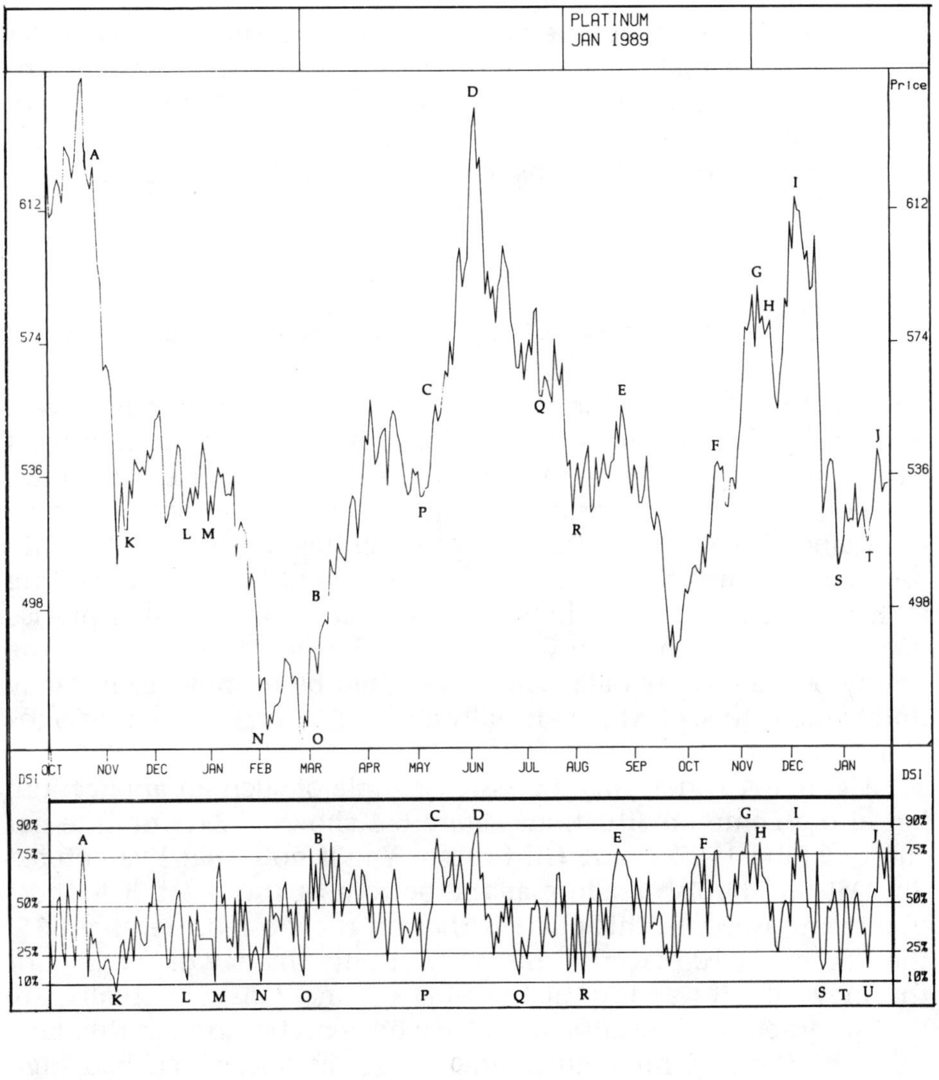

peaks and while some DSI lows will correlate with major bottoms, a majority of DSI peaks and troughs will correlate closely with short-term market swings due to the inherent nature of DSI.

4. The DSI extremes are not symmetrical. It often takes a lower DSI to signal a market upturn compared to the magnitude of DSI at market peaks. This is also due to the inherent nature of DSI and the respondent base. Now let's look at a few very short-term applications of raw DSI using intraday data.

Plotting Raw DSI Against Intraday Data

The examples I've given so far have shown raw DSI readings plotted against daily closing prices. This is not, however, the only way in which we may examine and employ the DSI. A closer examination of the relationship between DSI and market turning points can be ascertained from plotting the DSI against either half-hourly or hourly price data. By using such an approach you could employ DSI along with a variety of timing indicators in order to pinpoint a precise market turning point. Your first step would be to plot DSI against the hourly or half-hourly data. The next would be to move to intraday timing indicators, of which virtually all will suffice, to watch for signs of a turn.

Figure 6-4 is not only a classic example of such an application, but also a common situation. Figure 6-4 shows a sixty-minute bar chart of June 1992 Crude Oil futures. You'll note that I've entered the DSI "%" bullish reading at the bottom of the chart. The most significant aspect of this chart is that on the close of trading 4/15, the DSI was at 10 percent. This was not only the day of the low for this move, but it was also the lowest DSI in many days. Virtually any timing system or indicator would have been able to pick this turn once the DSI had highlighted the market as one which had high probability of changing trend.

For another example of DSI application with timing, consider Figure 6-5. Although it is a bit more complicated than the others, it quite clearly demonstrates the relationship between price turns and

Figure 6-4 Daily Sentiment, Lows and Highs in Crude Oil Futures

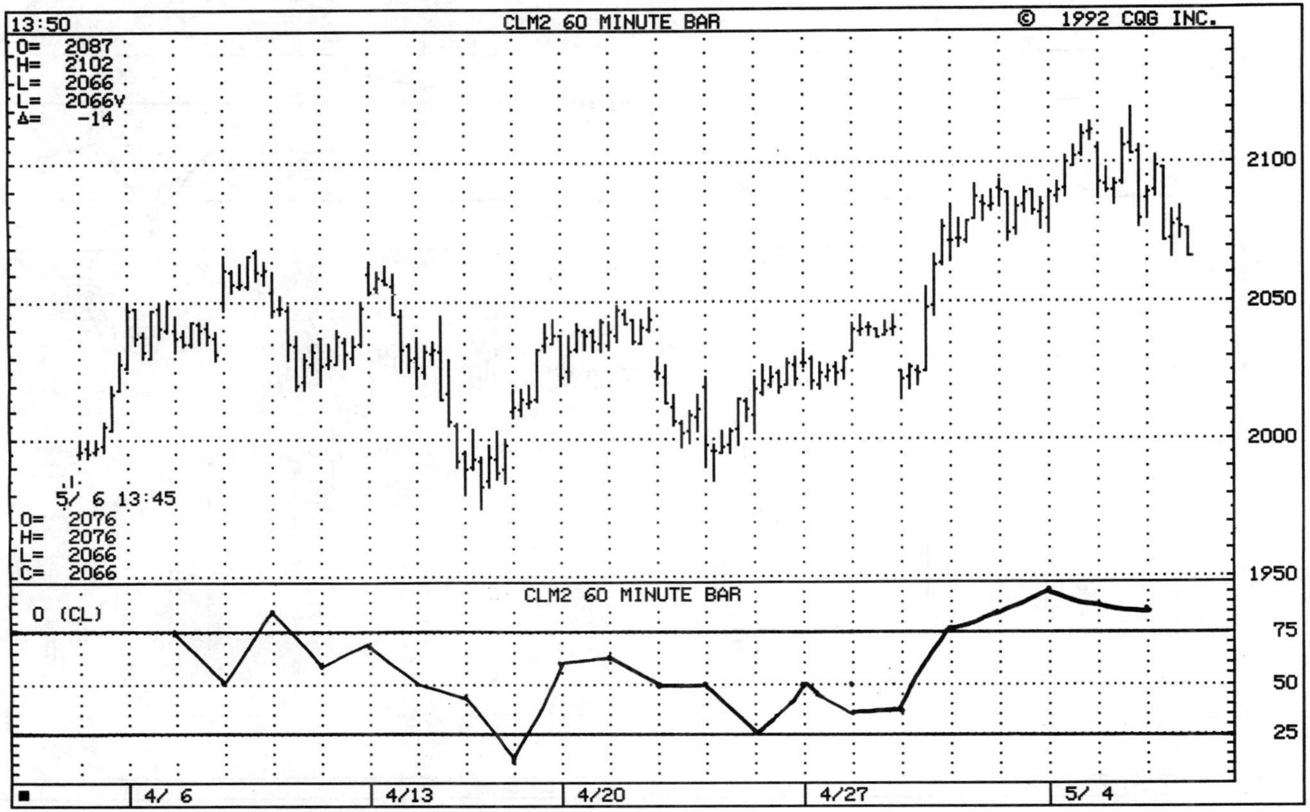

 (DSI added to chart manually.)

Figure 6-5 June 1992 60-Minute Swiss Franc and Daily DSI

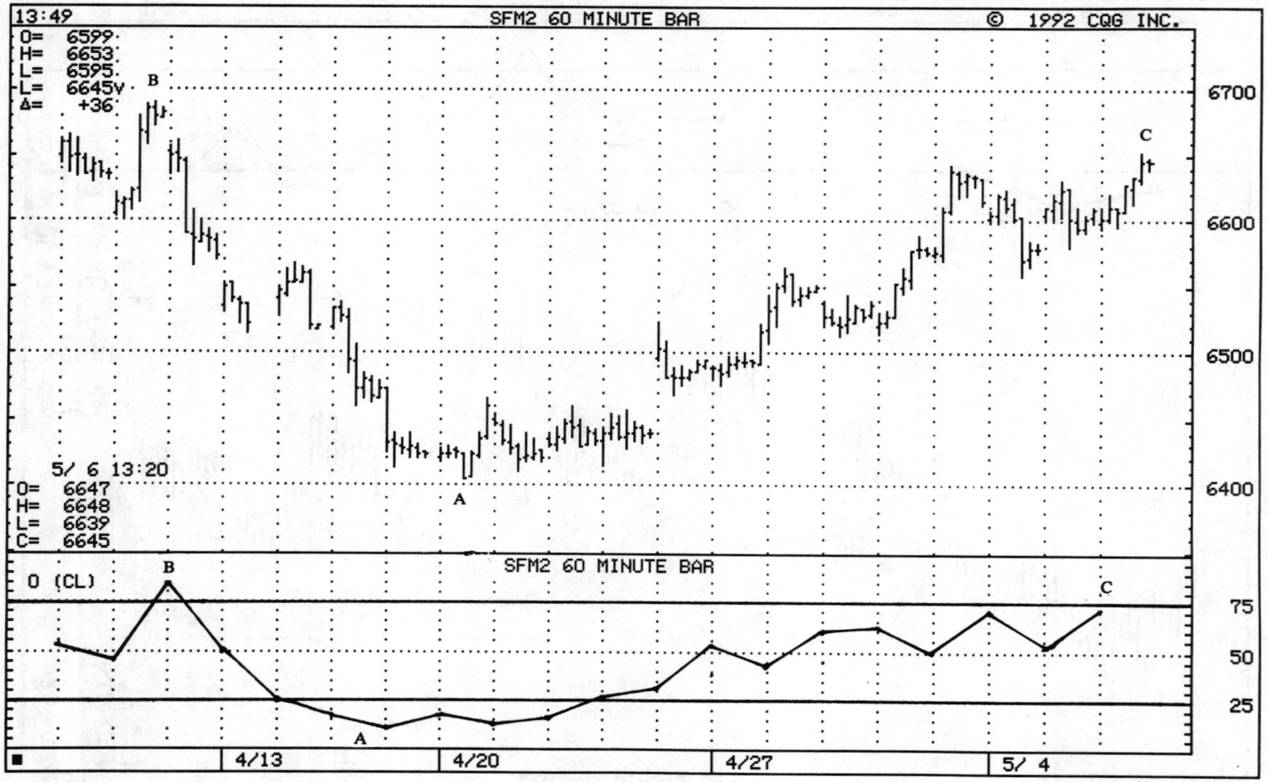

©1992 CQG Inc. Reprinted with permission. (DSI added to chart manually.)

DSI. First, note DSI low A and price low A. Note also top B in price and its correlation to DSI top B were in very close proximity. Finally, note that a persistent rally through point C was not accompanied by an excessively high DSI reading, suggesting that the move up was likely to continue. This is a classic situation in terms of DSI and short-term price swings.

Figure 6-6 shows the analysis of DSI and December 1992 corn futures, sixty-minute data versus daily DSI. The decline in corn prices from late March was persistent following a very high DSI on March 9, 1992 of 91 percent. The chart shows that although DSI fell to very low levels on several occasions, the market did not bottom. This is why DSI should be used in association with a timing indicator or indicators.

Using Raw DSI to Select Short-Term Trading Opportunities

If you're a short-term trader, then I suggest you consider using the raw DSI as an aid to selecting trading opportunities. Consider the following applications. DSI can:

1. Help you pinpoint markets which have a high probability of changing trend.

2. Help you avoid taking trades on the long side of markets which are reading too high on DSI or short positions in markets which are reading too low on DSI.

3. Help you be selective about markets, focusing on those markets which are most likely to make large moves and/or change direction very soon.

4. Help you develop new timing indicators using derivations of the DSI raw data (for example, moving averages of the DSI).

Figure 6-6 Hourly December 1992 Corn Futures versus DSI

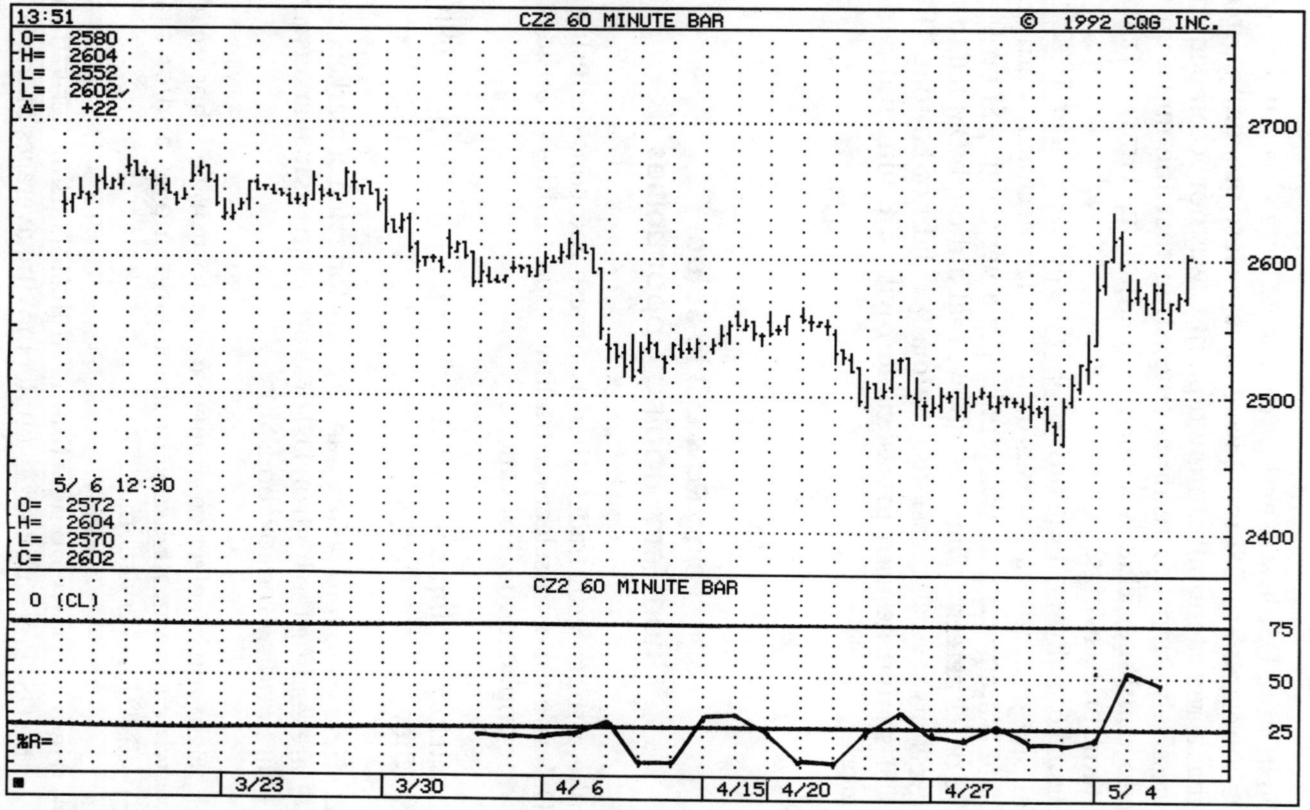

©1992 CQG Inc. Reprinted with permission. (DSI added to chart manually.)

Raw DSI and the News

As you can imagine, there is a close relationship between daily market sentiment and news. Based on DSI theory as stated herein, the DSI and news should relate to one another as follows:

1. *Bullish News.* There is bullish news and there is **bullish** news. News which is extraordinarily bullish often arouses emotional market reactions which correlate closely with high DSI readings. The combination of bullish news, already existing uptrend and high DSI, therefore, should result in a declining market as opposed to a rising one.

2. *DSI and Bearish News.* Conversely, bearish news, a declining market, and a low DSI reading is the combination of which important short-term lows are made.

I suggest that you take some time to observe the relationship between news, trend and DSI. I guarantee that you'll find some most interesting and profitable relationships. Remember, though, that these are primarily short-term conditions, in so far as the market is subject to the whims of traders and their expectations.

While there will be instances in which extreme sentiment will correlate exactly with important tops and bottoms, this is not a rule. Since markets are fueled by emotions, and since DSI is a derivative of emotions, it is not an exact indicator. As a guide to probable price direction, however, DSI is indispensable.

Finally, don't ignore the value of experience. Since the use of DSI is not a mechanical procedure, it requires an experienced trader to put it to its best use.

CHAPTER 7

A "Diamond in the Rough"

The raw DSI is like a diamond in the rough. It does not appear to have much value at first blush since it is unrefined, unpolished and has many jagged edges. In order to make the DSI shine, it must be changed from its raw form into any of several altered states. This process will allow us to view the DSI at peak performance. While there are several aspects of the raw DSI which have considerable value, the majority of DSI applications necessitate the use of derivations of the raw DSI data. In this chapter I will discuss some of these variations and illustrate the reasons for their use.

Slowing the DSI

The raw DSI is an unbridled index of trader emotion. Like emotion, it is highly variable, whimsical and subject to sudden change. While the emotional component of each futures market is precisely what we want to assess, we do not want to be caught in some of the positive and negative swings in emotion which are not significantly related to price movement. As I've indicated previously, one important use of the DSI is at market tops and bottoms, which often correlate with extremes in DSI readings. Figure 7-1 shows the raw DSI and nine-day MA of DSI for Eurodollar futures plotted against daily closing prices. As you can see, the raw DSI is highly variable, swinging repeatedly from one extreme to another. Some of the extremes do not correlate well with market tops and bottoms.

By slowing the raw DSI, however, we arrive at a much more "relaxed" picture of DSI versus price. In order to slow or mute the variability of DSI, I suggest using one of several moving averages of the raw DSI data. The trick is to use a moving average which will be slow enough to do the job without being so slow as to mask or entirely filter out the emotional component of DSI. I have found that either a three-, five-, or nine-day MA can do the job. Note that the longer the moving average you use, the more muted will be the DSI extremes. In other words, the use of moving averages will limit how high or how low the DSI can go. The larger the moving average, the smoother will be the continuous DSI plot, and the less likely it will be to move beyond 85 percent or 15 percent. Figure 7-2 shows July 1989 cotton versus a five- and nine-day MA of the DSI. As you can see, the tops and bottoms in price and DSI show a much closer correlation and there is less volatility in the DSI index, as we would expect. Note in particular the extremes which I've marked by letters A–L.

Indexing DSI

Yet another way to slow the DSI is to use an indexing method. In other words, the raw DSI readings are converted to index values, each of which correspond to a specific range of DSI values. To index by units of ten, for example, the following conversions would be used:

DSI	Index Value
0-10	1
11-20	2
21-30	3
31-40	4
41-50	5
51-60	6
61-70	7
71-80	8
81-90	9
91-100	10

Figure 7-1 Raw and 9-Day MA of DSI versus December 1991 Eurodollar Futures

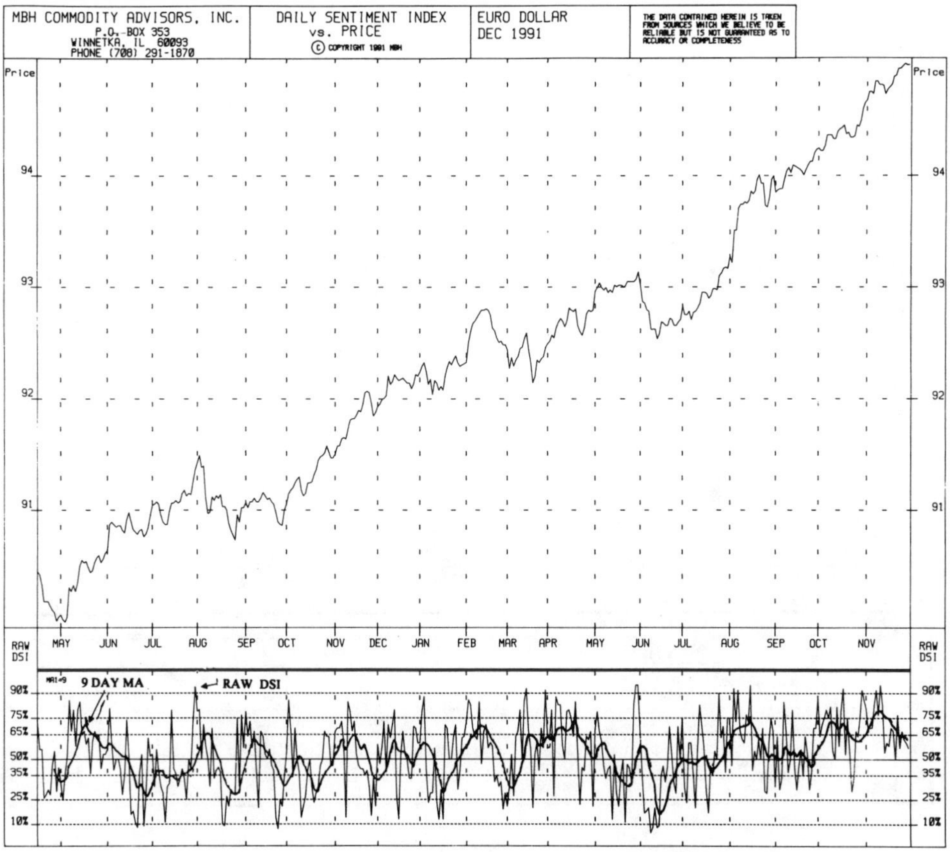

Figure 7-2 Slowed DSI versus July 1989 Cotton

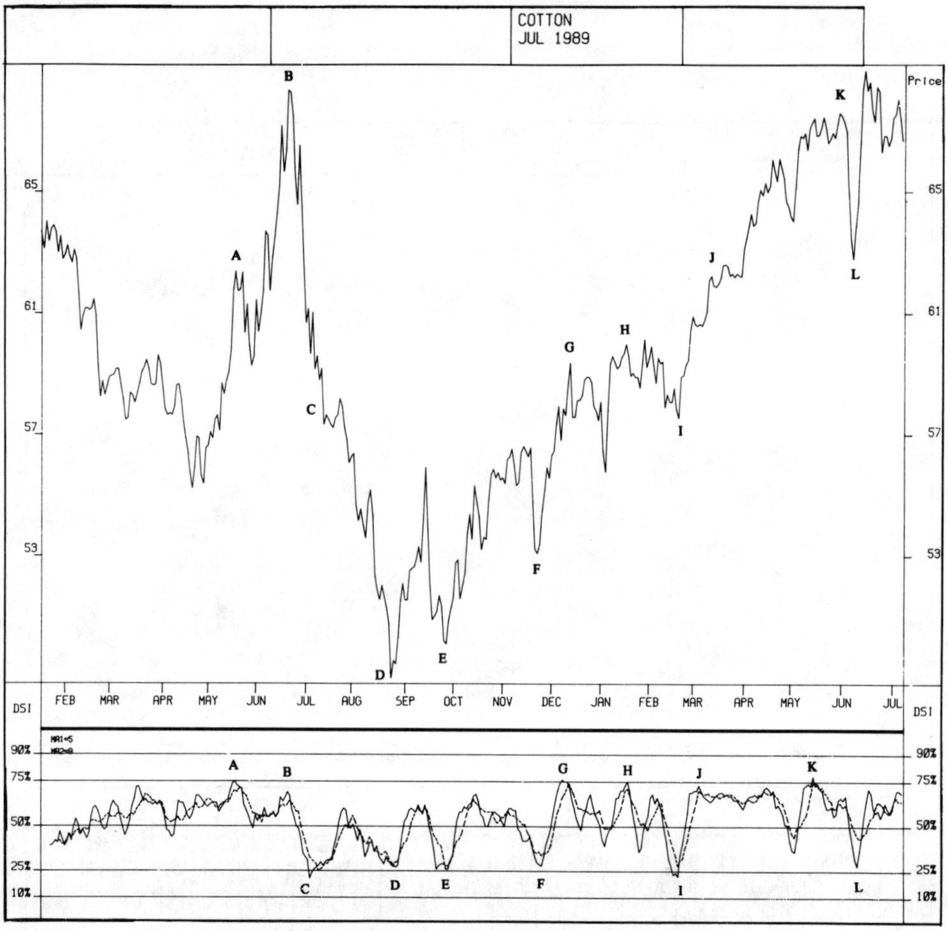

It's not perfect (see points C and J), but it *is* a valuable indicator.

This method eliminates the jagged day-to-day variations by assigning raw DSI readings to different quanta. You may also wish to experiment with different levels, such as five levels of twenty DSI units each. Another approach to indexing would be to use uneven levels, assigning more importance to readings within certain ranges. Figures 7-3 and 7-4 show a comparison between raw DSI, three-day MA of DSI, five-day MA of DSI, nine-day MA of DSI and the decile index of DSI for the same market.

Weekly DSI Readings

Another way to slow the DSI is to convert the daily readings into weekly readings and to then plot the weekly readings against price. As you can imagine, this will exert a significant slowing influence on the DSI, balancing off the intra-week extremes and allowing the DSI to climb or drop to extremes only when extreme optimism or pessimism have continued for a lengthy period of time. Such an application is ideal for longer term traders and should, theoretically, allow us to spot more important highs and lows.

Figures 7-5 and 7-6 show extreme weekly average DSI values (five-day simple average of daily DSI readings) at significant turning points.

Monthly DSI Readings

The use of monthly average DSI readings may also be beneficial to long-term traders; however, the current base of DSI data is not sufficiently lengthy to permit an evaluation of this application. This will be a good area for further investigation once we have accumulated several more years' worth of DSI readings. Using a monthly average, on the other hand, could result in so significant a slowing of DSI that emotional extremes could be entirely erased, so consider this in your studies if you decide to use a monthly approach.

Figure 7-3 Comparing DSI and MA's of DSI

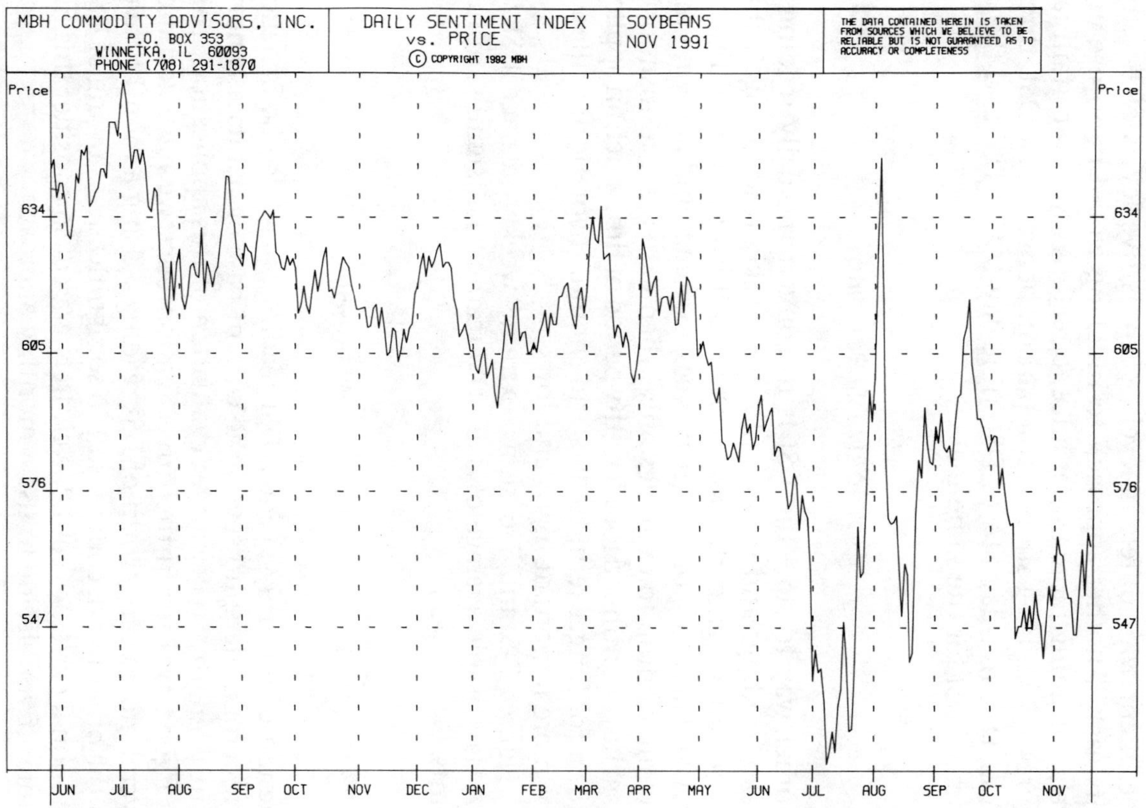

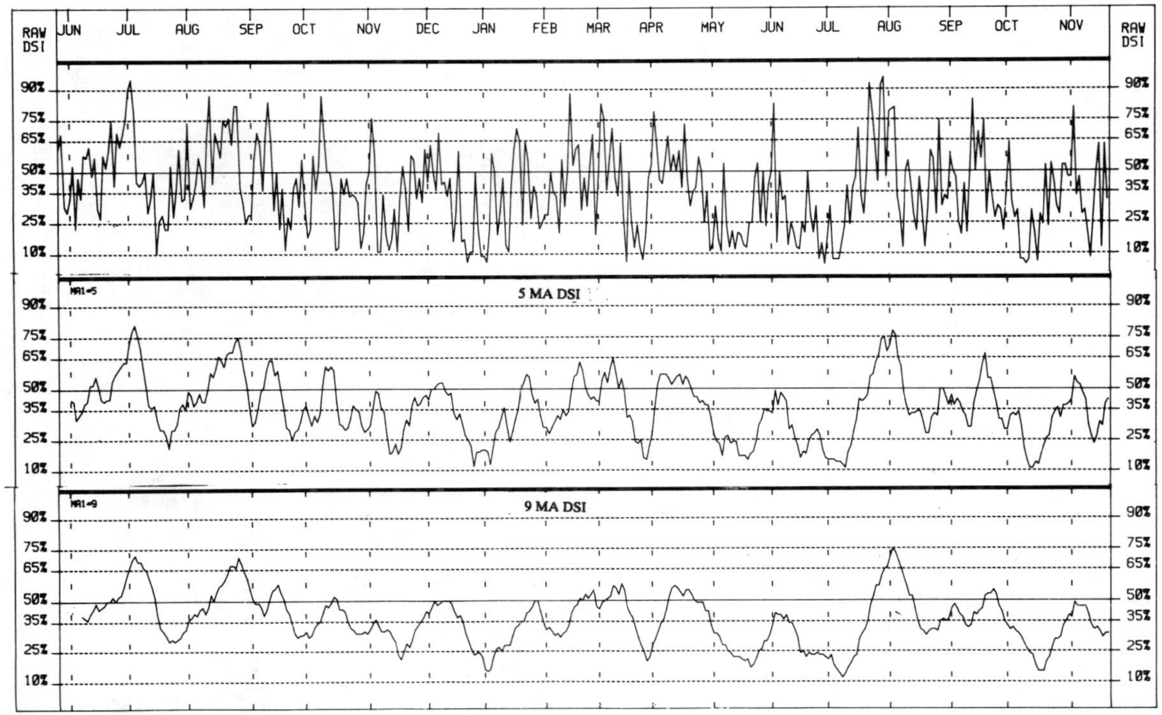
RAW DSI
JUN
JUL
AUG
SEP
OCT
NOV
DEC
JAN
FEB
MAR
APR
MAY
JUN
JUL
AUG
SEP
OCT
NOV
90%
75%
65%
50%
35%
25%
10%
5 MA DSI
MA1=5
9 MA DSI
MA1=9

Figure 7-4 Comparing DSI and MA's of DSI

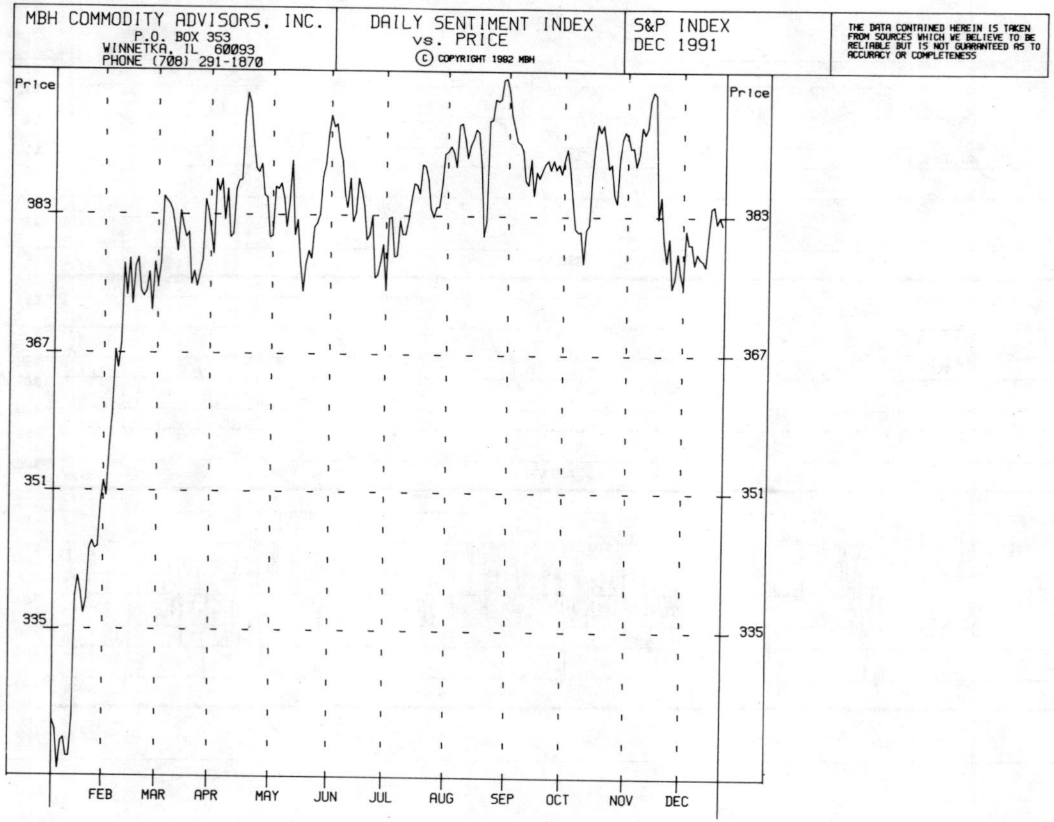

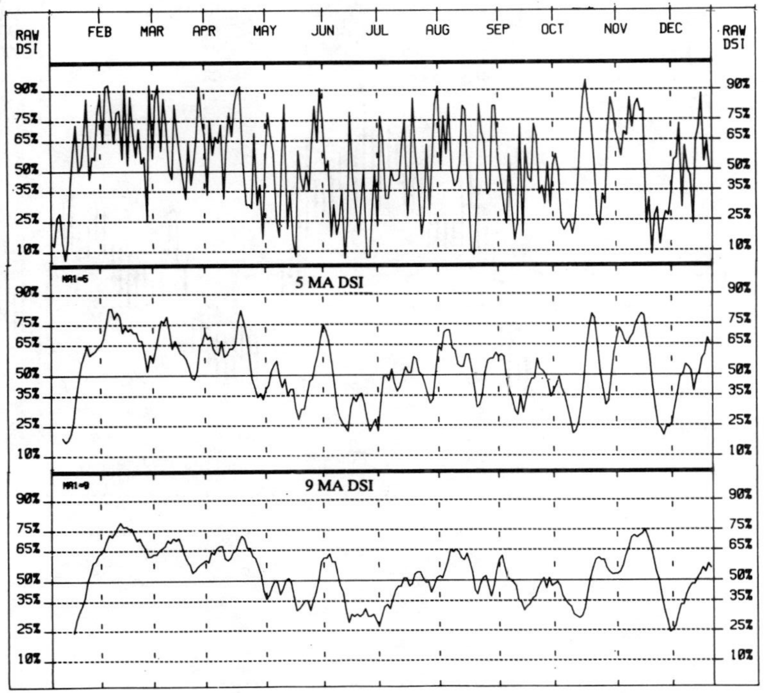

RAW DSI
FEB
MAR
APR
MAY
JUN
JUL
AUG
SEP
OCT
NOV
DEC
90%
75%
65%
50%
35%
25%
10%
5 MA DSI
9 MA DSI

Figure 7-5

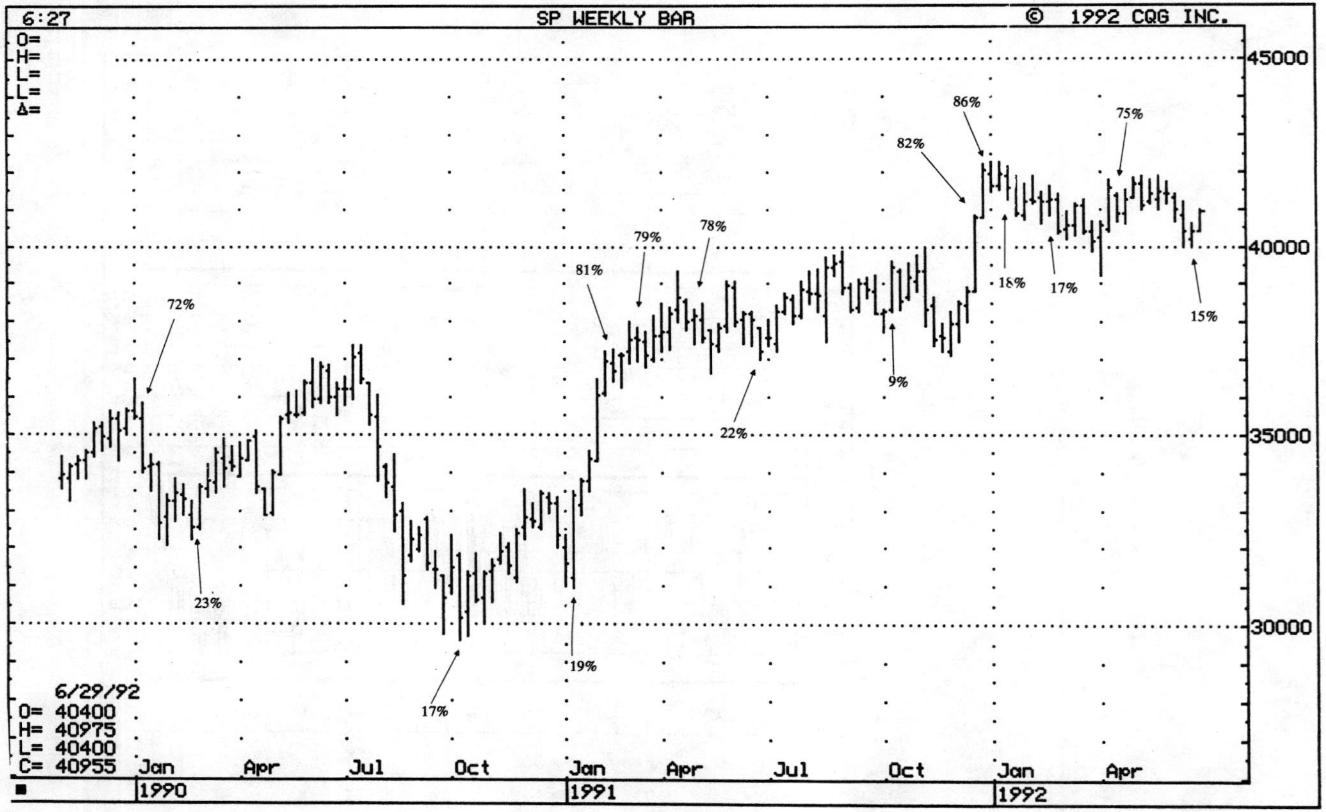
6:27
SP WEEKLY BAR
© 1992 CQG INC.
O=
H=
L=
L=
Δ=
45000
40000
35000
30000
72%
23%
17%
19%
81%
79%
78%
22%
9%
82%
86%
18%
17%
75%
15%
6/29/92
O= 40400
H= 40975
L= 40400
C= 40955
Jan
Apr
Jul
Oct
Jan
Apr
Jul
Oct
Jan
Apr
1990
1991
1992

Figure 7-6

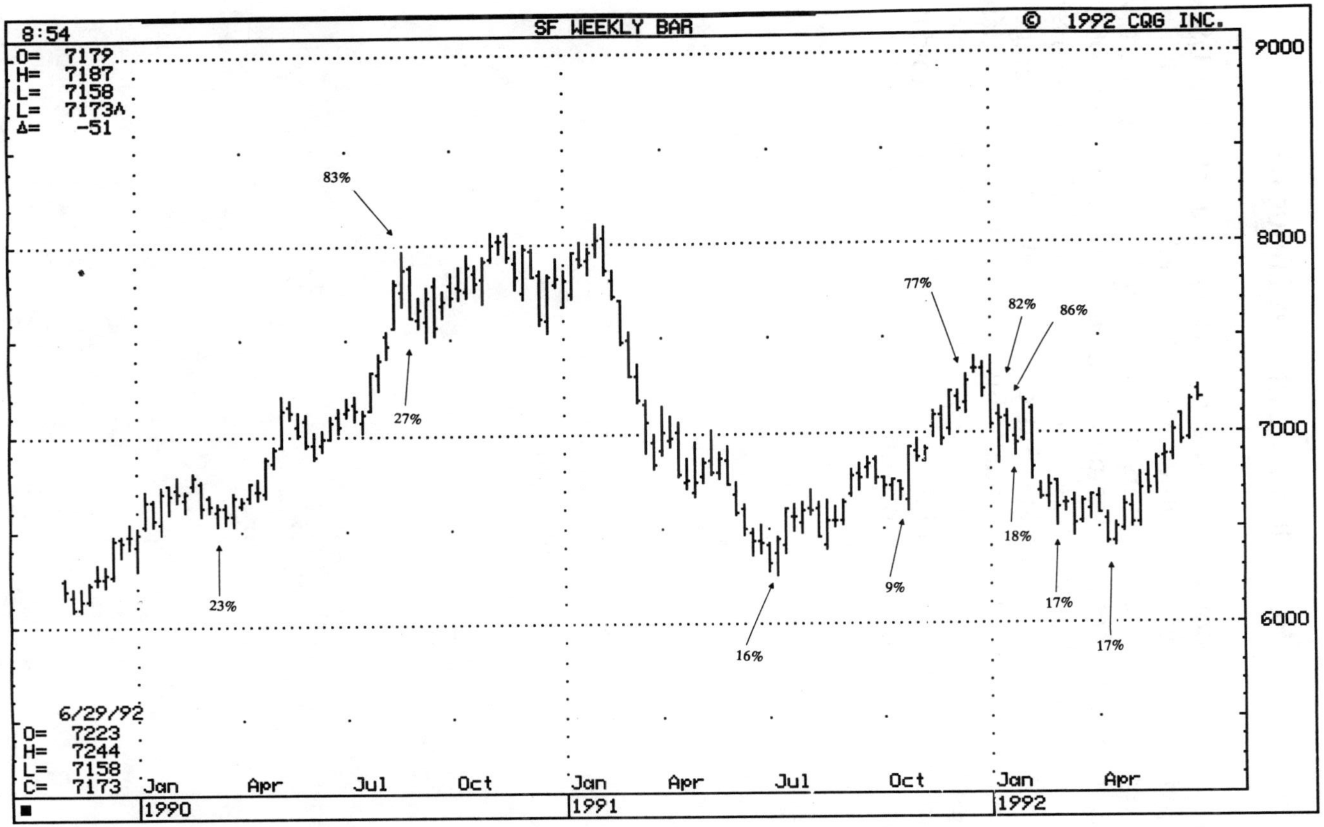
8:54
SF WEEKLY BAR
© 1992 CQG INC.
O= 7179
H= 7187
L= 7158
L= 7173A
Δ= -51
9000
8000
7000
6000
83%
27%
23%
16%
9%
77%
82%
86%
18%
17%
17%
6/29/92
O= 7223
H= 7244
L= 7158
C= 7173
Jan
Apr
Jul
Oct
Jan
Apr
Jul
Oct
Jan
Apr
1990
1991
1992

How Much Slowing Is Enough?

The degree of slowing or indexing which is applied to DSI is an individual matter, one which must be resolved by the individual trader within the constraints of his or her trading approach. While this chapter has described some specific methods of slowing DSI, there are others which may be used, including weighted moving averages, smoothed moving averages and exponential moving averages. Appendix I contains the entire daily history of DSI through the date this manuscript was completed. I encourage you to experiment with various methods of manipulating the raw data. The up-to-date DSI history is available from my office on computer disk or printout.

CHAPTER 8

Additional Application Principles of the DSI

DSI as an Indicator of "Overbought" or "Oversold"

Over the years, the terms "overbought" and "oversold" have been used to describe markets which, in the opinion of the trader or market analyst, have moved "too high" or "too low" in price. This is, of course, a subjective interpretation of markets which has often been supported by reference to various technical indicators. The very use of the terms tends to foster a psychological set which dissuades traders from buying when they suspect that a market is "overbought" or persuades them to sell short simply because they suspect that prices are too high. Conversely, when a market is considered "oversold," traders are dissuaded from selling short and are often encouraged to buy because they suspect that prices are too low and cannot, therefore, go much lower.

As I have indicated earlier, these terms are subjective. We find in practice that prices tend to continue even higher once they are overbought and even lower once they are considered oversold. A classic illustration derives from the use of stochastics, a popular indicator developed by George Lane.[1] Since the stochastic indicator (SI) is measured in percentage, its limits range from zero to 100. Typically, when stochastic reaches 75 percent or higher, traders become concerned that the SI is too high and that the particular market therefore, is too high or overbought. Thus, they are afraid to buy and, in fact, may be encouraged to sell short. In practice we find that when the SI reaches 75 percent or higher, prices tend frequently to continue to move higher—at times, considerably higher. Figure 8-1 illustrates this condition, which I have appropriately named the "POP" stochastic.

On the other hand, a market which reaches 25 percent on stochastic tends to continue lower regardless of how "oversold" traders feel it is. The fact that SI reads low does not in and of itself indicate that the market has made its low. Figure 8-2 illustrates another stochastic POP condition.

The DSI as an indicator of contrary opinion tends to behave in very much the same fashion as does SI; the correlation between persistently high DSI or low DSI readings and market tops and bottoms respectively is very high. This is true for the SI as well. However, with the DSI there is a marked tendency for high and low readings to be relatively short-lived and for the markets to respond in the direction of DSI rather quickly. In other words, when the DSI climbs to an 80 percent level or higher and then turns lower, price tends to follow suit quickly. And when DSI drops to the 20 percent level or lower and then turns higher, so do prices. As you know, the correlation between these events is not 100 percent; however, as can be seen, the evidence supports many claims that, in spite of its limitations—limitations which are inherent in every market indicator—the DSI is a very valuable tool.

Illustrations of the overbought and oversold relationship between price and DSI are shown in Figures 8-3 through 8-6. In particular, note the fairly short period of time that prices remain in an up or down trend once DSI has reached an extreme level. Remember that by an "extreme" level I mean specifically in excess of 80 percent or less than 20 percent.

---

1. Dr. George Lane, Investment Educators, 719 S. Fourth St., Watseka, IL 60970.

Figure 8-1 The Stochastic "POP" Indicator Showing Buy Signals (B), Sell Signals (S), Cover Short (CS), and Close (CL)

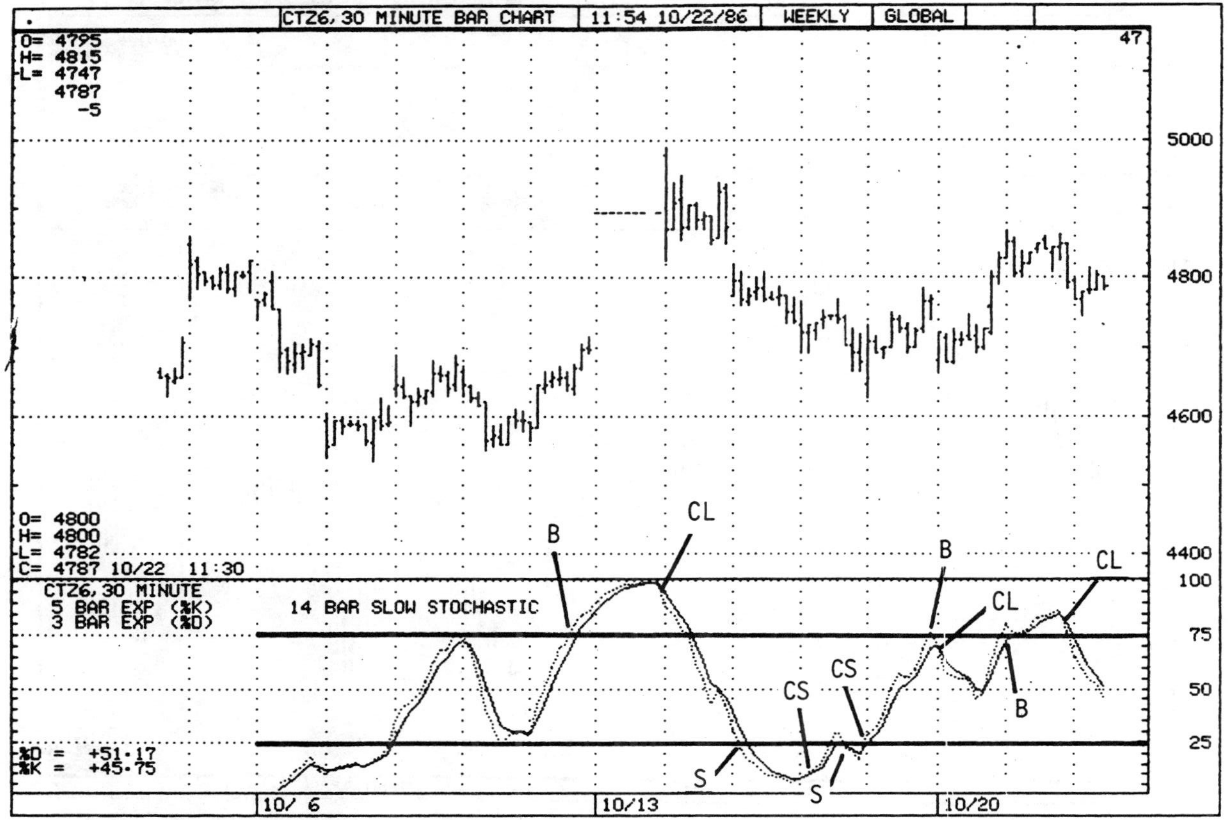

Chart reprinted with permission of CQG Inc.

Figure 8-2 Daily POP Signals S&P Futures

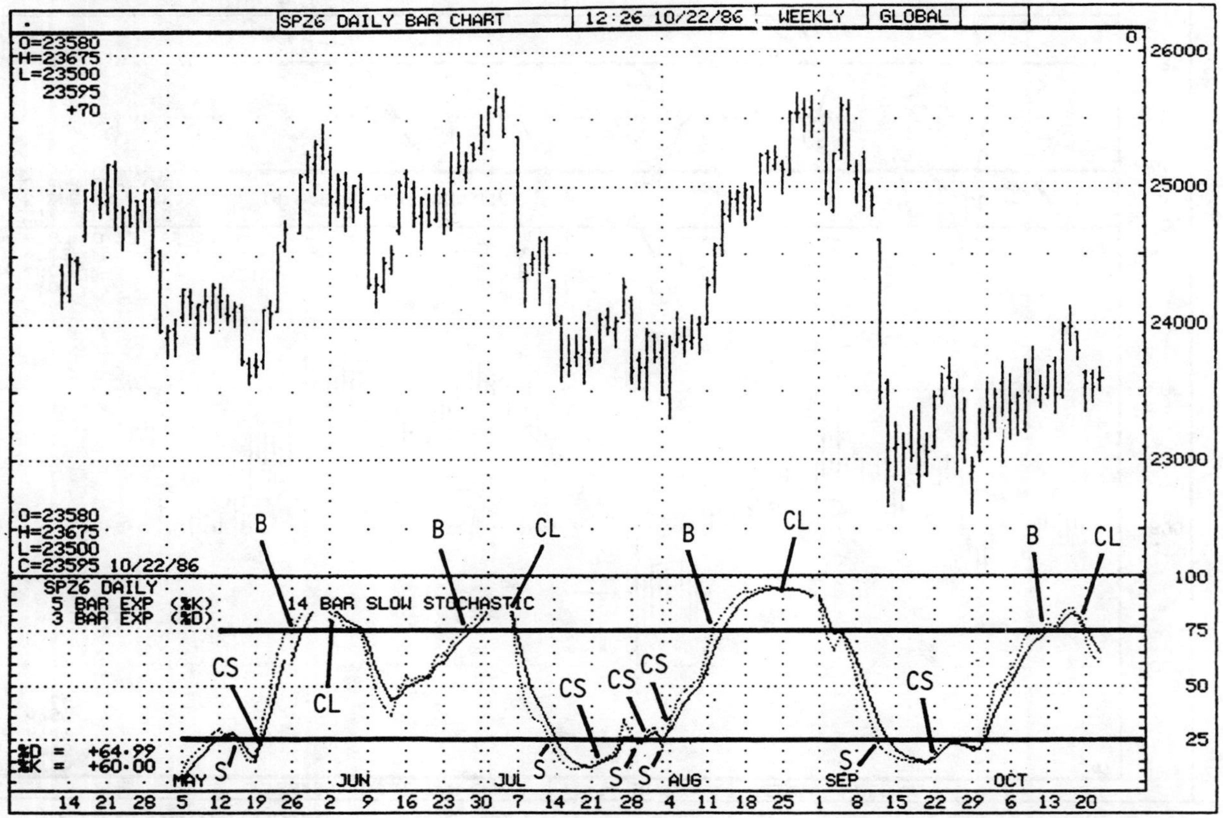

Note the tendency for prices to continue lower following a 25% stochastic.

Chart reprinted with permission of CQG Inc.

Figure 8-3 March 1992 Yen versus Raw DSI

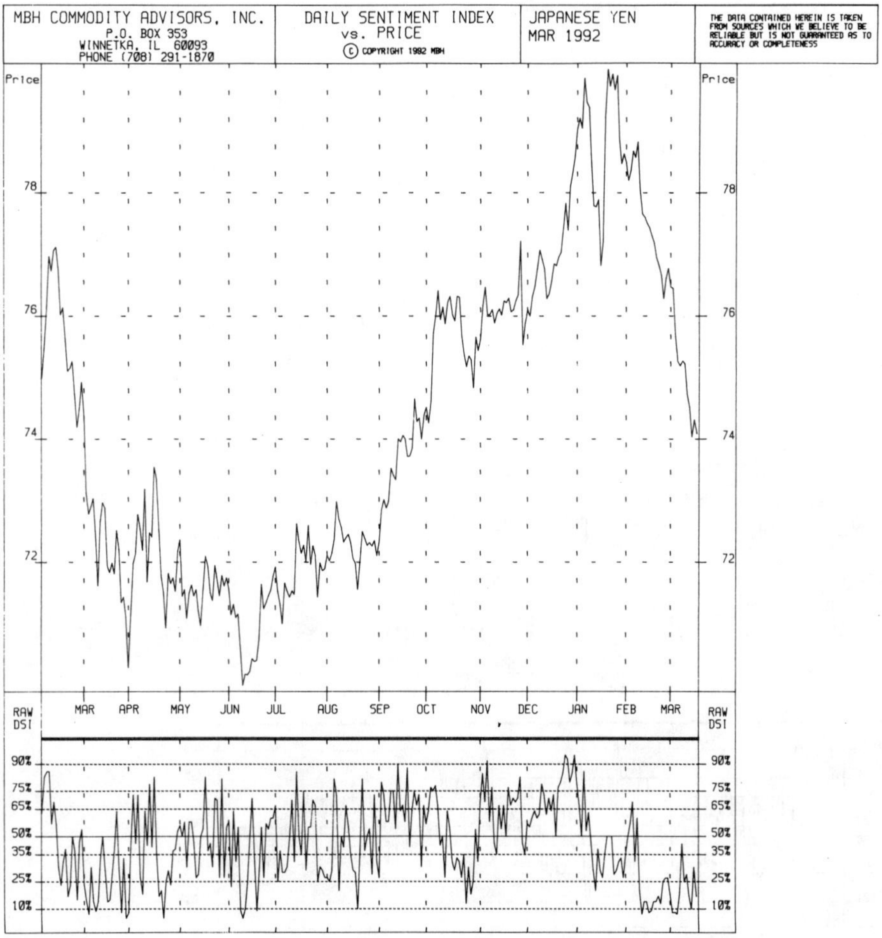

Figure 8-4 March 1992 S&P versus Raw DSI

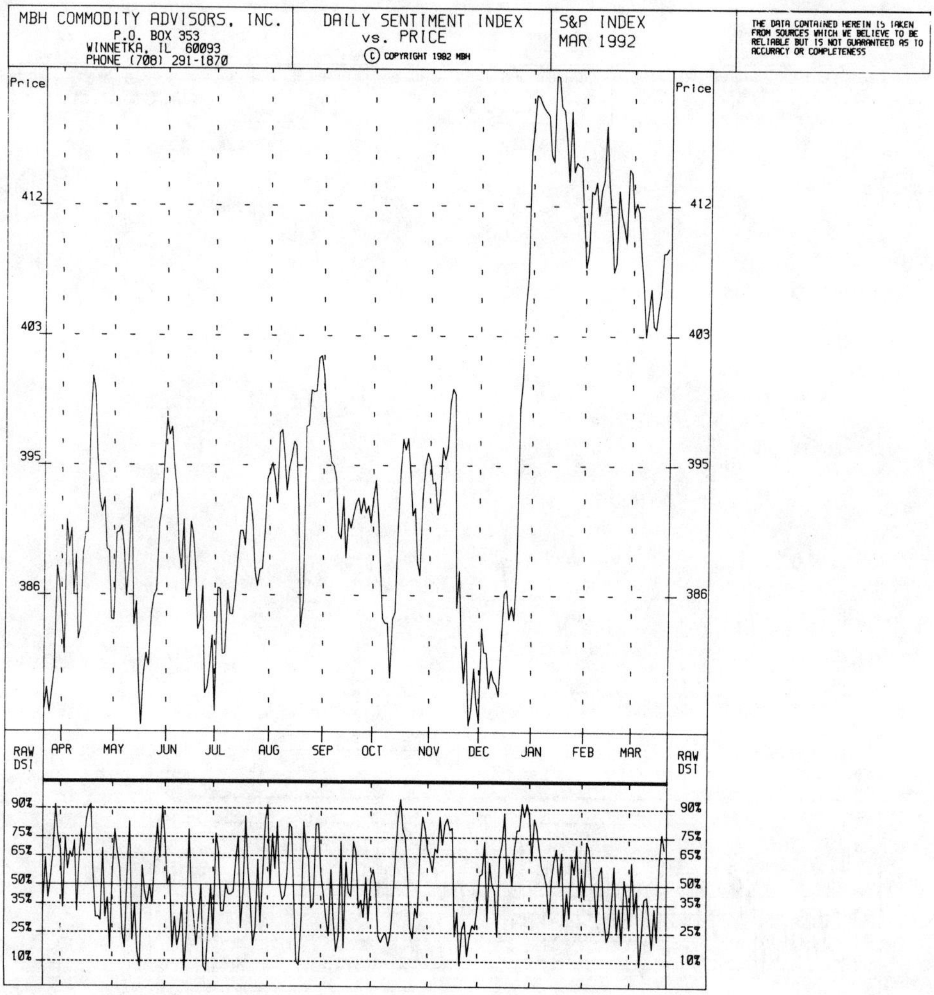

Figure 8-5 March 1992 T-Bonds versus Raw DSI

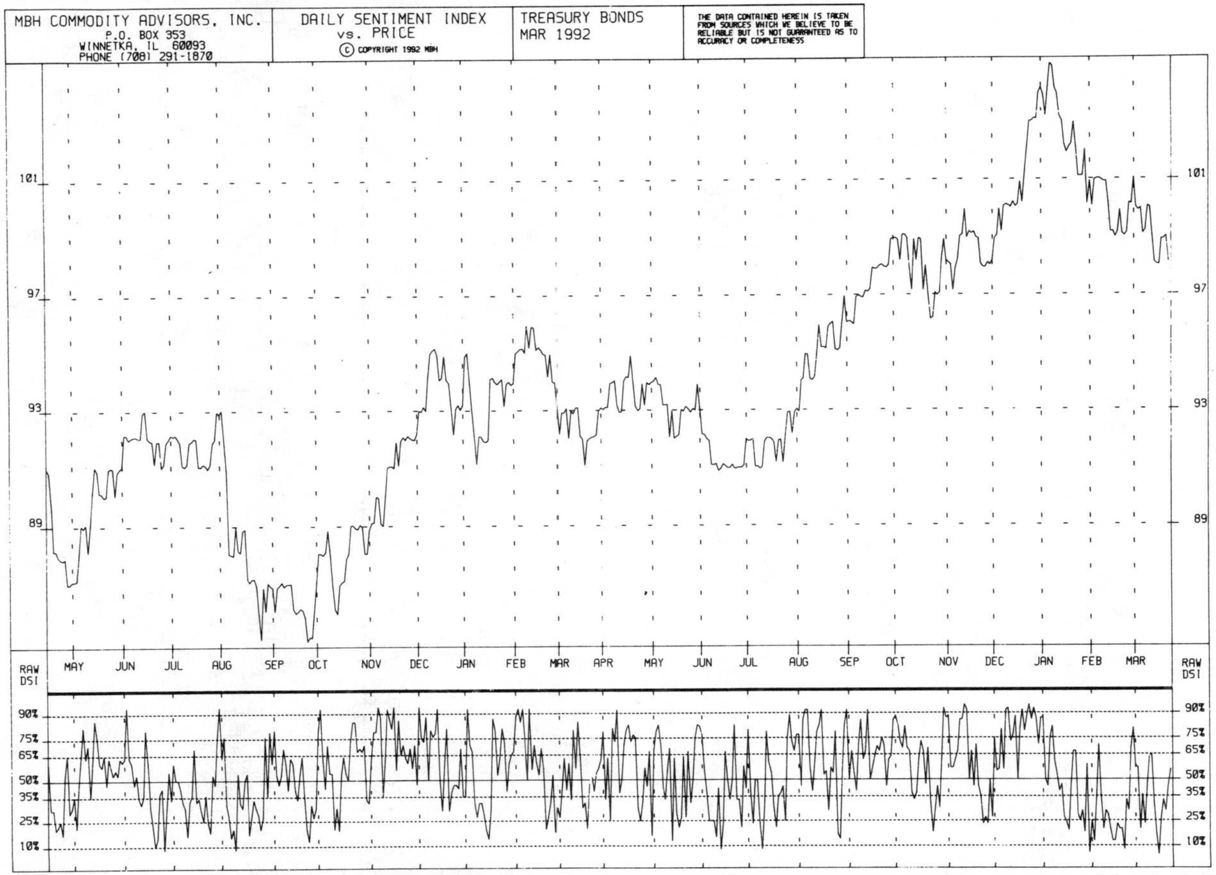

Figure 8-6 February 1992 Cattle versus Raw DSI

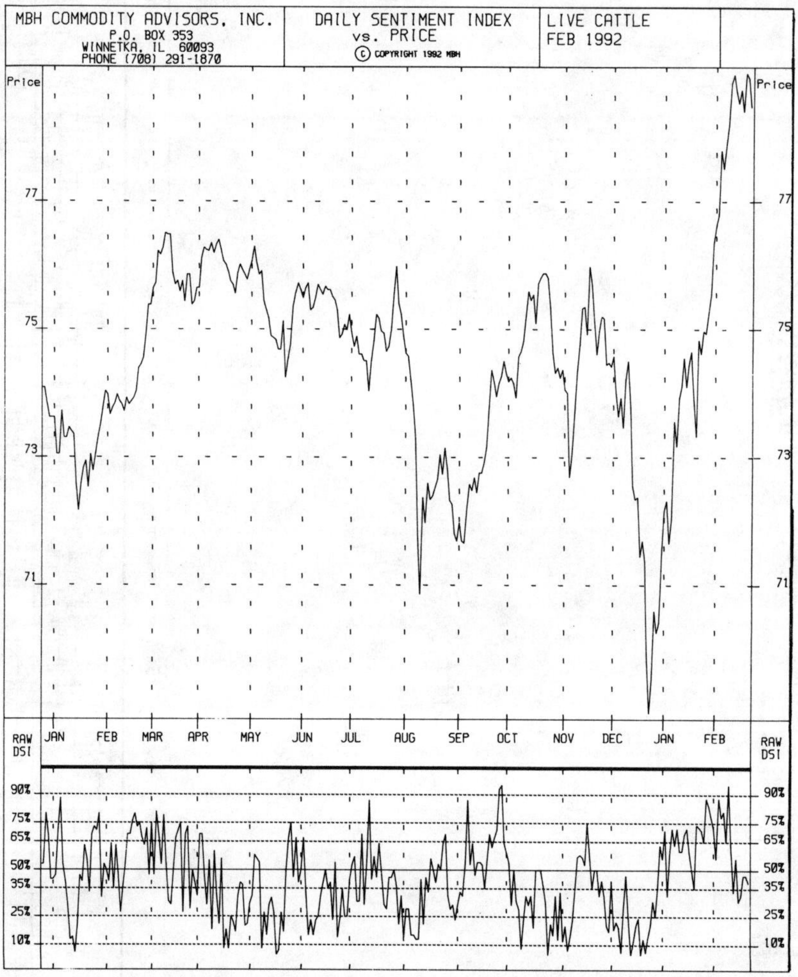

Smoothing DSI for Use as an Overbought/Oversold Index

Another method of application for DSI as an indicator of overbought or oversold markets is to convert the raw DSI readings into either three- or five-day moving averages. This tends to remove the jagged peaks and troughs of DSI and builds in a time lag factor in order to slow down its movement, peaks and troughs. Furthermore, it limits the effect of a one- or two-day sharp rise or drop. The result of slowing the movement of DSI is to avoid brief up or down moves in price and to concentrate upon more significant moves.

Figure 8-7 shows the ideal relationship between price, DSI, a three-day moving average of DSI and a five-day moving average of DSI. As you can see from this illustration, the application of a moving average tends to limit the number of times DSI climbs to an extreme. As you can also see from close examination of Figure 8-7, the extremes of DSI should be changed from 80 percent to 75 percent and from 20 percent to 25 percent if using the smoothing approach. Figures 8-8 and 8-9 show two price charts with moving averages of DSI. Take a few minutes to examine these charts in order to appreciate the very dramatic effect which moving average smoothing has upon the DSI. You may wish to experiment with moving averages and cutoff levels (i.e., the 80 percent and 20 percent levels) of your own, since this aspect of DSI has received less attention than other applications.

If you prefer to use the DSI as a monitoring device of overbought or oversold conditions, then I suggest the following procedure. Every afternoon when the readings are compiled (either by yourself or by my service), study them closely and highlight all readings of 20 percent and lower and all readings of 80 percent and higher. Then mark the three- and five-day moving averages 75 percent and above and 25 percent and below. Note the highest reading and the lowest reading. These are the markets which have the greatest probability of turning in the opposite direction. Once you have isolated the markets showing extreme readings, put them on your "watch list." You should monitor these markets very closely either in the EFP (overnight) markets or during the next day's trading. The advent of 24-hour trading through Globex could prove very helpful in maximizing DSI performance.

Figure 8-7 Ideal Relationship between Price, 5- and 9-Day MA of DSI

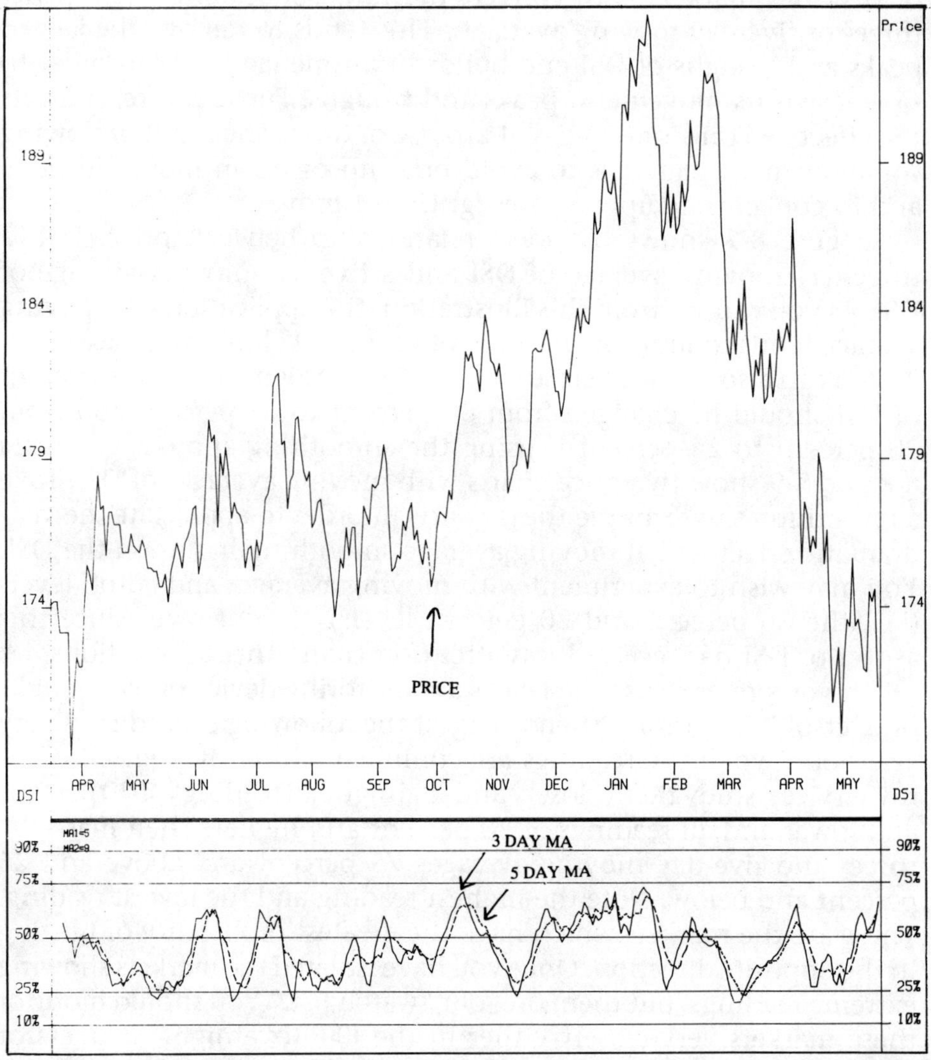

Figure 8-8 June Live Hogs versus 5- and 9-Day MA's of DSI

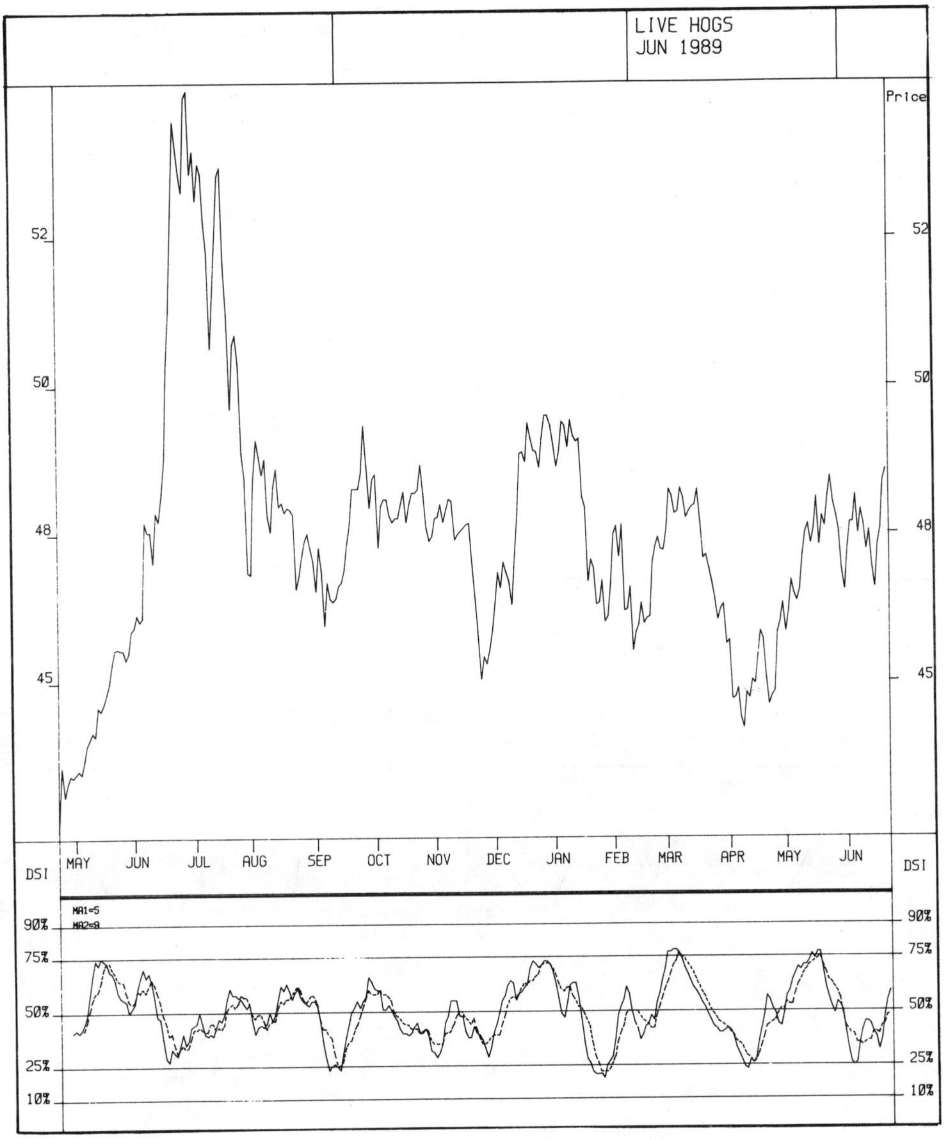

Note close correlation of tops and bottoms.

Figure 8-9 **March 1989 Coffee versus 5- and 9-Day MA's of DSI**

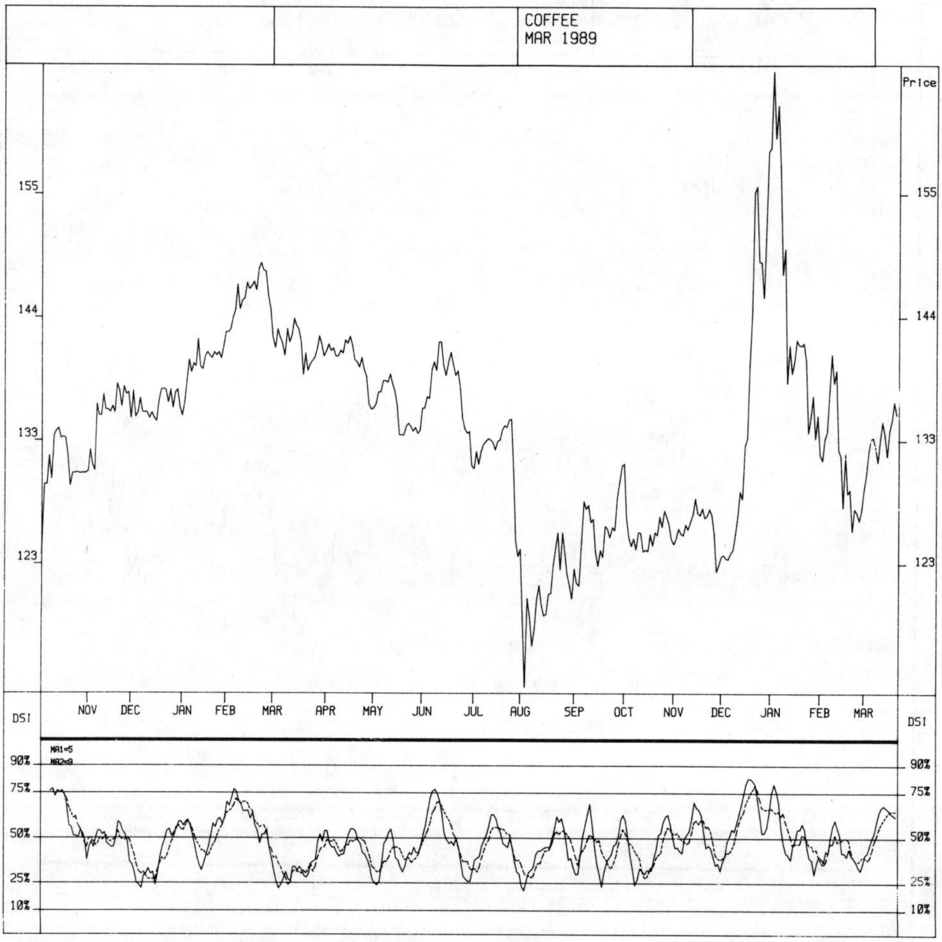

Note close correlation of tops and bottoms.

CHAPTER 9

The DSI, Bullish Divergence and Bearish Divergence

Perhaps one of the most promising applications of DSI is its ability to accurately pinpoint divergence tops and bottoms. Let's define bullish and bearish divergence. These definitions apply to raw as well as smoothed DSI.

Bullish DSI divergence is defined as a situation in which price has been in a declining trend and forms a low. This low is followed by another, lower low, shortly after the first low. At the same time, the DSI forms a first low, but then makes a second low which is higher than the first low. The divergence here is between the second price low (which is lower than the first low) and the second DSI low (which is higher than the first DSI low). This condition is illustrated in Figure 9-1, which shows several divergence lows.

Bearish DSI divergence is defined as a situation in which price has been in a rising trend and forms a top. This top is followed by another, higher top, shortly after the first top. At the same time, the DSI forms a first top but then makes a second top which is lower than the first top. The divergence here is between the second price top (which is higher than the first top) and the second DSI top (which

Figure 9-1 Divergence Bottoms (Bullish)

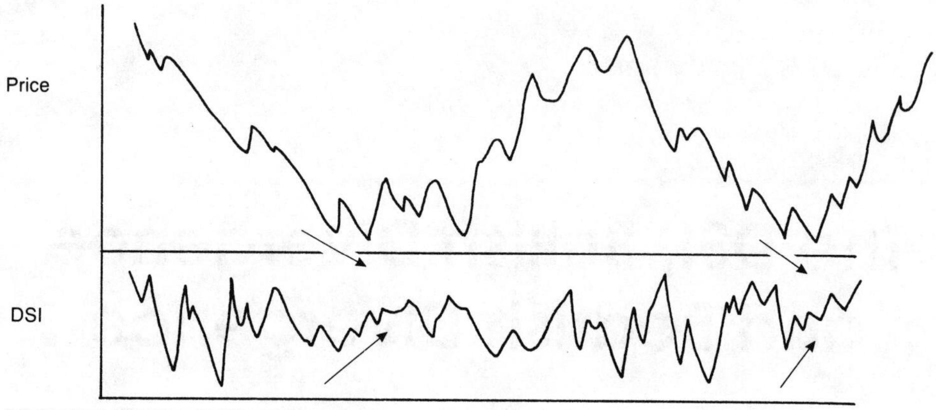

is lower than the first DSI top). This condition is illustrated in Figure 9-2 which shows several divergence tops.

Not all lows and tops are divergence lows and tops; and neither divergence lows nor tops are 100 percent reliable. However, as you study the DSI history and price charts, you must conclude, as have I, that divergence lows and tops, when they occur, are important.

Figure 9-2 Divergence Tops (Bearish)

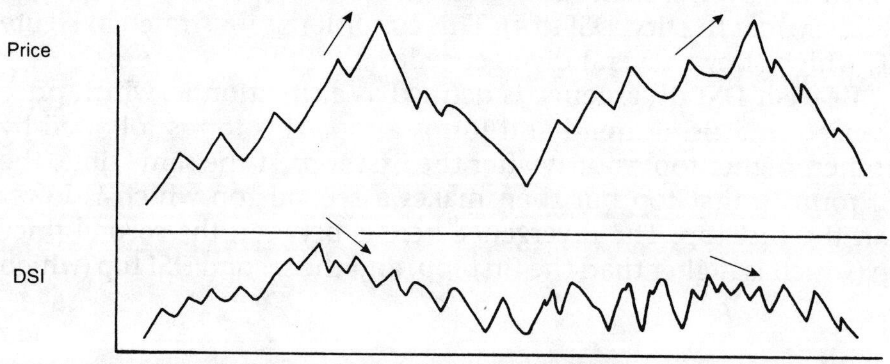

Other Divergence Conditions

It's difficult to know why DSI divergence works as well as it does. If you haven't already noticed, it seems as if the divergence scenarios I've presented are "backwards." In other words, it would seem that we would want to see a lower second DSI low correlated with a higher second price low, and vice versa. We want to see price fail to make a new low while the sentiment is more negative than it was at the first price low. While there are not many instances of this condition, they do occur, and I will point them out to you in my illustrations. In order to differentiate these two bullish divergence conditions, the second of which is illustrated in Figure 9-3, I will call this second form of bullish divergence Type B bullish divergence.

Another form of bearish divergence, which I will call Type B bearish divergence, is illustrated in Figure 9-4. As you can see, this type of divergence requires a lower second top in price accompanied by a higher second top in DSI. In other words, the sentiment is more bullish at the second top which, as you know from DSI theory, is bearish.

Figure 9-3 Type B Bullish Divergence

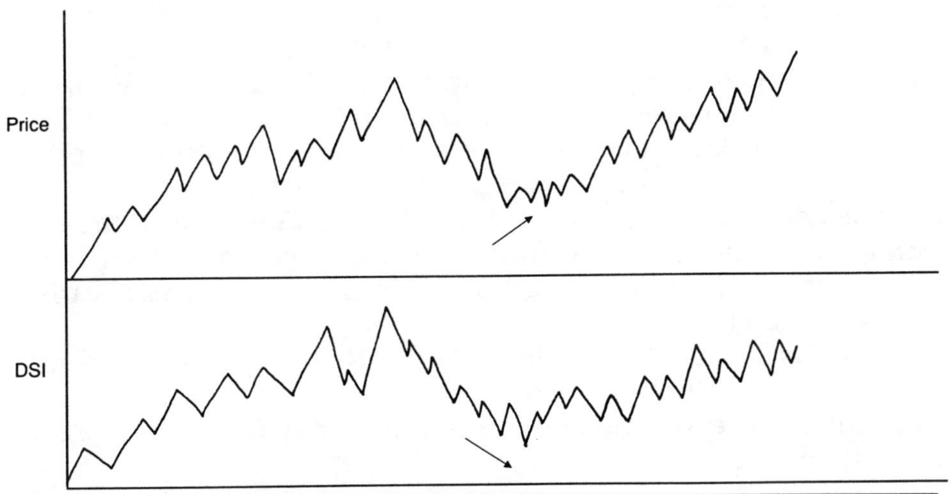

Figure 9-4 Type B Bearish Divergence

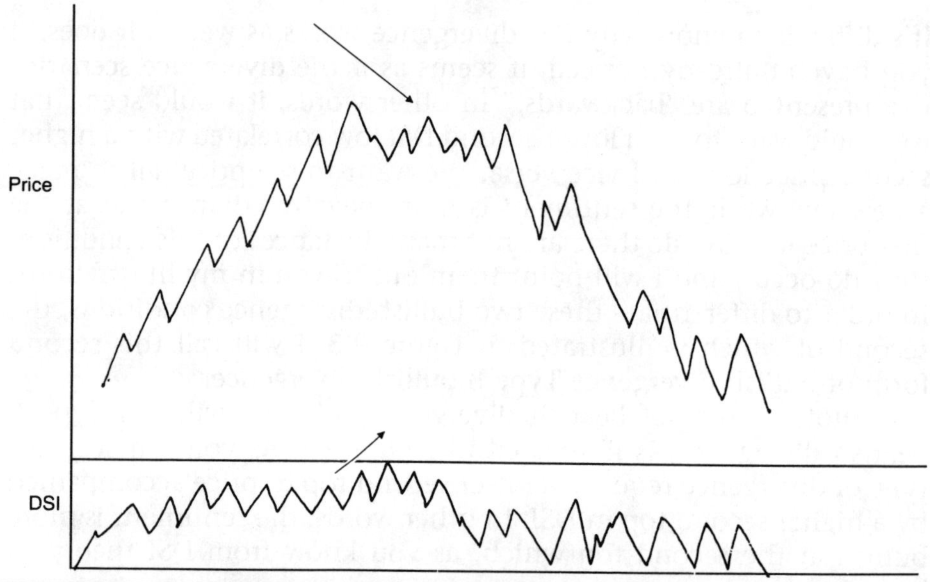

Looking at Type A and B Divergence Tops and Bottoms

Figure 9-5 shows a daily closing price chart of September 1990 cocoa futures versus a five-day MA of DSI. I've marked several divergence tops and bottoms of both types on the chart. My analysis follows.

1 shows a divergence bottom which failed to produce an upswing. As you can see, price made a new low while DSI did not. An upswing was expected; however, it failed to occur.

2 shows a classic bullish divergence bottom. Not only did price make a new low, but it was also a new contract low following an extended decline. At the same time, DSI made a higher low, thereby setting up the bullish divergence. As you can see, the market went on to rally very strongly for five months until it made a classic bearish divergence top (4).

3 shows a type B bullish divergence, but it requires some "bending" of the rules since the market was not in a declining trend prior to the divergence. (I include this example merely for the purpose of illustration.)

Figure 9-5

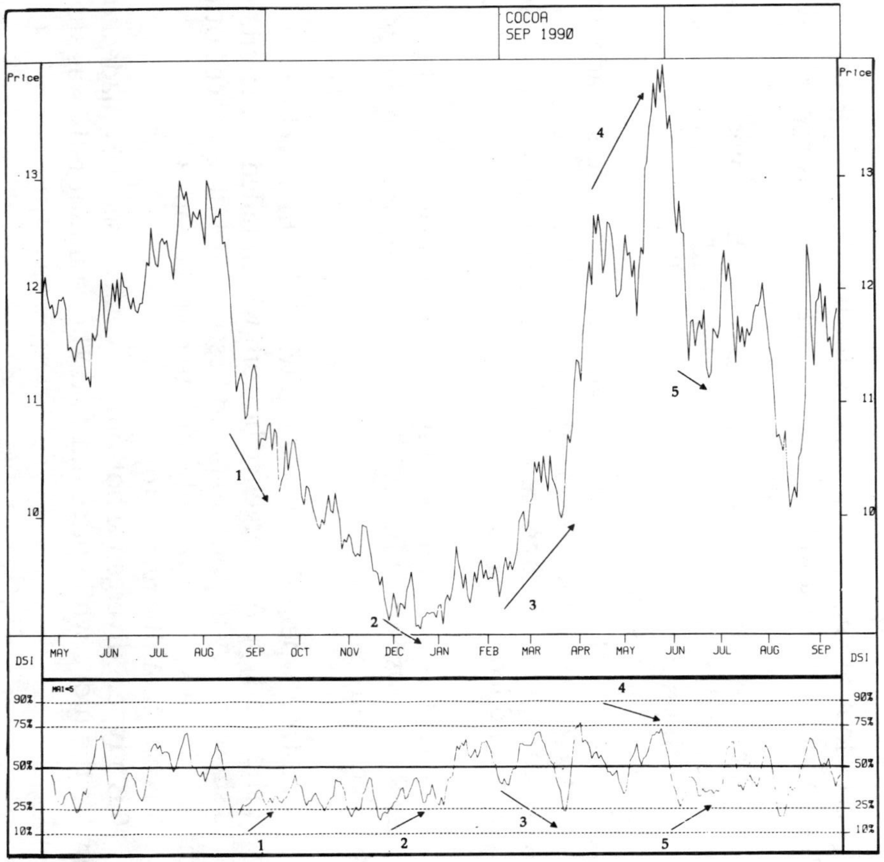

COCOA
SEP 1990
Price
13
12
11
10
DSI
MAY
JUN
JUL
AUG
SEP
OCT
NOV
DEC
JAN
FEB
MAR
APR
MAY
JUN
JUL
AUG
SEP
90%
75%
50%
25%
10%
1
2
3
4
5

4 is a classic bearish divergence top, type A. As you can see, price made a new contract high and a second higher high; however, the DSI did not, thereby setting up a bearish divergence which was followed by a strong decline lasting several months.

5 is another type A divergence bottom which resulted in a minor uptrend.

Let's look at another example. Figure 9-6 shows September 1990 Orange Juice futures and five-day MA of DSI. Here is my analysis:

1 is a classic type A divergence bottom which preceded one of the largest bull markets in OJ history. You will also note that about one month prior to the bottom, DSI was reading very low—an indication that a low was likely.

2 is a classic type A top. As you can see, prices made three successive peaks, while DSI made a lower second peak. This set up the potential for a divergence top which, as you can see, developed correctly and led to a sustained decline.

Now let's look at a third example of divergence tops and bottoms. Figure 9-7 shows September 1990 copper futures and five-day MA of DSI. Here is my analysis:

1 shows a type A divergence top which led to a decline.

2 shows a type A divergence bottom which failed to materialize.

3 shows a very important, broad-based type A divergence bottom which led to a substantial rally and divergence top, 4.

5 is a type A divergence top.

6 is a type B divergence bottom. As you can see, DSI made a new low for the move while price did not. The resultant rally was significant.

Figure 9-6

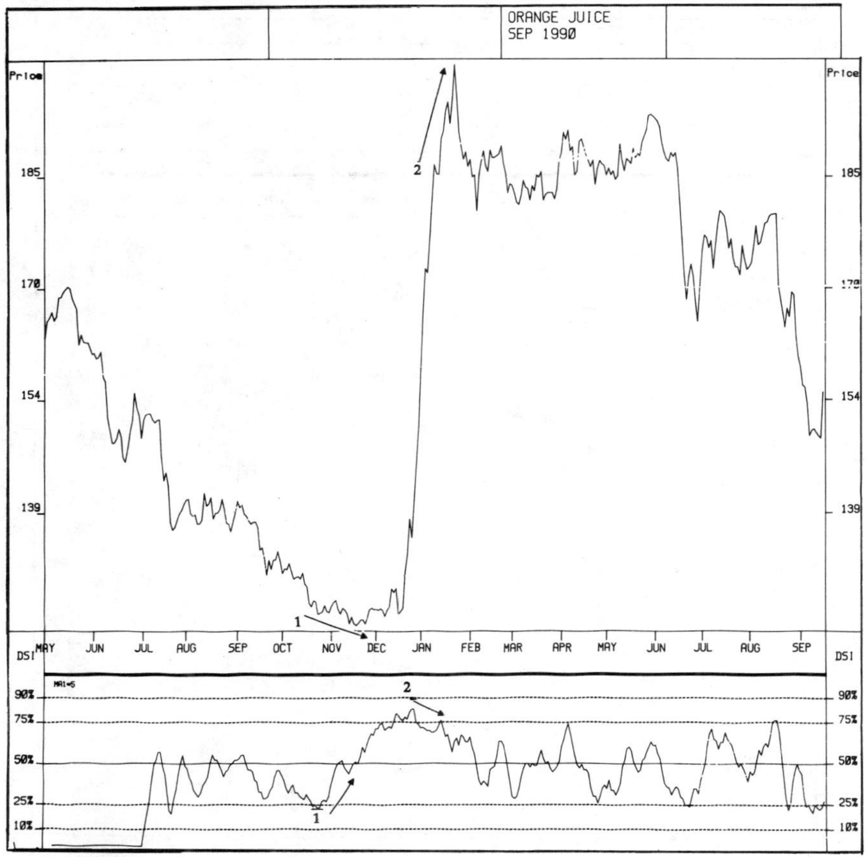
ORANGE JUICE
SEP 1990
Price
185
170
154
139
MAY
JUN
JUL
AUG
SEP
OCT
NOV
DEC
JAN
FEB
MAR
APR
MAY
JUN
JUL
AUG
SEP
DSI
90%
75%
50%
25%
10%
1
2

Figure 9-7

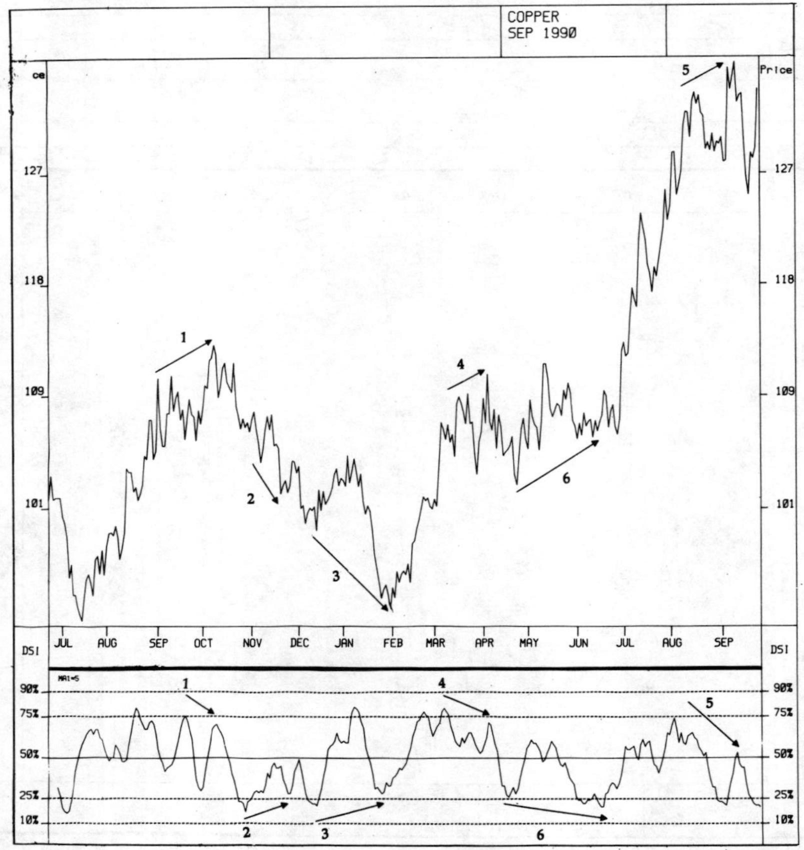
COPPER
SEP 1990
Price
127
118
109
101
1
2
3
4
5
6
JUL
AUG
SEP
OCT
NOV
DEC
JAN
FEB
MAR
APR
MAY
JUN
JUL
AUG
SEP
DSI
90%
75%
50%
25%
10%

Summary and Conclusions Regarding DSI Divergence

1. There are two basic types of DSI divergence tops and bottoms.

2. Not all bottoms or tops are divergence tops or bottoms.

3. Divergence tops and bottoms are not 100 percent reliable; however, they are sufficiently reliable to warrant attention from all traders.

4. Divergence tops and bottoms can only be spotted after they occur. A lengthy wait is not necessary. Typically, divergence tops and bottoms can be identified within a day or two after they occur.

5. Divergence tops and bottoms can be identified using raw DSI or smoothed DSI.

6. Divergence tops or bottoms are more reliable if at least one of the lows or highs is in the extreme range.

7. To fine-tune divergence tops and bottoms for short-term market moves, use intra-day data (as shown in the examples).

What DSI Cannot Do for You

Perhaps the single most grievous error a futures trader can commit is to use a system, method or trading approach in a fashion which is not consistent with its intended application—provided, of course, that such application has been proven valid. While there are certain unique applications of timing indicators which are not used in their original form, they are applications which, to one extent or another, have been found profitable by their users. In the final analysis it is up to the individual to use a system, method or indicator in the way which proves beneficial; however, it is important that you know the limitations of DSI in its current state of development. Once you do, you are free to pursue your own applications. Though my research has been very thorough, it has not explored every possible application.

DSI Can Continue to Read Very High for an Extended Period of Time

The mere fact that raw DSI is at 80 percent or higher does not in and of itself signal that a top or a downside reaction are imminent. A high DSI reading indicates only one thing: a majority of respondents to the DSI survey is bullish. While a high degree of bullish consensus strongly suggests that a top or a downside reaction are developing, the correlation between these two events is not 100 percent. DSI is merely an early warning indicator which should alert you to a possible change in trend.

PART IIIA

Daily DSI History 1987-1991*

The data history which follows is arranged by calendar date and market. Not all markets were monitored from the very first day of data collection.

DSI Symbol Listing

TR	T-Bonds	W	Wheat
ED	EuroDollar	O	Oats
SP	S&P	S	Soybeans
SF	Swiss Franc	BO	Soybean Oil
DM	Deutschemark	SM	Soybean Meal
JY	Japanese Yen	OJ	Orange Juice
BP	British Pound	CF	Coffee
CD	Canadian Dollar	CO	Cocoa
DX	U.S. Dollar Index	SU	Sugar
CL	Crude Light Oil	LB	Lumber
HO	Heating Oil	NY	Cotton
UR	Unleaded Gas	LC	Live Cattle
SU	Silver	LH	Live Hogs
PL	Platinum	PB	Pork Bellies
CP	Copper	CR	CRB Index
C	Corn		

*Data updates either in printout form and/or computer disk can be obtained from my office. For price and additional details, contact MBH, P.O. Box 353, Winnetka, IL, 60093.

DSI Data for April 1987

DAY	TR	ED	SP	SF	DM	JY	BP	CD	DX	CL	HO	UR	GC	SV	PL	CP	C	W	O	S	BO	SM	OJ	CF	CO	SU	LB	NY	LC	LH	PB	CR
13	31	0	44	38	0	44	47	50	0	31	0	0	35	35	41	25	93	33	0	79	57	67	0	60	50	64	47	86	60	57	79	0
14	44	0	38	56	0	56	64	50	0	25	0	0	53	47	63	29	75	44	0	76	50	77	0	64	60	47	14	93	38	38	50	0
15	74	0	93	43	0	44	50	23	0	38	0	0	34	53	40	20	71	75	0	60	38	42	0	75	73	74	31	73	46	54	69	0
16	62	0	81	40	0	33	46	54	0	50	0	0	31	30	38	31	67	61	0	75	54	57	0	75	77	54	43	86	47	71	72	0
20	28	0	37	44	0	43	60	53	0	31	0	0	56	55	64	61	71	37	0	83	73	79	0	86	81	57	37	93	33	50	56	0
21	58	0	74	44	0	37	54	53	0	48	0	0	47	53	56	47	78	39	0	72	62	60	0	73	75	47	53	64	56	69	87	0
22	47	0	55	33	0	39	47	47	0	22	0	0	42	55	53	32	65	29	0	67	50	72	0	74	47	57	50	60	47	50	56	0
23	32	0	42	61	0	63	76	38	0	58	0	0	74	84	82	29	82	54	0	94	69	80	0	75	60	72	44	50	69	79	77	0
24	17	0	30	78	0	79	88	44	0	61	0	0	70	80	77	37	76	63	0	94	73	96	0	73	80	93	6	71	75	87	65	0
27	76	0	77	20	0	20	36	38	0	56	0	0	33	31	33	29	60	47	0	56	50	38	0	54	64	77	47	69	50	71	69	0
28	68	0	74	39	0	39	47	31	0	56	0	0	42	47	39	30	62	36	0	82	74	86	0	71	43	54	47	69	68	80	67	0
29	45	0	60	37	0	38	50	29	0	37	0	0	25	40	21	16	75	47	0	94	67	85	0	80	40	93	47	64	63	41	31	0
30	79	0	95	50	0	44	81	40	0	52	0	0	55	53	58	37	87	62	0	88	80	87	0	47	53	57	75	86	76	80	82	0

DSI Data for May 1987

DAY	TR	ED	SP	SF	DM	JY	BP	CD	DX	CL	HO	UR	GC	SV	PL	CP	C	W	O	S	BO	SM	OJ	CF	CO	SU	LB	NY	LC	LH	PB	CR
1	44	0	69	60	0	63	84	50	0	60	0	0	63	56	62	44	93	73	0	94	93	92	0	54	77	42	72	82	81	71	62	0
4	17	0	61	71	0	76	75	14	0	61	0	0	72	73	67	78	93	94	0	97	98	86	0	67	80	64	69	43	89	81	87	0
5	38	0	73	47	0	57	64	54	0	56	0	0	69	67	70	81	71	67	0	80	77	83	0	78	85	50	64	69	94	87	98	0
6	56	0	68	59	0	57	60	31	0	58	0	0	47	45	50	68	76	78	0	89	93	87	0	47	60	67	47	80	79	89	81	0
7	75	0	55	42	0	40	47	62	0	55	0	0	45	50	45	70	94	93	0	95	88	87	0	37	71	53	61	67	70	42	33	0
8	81	0	57	30	0	25	42	56	0	62	0	0	36	38	38	57	83	89	0	91	82	88	0	25	71	60	63	93	84	79	61	0
11	53	0	65	27	0	25	28	35	0	70	0	0	50	55	45	70	94	95	0	96	94	99	0	60	71	93	78	98	83	84	94	0
12	74	0	80	58	0	53	61	45	0	60	0	0	55	65	55	50	59	67	0	66	59	63	0	62	75	67	59	64	56	61	53	0
13	53	0	60	45	0	43	36	38	0	74	0	0	35	40	37	50	71	56	0	78	75	73	0	63	40	81	75	98	37	39	29	0
14	39	0	50	62	0	61	69	47	0	70	0	0	50	55	50	60	88	56	0	83	94	87	0	56	47	81	76	87	32	42	28	0
15	11	0	21	67	0	61	56	29	0	84	0	0	79	84	78	89	65	41	0	72	81	74	0	73	33	82	41	93	50	59	56	0
18	75	0	62	27	0	29	41	56	0	67	0	0	38	34	43	45	39	17	0	37	35	31	0	60	53	62	61	53	60	63	61	0
19	25	0	19	50	0	53	44	50	0	43	0	0	52	62	52	55	56	47	0	65	53	56	0	73	60	81	39	87	40	79	67	0
20	37	0	30	50	0	47	50	24	0	26	0	0	24	20	30	40	50	61	0	58	65	44	0	55	50	53	50	94	21	37	28	0
21	61	0	58	18	0	12	25	38	0	42	0	0	25	27	32	26	87	63	0	88	87	79	0	64	58	67	44	87	56	59	38	0
22	78	0	68	18	0	16	20	37	0	43	0	0	16	11	21	26	88	53	0	67	69	80	0	50	46	71	25	60	67	76	31	0
26	79	0	81	9	0	7	11	44	0	60	0	0	23	20	15	20	61	51	0	49	35	37	0	30	28	31	47	75	79	89	67	0
27	60	0	70	28	0	44	24	35	0	40	0	0	34	37	35	45	83	50	0	79	62	78	0	50	21	53	39	80	68	94	83	0
28	47	0	53	47	0	49	50	44	0	39	0	0	53	58	56	63	59	35	0	56	40	53	0	57	43	45	56	51	72	59	62	0
29	58	0	52	23	0	25	44	62	0	58	0	0	21	26	23	25	62	25	0	61	66	76	0	17	33	47	44	75	67	61	71	0

DSI Data for June 1987

DAY	TR	ED	SP	SF	DM	JY	BP	CD	DX	CL	HO	UR	GC	SV	PL	CP	C	W	O	S	BO	SM	OJ	CF	CO	SU	LB	NY	LC	LH	PB	CR
1	45	0	50	34	0	32	47	38	0	78	0	0	56	53	50	70	47	41	0	50	56	58	0	25	23	25	76	67	71	88	85	0
2	20	0	35	75	0	78	71	31	0	75	0	0	65	60	65	79	77	29	0	84	94	93	0	25	36	53	33	26	47	74	82	0
3	52	0	71	32	0	35	41	33	0	71	0	0	30	33	24	52	79	68	0	80	83	82	0	20	37	35	53	59	50	58	72	0
4	70	0	80	35	0	38	37	53	0	60	0	0	53	55	40	75	72	39	0	79	87	86	0	31	7	27	61	64	75	78	76	0
5	75	0	65	28	0	35	33	44	0	55	0	0	45	40	49	45	79	37	0	84	88	92	0	31	38	29	53	63	70	84	89	0
8	65	0	81	39	0	33	56	39	0	71	0	0	40	32	39	62	63	32	0	55	50	53	0	37	49	44	51	56	55	69	67	0
9	41	0	64	79	0	74	83	67	0	53	0	0	66	75	72	65	48	39	0	74	53	82	0	40	71	43	46	54	52	49	71	0
10	68	0	63	51	0	44	53	56	0	47	0	0	43	46	63	47	41	47	0	67	49	79	0	51	64	20	59	60	78	59	56	0
11	56	0	61	47	0	41	56	69	0	62	0	0	66	72	78	76	69	43	0	88	79	92	0	57	61	47	68	78	70	69	73	0
12	79	0	89	22	0	19	38	71	0	68	0	0	37	39	42	53	87	35	0	89	52	93	0	49	37	33	71	87	76	87	84	0
15	83	0	72	26	0	23	31	56	0	78	0	0	43	47	56	67	93	75	0	94	81	93	0	15	51	73	63	85	51	88	93	0
16	65	0	59	44	0	49	47	45	0	76	0	0	35	38	41	47	92	63	0	82	80	77	0	8	67	54	67	53	63	60	57	0
17	72	0	65	26	0	28	33	56	0	70	0	0	38	37	42	40	65	54	0	72	65	63	0	20	80	75	61	38	64	56	59	0
18	53	0	42	44	0	39	47	59	0	75	0	0	51	48	56	47	59	56	0	67	51	53	0	29	79	33	38	67	89	82	74	0
19	47	0	53	45	0	43	52	65	0	68	0	0	23	19	21	31	53	59	0	50	44	40	0	21	80	51	62	66	69	71	63	0
22	74	0	83	18	0	9	12	69	0	45	0	0	20	13	11	21	32	25	0	29	30	27	0	15	86	49	53	23	82	29	31	0
23	59	0	51	44	0	35	53	47	0	42	0	0	35	40	32	48	76	70	0	65	56	60	0	47	81	50	38	64	83	59	52	0
24	35	0	40	58	0	55	61	59	0	21	0	0	43	49	52	65	78	67	0	63	66	64	0	38	88	25	39	37	53	31	34	0
25	58	0	53	39	0	28	47	81	0	42	0	0	27	25	23	68	47	53	0	44	52	56	0	33	82	43	45	54	67	59	56	0
26	25	0	42	28	0	21	33	56	0	70	0	0	41	45	48	60	51	50	0	58	56	59	0	46	87	92	43	62	32	23	25	0
29	48	0	43	35	0	20	28	53	0	63	0	0	48	62	53	57	39	48	0	28	32	35	0	59	61	25	19	75	30	17	18	0
30	26	0	26	72	0	53	69	71	0	52	0	0	53	55	58	74	58	53	0	49	47	44	0	33	50	69	22	67	56	53	41	0

DSI Data for July 1987

DAY	TR	ED	SP	SF	DM	JY	BP	CD	DX	CL	HO	UR	GC	SV	PL	CP	C	W	O	S	BO	SM	OJ	CF	CO	SU	LB	NY	LC	LH	PB	CR
1	32	0	21	58	0	33	49	65	0	61	0	0	47	58	53	83	41	56	0	38	59	31	0	42	67	55	13	40	32	61	64	0
2	49	0	56	33	0	14	42	43	0	52	0	0	48	51	60	87	57	73	0	46	61	44	0	33	84	53	62	83	65	72	70	0
6	42	0	33	31	0	28	41	59	0	74	0	0	68	73	71	88	45	82	0	65	68	66	0	40	72	64	57	69	74	76	87	0
7	63	0	66	37	0	34	67	83	0	45	0	0	51	60	58	84	56	74	0	82	76	81	0	19	61	57	38	73	68	71	69	0
8	38	0	43	47	0	45	71	62	0	63	0	0	42	65	61	44	22	50	0	35	39	24	0	38	45	48	53	59	75	79	83	0
9	31	0	58	29	0	35	75	68	0	79	0	0	37	68	52	57	38	65	0	67	50	53	0	44	66	81	40	47	78	75	82	0
10	59	0	55	36	0	33	56	61	0	70	0	0	30	39	35	41	47	52	0	33	29	34	0	35	71	67	54	62	26	32	42	0
13	18	0	36	45	0	42	70	74	0	62	0	0	53	68	59	47	26	65	0	30	32	45	0	69	58	72	39	44	35	37	43	0
14	67	0	61	25	0	24	37	56	0	73	0	0	44	51	39	45	43	58	0	53	56	47	0	40	54	25	27	57	23	21	17	0
15	27	0	32	76	0	71	80	51	0	69	0	0	73	64	68	36	45	67	0	50	58	66	0	53	69	29	24	65	30	35	47	0
16	50	0	59	48	0	43	52	71	0	68	0	0	59	54	63	55	25	56	0	38	40	47	0	58	53	28	39	77	61	65	74	0
17	60	0	64	22	0	21	38	50	0	54	0	0	31	33	26	25	21	55	0	27	26	29	0	83	41	30	34	59	27	32	28	0
20	28	0	31	38	0	29	30	52	0	64	0	0	58	60	53	37	62	47	0	74	67	83	0	53	45	39	44	59	37	61	72	0
21	14	0	19	60	0	58	63	47	0	38	0	0	73	69	67	61	47	34	0	45	47	58	0	44	35	22	18	71	36	45	67	0
22	24	0	38	35	0	37	47	53	0	57	0	0	77	68	73	76	67	62	0	58	63	61	0	56	29	49	24	65	47	78	83	0
23	40	0	43	37	0	48	39	27	0	42	0	0	52	48	46	65	46	56	0	54	50	59	0	75	45	22	19	57	28	44	61	0
24	35	0	58	53	0	50	48	21	0	40	0	0	38	51	70	61	55	66	0	72	75	64	0	65	59	41	21	82	42	56	69	0
27	42	0	60	37	0	42	39	50	0	31	0	0	52	55	71	40	62	79	0	78	84	87	0	37	41	59	13	56	66	61	63	0
28	32	0	59	48	0	52	45	50	0	64	0	0	69	65	77	68	75	73	0	84	80	79	0	28	12	25	28	59	35	37	58	0
29	63	0	79	64	0	50	43	43	0	57	0	0	43	50	47	33	40	53	0	44	50	40	0	38	33	62	20	91	64	79	79	0
30	75	0	80	67	0	73	46	43	0	33	0	0	50	53	56	53	56	69	0	65	75	69	0	57	43	54	54	73	76	88	63	0
31	57	0	62	33	0	38	34	67	0	27	0	0	53	54	60	50	69	83	0	54	62	45	0	46	42	40	62	40	64	57	62	0

DSI Data for August 1987

DAY	TR	ED	SP	SF	DM	JY	BP	CD	DX	CL	HO	UR	GC	SV	PL	CP	C	W	O	S	BO	SM	OJ	CF	CO	SU	LB	NY	LC	LH	PB	CR
3	19	0	52	15	0	25	26	74	0	62	0	0	89	91	95	57	29	68	0	38	53	30	0	72	18	47	42	83	50	54	67	0
4	30	0	25	16	0	21	28	73	0	50	0	0	71	76	85	55	15	72	0	29	30	21	0	94	35	45	44	41	68	43	65	0
5	62	0	57	45	0	47	44	48	0	29	0	0	46	41	48	40	57	65	0	63	71	65	0	47	64	42	74	50	55	42	71	0
6	57	0	63	30	0	34	42	69	0	28	0	0	64	55	53	47	38	69	0	41	45	58	0	67	42	48	43	53	70	59	61	0
7	61	0	64	35	0	41	32	52	0	19	0	0	34	30	28	48	33	45	0	43	35	37	0	70	23	67	61	34	89	78	62	0
10	53	0	84	39	0	58	61	38	0	10	0	0	53	52	68	74	50	79	0	50	46	69	0	56	6	76	44	28	56	94	87	0
11	71	0	81	37	0	42	50	45	0	49	0	0	67	65	75	72	59	86	0	62	63	66	0	45	59	33	32	31	50	26	28	0
12	54	0	68	29	0	33	55	42	0	23	0	0	41	49	54	45	48	87	0	36	35	63	0	70	67	26	65	72	66	75	79	0
13	85	0	87	32	0	23	43	57	0	20	0	0	19	13	18	17	41	70	0	52	38	60	0	33	16	63	47	89	43	50	45	0
14	83	0	69	44	0	56	64	41	0	17	0	0	26	25	27	47	61	78	0	56	29	68	0	31	47	50	64	69	39	47	44	0
17	76	0	57	80	0	78	84	37	0	15	0	0	58	67	56	63	65	86	0	58	53	51	0	50	52	56	89	78	43	55	53	0
18	27	0	32	67	0	68	80	30	0	31	0	0	61	57	55	29	42	73	0	46	52	45	0	31	42	60	55	50	36	52	30	0
19	29	0	62	65	0	67	74	39	0	19	0	0	50	59	54	45	85	81	0	89	82	70	0	28	41	25	63	71	47	68	64	0
20	71	0	89	50	0	41	53	79	0	11	0	0	19	23	20	52	43	54	0	45	57	35	0	58	20	24	70	76	49	74	78	0
21	37	0	53	61	0	67	71	69	0	21	0	0	52	50	45	11	68	85	0	79	63	47	0	33	56	41	64	56	58	67	59	0
24	47	0	58	50	0	56	52	75	0	26	0	0	55	51	59	45	47	70	0	54	57	44	0	65	71	22	31	25	68	79	77	0
25	74	0	83	36	0	32	33	63	0	30	0	0	32	33	31	25	64	83	0	72	86	50	0	91	60	28	52	32	59	57	55	0
26	36	0	51	53	0	51	55	80	0	54	0	0	52	48	61	47	77	78	0	65	47	79	0	80	89	17	25	88	90	65	52	0
27	30	0	41	58	0	55	53	68	0	52	0	0	43	41	57	66	71	86	0	64	57	70	0	84	47	39	17	72	56	50	37	0
28	25	0	18	32	0	37	56	61	0	25	0	0	38	33	43	29	50	52	0	43	30	42	0	89	29	28	59	25	35	26	28	0
31	70	0	66	41	0	43	51	44	0	55	0	0	43	52	42	53	42	45	0	40	44	28	0	85	67	43	56	17	70	75	78	0

DSI Data for September 1987

DAY	TR	ED	SP	SF	DM	JY	BP	CD	DX	CL	HO	UR	GC	SV	PL	CP	C	W	O	S	BO	SM	OJ	CF	CO	SU	LB	NY	LC	LH	PB	CR
1	36	0	41	60	0	75	68	79	0	27	0	0	61	48	56	42	37	73	0	44	33	57	0	62	17	70	29	35	59	81	45	0
2	22	0	23	76	0	77	85	75	0	28	0	0	57	56	70	36	71	82	0	77	62	80	0	86	47	61	25	15	68	72	30	0
4	35	0	52	45	0	41	52	69	0	25	0	0	48	47	52	57	53	55	0	67	48	75	0	79	44	25	31	47	74	53	32	0
8	29	0	33	67	0	72	80	42	0	20	0	0	43	34	36	86	85	82	0	87	50	86	0	40	16	67	14	18	66	52	25	0
9	30	0	35	36	0	39	37	17	0	38	0	0	32	36	23	41	80	83	0	57	60	58	0	67	22	84	58	16	62	50	37	0
10	52	0	61	42	0	37	50	53	0	57	0	0	72	74	59	64	81	67	0	80	55	89	0	60	35	68	28	47	56	35	32	0
11	72	0	81	21	0	20	23	52	0	24	0	0	36	41	27	89	67	64	0	91	62	90	0	63	45	43	47	61	63	38	45	0
14	33	0	52	29	0	35	41	65	0	56	0	0	22	28	17	37	93	85	0	88	59	87	0	35	44	25	27	43	34	25	19	0
15	31	0	47	49	0	50	67	61	0	58	0	0	46	53	42	50	56	63	0	65	52	59	0	24	13	53	47	21	33	51	56	0
16	19	0	17	35	0	47	65	42	0	36	0	0	28	22	31	72	81	82	0	83	64	80	0	16	36	75	25	67	18	47	50	0
17	36	0	37	45	0	67	72	46	0	29	0	0	58	53	51	77	63	61	0	58	52	56	0	59	33	82	29	48	17	23	25	0
18	65	0	50	41	0	62	74	63	0	45	0	0	22	15	21	60	55	73	0	62	47	64	0	61	35	53	27	62	71	65	49	0
21	20	0	18	30	0	32	58	61	0	65	0	0	62	57	53	50	48	81	0	47	50	56	0	49	77	60	13	39	74	61	59	0
22	70	0	79	21	0	23	44	47	0	50	0	0	47	43	45	25	50	62	0	43	78	25	0	26	53	59	17	24	40	22	29	0
23	44	0	63	19	0	33	46	20	0	78	0	0	55	50	42	63	54	37	0	56	55	53	0	38	31	39	41	77	56	18	37	0
24	34	0	57	44	0	56	70	78	0	43	0	0	61	53	50	49	55	46	0	54	79	42	0	45	47	40	16	52	46	54	61	0
25	43	0	56	41	0	43	65	81	0	38	0	0	47	42	39	67	53	63	0	48	76	41	0	72	43	81	20	46	75	44	60	0
28	47	0	89	23	0	21	30	82	0	59	0	0	55	46	50	41	70	29	0	65	81	56	0	47	53	71	60	20	18	12	16	0
29	17	0	50	18	0	16	22	72	0	69	0	0	40	49	42	32	81	70	0	74	72	83	0	71	24	83	30	22	32	56	29	0
30	48	0	71	15	0	24	40	68	0	62	0	0	19	21	18	24	41	27	0	67	53	64	0	35	18	47	21	50	22	55	42	0

DSI Data for October 1987

DAY	TR	ED	SP	SF	DM	JY	BP	CD	DX	CL	HO	UR	GC	SV	PL	CP	C	W	O	S	BO	SM	OJ	CF	CO	SU	LB	NY	LC	LH	PB	CR
1	47	0	79	42	0	43	39	78	0	44	0	0	16	17	22	23	78	80	0	91	67	83	0	87	33	84	43	29	41	76	75	0
2	50	0	78	14	0	18	22	53	0	84	0	0	47	39	53	50	63	72	0	61	70	47	0	86	36	61	68	52	33	44	20	0
5	42	0	53	67	0	61	60	70	0	63	0	0	49	52	55	58	54	56	0	60	61	59	0	88	25	78	62	39	19	67	64	0
6	36	0	27	52	0	33	54	79	0	23	0	0	38	24	28	47	53	57	0	51	48	57	0	60	24	86	27	34	52	80	78	0
7	25	0	40	53	0	47	58	52	0	45	0	0	36	35	20	73	79	78	0	73	67	77	0	65	44	63	28	32	35	79	77	0
8	19	0	16	78	0	80	76	60	0	43	0	0	71	57	62	70	81	93	0	72	64	45	0	84	39	57	11	37	55	42	37	0
9	15	0	20	79	0	77	84	47	0	54	0	0	65	45	47	68	52	49	0	61	53	37	0	88	23	58	12	33	60	68	56	0
12	26	0	27	56	0	72	44	55	0	34	0	0	42	37	33	78	53	62	0	48	47	35	0	69	19	72	43	28	63	67	53	0
13	65	0	57	33	0	35	45	74	0	43	0	0	29	27	20	55	81	76	0	80	78	69	0	78	24	56	26	27	57	54	48	0
14	29	0	27	70	0	71	76	59	0	48	0	0	50	56	58	87	77	83	0	78	87	85	0	60	31	75	48	50	28	27	30	0
15	42	0	51	37	0	36	58	77	0	48	0	0	45	42	55	74	75	70	0	61	47	58	0	87	32	63	62	44	52	31	22	0
16	27	0	14	60	0	52	70	80	0	86	0	0	78	81	79	89	57	62	0	84	85	79	0	78	11	90	32	21	23	26	17	0
19	35	0	7	75	0	73	84	75	0	32	0	0	68	74	63	44	17	19	0	12	20	18	0	39	28	50	11	6	9	13	11	0
20	69	0	43	24	0	19	25	27	0	25	0	0	44	18	14	7	70	64	0	53	27	73	0	22	42	46	28	24	17	37	40	0
21	77	0	44	17	0	16	28	41	0	58	0	0	53	47	39	30	43	52	0	42	38	61	0	56	44	53	49	40	29	39	47	0
22	62	0	15	50	0	32	45	21	0	61	0	0	46	30	31	49	33	47	0	52	55	51	0	62	35	56	42	16	20	23	21	0
23	45	0	31	68	0	63	77	58	0	60	0	0	59	50	34	47	21	48	0	50	46	62	0	76	65	84	61	28	63	54	50	0
26	76	0	11	65	0	36	60	29	0	38	0	0	48	24	25	15	43	45	0	66	50	71	0	34	43	59	13	16	15	24	31	0
27	45	0	32	63	0	58	67	26	0	64	0	0	41	17	19	37	40	32	0	62	26	74	0	42	39	47	27	29	24	39	38	0
28	47	0	26	67	0	71	68	32	0	41	0	0	45	22	18	28	18	23	0	22	25	30	0	55	58	64	60	54	57	43	32	0
29	68	0	49	59	0	62	55	37	0	30	0	0	34	26	22	23	44	39	0	43	33	52	0	40	45	41	38	57	51	54	50	0
30	69	0	52	54	0	45	56	47	0	26	0	0	31	22	23	34	26	40	0	44	38	55	0	20	16	68	62	64	19	21	20	0

DSI Data for November 1987

DAY	TR	ED	SP	SF	DM	JY	BP	CD	DX	CL	HO	UR	GC	SV	PL	CP	C	W	O	S	BO	SM	OJ	CF	CO	SU	LB	NY	LC	LH	PB	CR
2	57	0	38	74	0	79	73	47	0	16	0	0	35	15	16	70	21	18	0	23	17	36	0	68	53	34	63	75	9	12	14	0
3	77	0	23	43	0	48	62	15	0	24	0	0	22	18	14	30	17	15	0	16	23	25	0	57	26	19	27	47	65	53	58	0
4	73	0	27	56	0	61	57	10	0	26	0	0	9	7	6	78	33	45	0	41	44	40	0	41	12	23	58	60	46	25	26	0
5	53	0	42	73	0	70	74	33	0	21	0	0	23	20	16	71	65	62	0	66	63	78	0	64	37	58	62	61	55	60	59	0
6	40	0	25	64	0	53	55	47	0	20	0	0	35	33	30	75	55	59	0	83	85	84	0	42	25	50	46	52	75	63	66	0
9	43	0	4	59	0	64	60	52	0	21	0	0	23	22	33	47	43	46	0	76	45	65	0	66	48	79	40	45	54	56	60	0
10	48	0	20	34	0	33	36	43	0	44	0	0	32	30	21	73	67	63	0	85	72	86	0	50	77	54	55	23	74	69	72	0
11	45	0	22	50	0	49	52	53	0	36	0	0	30	33	28	60	68	66	0	78	75	80	0	45	75	57	75	37	59	45	47	0
12	47	0	38	42	0	45	41	34	0	30	0	0	29	37	39	40	43	47	0	79	66	81	0	34	40	43	38	62	56	52	45	0
13	35	0	26	49	0	52	60	50	0	28	0	0	36	34	22	39	52	32	0	77	48	70	0	36	30	51	49	77	52	61	68	0
16	58	0	32	30	0	35	34	59	0	17	0	0	41	32	45	33	48	59	0	47	38	35	0	60	14	41	70	67	65	60	32	0
17	52	0	17	64	0	57	59	55	0	16	0	0	43	47	41	45	82	68	0	79	43	76	0	51	28	38	67	83	81	69	57	0
18	55	0	52	65	0	61	63	79	0	48	0	0	42	40	33	72	53	62	0	50	34	55	0	71	59	80	22	29	63	32	24	0
19	65	0	34	46	0	44	50	71	0	25	0	0	26	19	30	81	60	39	0	78	37	86	0	78	38	56	39	32	61	42	40	0
20	57	0	50	48	0	42	56	39	0	60	0	0	52	47	31	46	78	82	0	84	77	87	0	32	41	66	30	29	68	78	57	0
23	73	0	38	76	0	73	80	75	0	50	0	0	53	55	52	63	81	76	0	54	62	47	0	41	55	43	56	74	79	62	78	0
24	21	0	63	59	0	57	65	62	0	43	0	0	52	48	50	68	69	70	0	77	76	75	0	42	60	54	82	91	57	86	81	0
25	20	0	39	50	0	46	67	74	0	41	0	0	58	51	67	73	64	60	0	72	68	73	0	47	52	75	85	33	59	76	62	0
27	20	0	39	50	0	46	67	74	0	41	0	0	58	51	67	73	64	60	0	72	68	73	0	47	52	75	85	33	59	76	62	0
30	63	0	13	58	0	56	64	57	0	22	0	0	52	44	51	38	58	92	0	59	50	57	0	27	55	81	43	49	51	42	52	0

DSI Data for December 1987

DAY	TR	ED	SP	SF	DM	JY	BP	CD	DX	CL	HO	UR	GC	SV	PL	CP	C	W	O	S	BO	SM	OJ	CF	CO	SU	LB	NY	LC	LH	PB	CR
1	45	31	27	38	0	35	46	40	0	36	0	0	39	35	37	68	54	83	0	75	72	74	0	21	56	83	70	33	46	50	45	0
2	64	55	42	35	0	33	28	44	0	49	0	0	34	41	40	36	37	50	0	35	36	32	0	18	38	61	45	73	58	52	41	0
3	75	68	16	41	0	52	38	57	0	75	0	0	44	32	41	35	71	67	0	54	43	48	0	13	42	30	50	24	31	27	23	0
4	56	54	17	29	0	46	37	26	0	36	0	0	37	26	20	22	21	36	0	20	24	19	0	41	63	37	68	14	22	24	19	0
7	17	27	56	21	0	28	22	36	0	15	0	0	30	19	21	65	55	48	0	66	78	69	0	21	25	68	54	67	56	64	62	0
8	16	18	64	45	0	54	50	73	0	11	0	0	49	33	36	77	39	42	0	34	65	33	0	55	19	36	74	66	28	62	60	0
9	56	52	63	48	0	55	59	68	0	46	0	0	54	50	45	35	61	58	0	60	37	62	0	24	32	79	62	47	69	61	54	0
10	13	17	40	69	0	73	77	75	0	44	0	0	70	56	55	65	57	37	0	71	64	68	0	28	50	78	36	33	81	65	59	0
11	28	25	46	71	0	75	67	61	0	24	0	0	66	42	58	62	32	51	0	38	52	30	0	24	32	53	71	24	70	52	58	0
14	59	47	76	49	0	50	48	43	0	10	0	0	47	43	41	36	45	67	0	46	77	27	0	26	17	65	84	16	89	70	68	0
15	70	72	65	32	0	36	31	37	0	16	0	0	24	23	18	37	35	55	0	43	71	29	0	19	24	67	69	44	68	59	44	0
16	71	74	68	64	0	61	63	67	0	9	0	0	42	36	12	57	26	35	0	37	79	30	0	53	47	86	61	50	47	52	26	0
17	50	36	39	76	0	73	75	76	0	30	0	0	41	48	45	64	78	69	0	75	68	76	0	77	58	91	84	79	81	66	68	0
18	66	73	69	32	0	36	30	40	0	31	0	0	27	25	41	76	52	74	0	69	72	56	0	53	57	87	88	55	58	70	47	0
21	44	50	73	64	0	65	60	58	0	19	0	0	18	33	24	80	50	65	0	77	75	67	0	46	65	54	56	73	42	78	45	0
22	56	52	58	67	0	71	58	63	0	55	0	0	42	46	48	74	63	71	0	58	52	61	0	42	47	66	40	63	27	29	15	0
23	95	88	80	42	0	47	37	43	0	46	0	0	26	31	33	73	76	67	0	83	74	79	0	59	18	85	83	81	42	47	38	0
24	95	88	80	42	0	47	37	43	0	46	0	0	26	31	33	73	76	67	0	83	74	79	0	59	18	85	83	81	42	47	38	0
28	95	88	80	42	0	47	37	43	0	46	0	0	26	31	33	73	76	67	0	83	74	79	0	59	18	85	83	81	42	47	38	0
29	95	88	80	42	0	47	37	43	0	46	0	0	26	31	33	73	76	67	0	83	74	79	0	59	18	85	83	81	42	47	38	0
30	95	88	80	42	0	47	37	43	0	46	0	0	26	31	33	73	76	67	0	83	74	79	0	59	18	85	83	81	42	47	38	0
31	95	88	80	42	0	47	37	43	0	46	0	0	26	31	33	73	76	67	0	83	74	79	0	59	18	85	83	81	42	47	38	0

DSI Data for January 1988

DAY	TR	ED	SP	SF	DM	JY	BP	CD	DX	CL	HO	UR	GC	SV	PL	CP	C	W	O	S	BO	SM	OJ	CF	CO	SU	LB	NY	LC	LH	PB	CR
4	65	44	76	36	0	38	30	67	0	82	0	0	20	19	11	41	78	74	0	91	90	86	0	52	81	87	89	63	90	80	50	0
5	74	59	63	23	0	26	28	65	0	73	0	0	61	65	64	45	57	81	0	54	77	43	0	69	70	73	45	26	71	78	62	0
6	48	47	60	17	0	15	19	57	0	52	0	0	64	78	72	13	77	79	0	87	86	68	0	61	80	37	43	40	83	86	85	0
7	67	62	76	28	0	19	20	71	0	20	0	0	47	56	51	15	71	54	0	50	66	43	0	45	57	58	52	25	72	81	80	0
8	26	23	30	46	0	55	52	62	0	27	0	0	51	69	56	32	68	69	0	78	76	45	0	35	60	77	33	42	57	71	65	0
11	54	58	46	23	0	26	28	50	0	26	0	0	27	46	31	65	84	61	0	63	58	39	0	22	48	35	39	46	76	63	56	0
12	32	43	28	33	0	37	38	64	0	35	0	0	24	25	33	30	48	60	0	36	54	23	0	37	38	47	64	38	62	66	54	0
13	47	42	29	37	0	41	43	65	0	38	0	0	21	34	29	16	93	89	0	82	87	60	0	39	47	61	62	50	57	60	73	0
14	33	33	30	58	0	66	62	53	0	71	0	0	60	55	54	31	69	67	0	58	59	56	0	31	48	75	28	29	66	71	68	0
15	80	74	72	16	0	12	15	61	0	36	0	0	19	15	21	28	65	50	0	63	65	53	0	52	57	64	63	47	79	82	80	0
18	56	47	52	44	0	48	45	46	0	67	0	0	61	65	64	61	85	56	0	65	84	32	0	71	64	41	59	40	76	83	81	0
19	68	56	43	55	0	57	53	60	0	59	0	0	46	47	58	50	67	48	0	56	73	45	0	50	77	79	42	38	72	63	55	0
20	77	69	31	61	0	60	65	81	0	52	0	0	29	25	37	17	50	49	0	38	76	16	0	57	73	59	25	22	53	57	52	0
21	71	64	62	26	0	37	25	66	0	39	0	0	55	51	52	25	54	42	0	44	47	34	0	69	72	58	53	49	82	75	80	0
22	73	72	60	35	0	42	30	65	0	28	0	0	42	54	38	44	62	41	0	70	52	53	0	65	59	82	55	54	71	81	72	0
25	69	52	73	15	0	18	14	79	0	54	0	0	19	16	17	22	76	64	0	53	69	39	0	40	26	73	52	50	43	39	38	0
26	51	47	45	41	0	42	30	46	0	37	0	0	18	20	26	48	77	73	0	47	50	28	0	71	23	70	59	32	58	49	45	0
27	75	72	49	42	0	58	45	50	0	25	0	0	20	32	29	21	52	40	0	19	17	29	0	62	16	63	78	53	69	56	57	0
28	67	60	78	39	0	47	38	61	0	58	0	0	28	22	24	39	42	36	0	20	37	21	0	55	20	46	85	28	30	43	36	0
29	83	74	72	16	0	12	19	75	0	21	0	0	15	19	11	17	35	54	0	36	40	27	0	80	9	36	81	36	29	42	18	0

DSI Data for February 1988

DAY	TR	ED	SP	SF	DM	JY	BP	CD	DX	CL	HO	UR	GC	SV	PL	CP	C	W	O	S	BO	SM	OJ	CF	CO	SU	LB	NY	LC	LH	PB	CR
1	47	40	25	17	0	15	18	74	0	20	0	0	19	32	28	7	43	62	0	33	45	48	0	84	17	10	64	56	62	64	42	0
2	71	68	42	57	0	61	54	52	0	38	0	0	36	33	44	49	51	44	0	28	30	32	0	63	45	39	62	57	65	61	41	0
3	43	30	29	28	0	30	32	57	0	66	0	0	16	21	25	48	41	65	0	47	42	49	0	78	23	38	76	35	78	69	59	0
4	56	58	28	62	0	57	59	79	0	80	0	0	64	61	58	55	80	84	0	73	59	75	0	83	22	85	58	66	63	60	45	0
5	46	45	27	38	0	36	35	73	0	71	0	0	40	39	43	45	62	67	0	54	52	61	0	76	53	57	68	60	85	76	50	0
8	38	43	29	42	0	33	25	71	0	74	0	0	50	45	46	37	75	71	0	50	47	43	0	55	32	30	89	41	69	52	31	0
9	46	52	42	43	0	49	36	60	0	58	0	0	46	27	44	54	81	52	0	69	74	45	0	53	44	47	77	32	71	84	77	0
10	54	62	47	40	0	31	36	51	0	37	0	0	25	29	37	76	67	58	0	75	57	59	0	60	41	39	65	45	56	57	85	0
11	57	48	33	21	0	25	22	70	0	44	0	0	40	42	58	41	64	57	0	80	73	86	0	81	63	65	72	55	35	34	27	0
12	25	22	54	17	0	24	21	52	0	25	0	0	58	59	62	65	66	83	0	87	74	91	0	79	27	42	71	43	52	35	36	0
16	52	45	61	41	0	43	40	53	0	28	0	0	43	34	44	71	36	50	0	31	35	40	0	32	28	66	74	55	57	38	25	0
17	36	41	45	43	0	47	44	68	0	24	0	0	57	51	48	50	70	65	0	80	72	79	0	69	47	61	48	81	71	49	48	0
18	44	46	41	32	0	34	31	58	0	24	0	0	28	30	31	29	42	23	0	51	48	38	0	26	41	73	68	69	20	17	18	0
19	47	40	62	48	0	47	39	19	0	55	0	0	58	54	52	49	63	62	0	75	68	65	0	67	23	54	51	57	69	35	31	0
22	32	26	53	56	0	54	59	30	0	15	0	0	34	35	30	31	29	24	0	42	36	23	0	43	55	37	19	36	35	25	24	0
23	64	60	51	28	0	39	53	55	0	50	0	0	23	20	19	12	31	33	0	46	40	49	0	58	21	42	65	35	38	24	20	0
24	33	35	38	34	0	43	47	53	0	14	0	0	18	15	14	47	36	35	0	48	29	52	0	66	25	27	32	53	65	45	47	0
25	31	32	22	56	0	59	77	54	0	21	0	0	47	49	56	43	39	37	0	34	18	33	0	45	54	22	11	60	68	59	43	0
26	43	42	39	50	0	58	76	44	0	47	0	0	28	29	32	27	62	45	0	79	63	72	0	16	20	39	29	62	65	56	36	0
29	42	27	54	29	0	51	53	61	0	57	0	0	60	56	79	71	78	42	0	81	80	83	0	14	17	56	30	68	29	25	26	0

DSI Data for March 1988

DAY	TR	ED	SP	SF	DM	JY	BP	CD	DX	CL	HO	UR	GC	SV	PL	CP	C	W	O	S	BO	SM	OJ	CF	CO	SU	LB	NY	LC	LH	PB	CR
1	50	35	37	30	0	33	65	77	0	29	0	0	46	40	52	56	67	30	0	74	52	85	0	22	47	62	49	63	66	50	41	0
2	52	38	35	32	0	34	48	69	0	43	0	0	50	54	71	68	40	20	0	52	39	61	0	37	30	66	67	68	65	39	50	0
3	45	26	36	25	0	46	63	79	0	30	0	0	31	46	48	57	44	28	0	32	33	38	0	25	32	55	64	52	22	30	31	0
4	25	23	29	48	0	56	65	62	0	67	0	0	56	64	79	82	42	33	0	29	26	45	0	23	65	76	63	54	28	32	46	0
7	18	22	34	71	0	77	79	84	0	31	0	0	45	58	66	59	69	43	0	40	36	47	0	29	43	81	30	38	62	63	80	0
8	35	36	56	82	0	64	76	55	0	54	0	0	33	41	60	40	43	21	0	44	45	62	0	44	55	54	22	42	67	62	43	0
9	53	50	58	64	0	63	83	76	0	47	0	0	46	52	61	73	44	18	0	21	22	24	0	14	35	63	34	39	60	38	36	0
10	31	28	23	57	0	60	66	38	0	63	0	0	54	45	82	68	37	22	0	32	24	38	0	23	65	56	17	70	61	33	28	0
11	36	40	45	75	0	76	70	40	0	68	0	0	18	22	43	42	46	53	0	62	57	75	0	64	63	72	45	78	56	50	44	0
14	66	52	33	53	0	67	56	38	0	34	0	0	48	46	62	43	70	64	0	75	68	84	0	29	28	35	58	77	81	72	63	0
15	49	67	28	36	0	45	50	73	0	64	0	0	59	58	76	33	47	48	0	52	45	70	0	30	61	38	35	62	57	49	32	0
16	40	42	32	50	0	53	51	60	0	76	0	0	34	23	44	57	38	28	0	46	40	55	0	24	29	77	68	75	74	61	50	0
17	48	77	59	9	0	22	26	78	0	69	0	0	40	31	52	50	57	59	0	77	62	76	0	17	38	82	55	71	73	76	75	0
18	16	24	57	23	0	34	42	53	0	86	0	0	43	45	59	52	41	48	0	54	38	56	0	47	49	61	50	55	58	70	79	0
21	59	56	36	45	0	54	53	55	0	38	0	0	57	46	56	37	66	32	0	80	63	75	0	22	71	48	77	60	39	35	40	0
22	47	50	27	21	0	42	48	70	0	63	0	0	40	45	63	52	54	65	0	73	48	79	0	44	66	94	35	67	76	78	75	0
23	41	39	50	46	0	63	71	77	0	76	0	0	59	70	68	75	49	34	0	59	31	60	0	51	68	43	41	65	62	50	42	0
24	54	55	10	56	0	75	64	72	0	53	0	0	52	66	51	76	47	39	0	74	48	78	0	23	57	56	39	70	63	67	61	0
25	59	62	9	43	0	73	60	68	0	65	0	0	53	61	48	67	68	31	0	62	61	57	0	54	55	76	56	52	77	68	72	0
28	38	33	35	71	0	79	75	58	0	66	0	0	59	63	68	44	61	30	0	77	84	82	0	72	46	69	37	61	79	62	54	0
29	46	40	42	51	0	54	52	67	0	48	0	0	47	58	65	62	76	53	0	57	36	49	0	60	52	50	61	62	65	63	46	0
30	40	49	30	62	0	68	67	69	0	56	0	0	48	46	55	70	54	34	0	45	50	41	0	32	53	72	56	75	51	43	47	0
31	55	57	26	42	0	45	56	54	0	47	0	0	35	40	41	46	59	40	0	60	61	53	0	52	46	53	45	57	54	50	51	0

DSI Data for April 1988

DAY	TR	ED	SP	SF	DM	JY	BP	CD	DX	CL	HO	UR	GC	SV	PL	CP	C	W	O	S	BO	SM	OJ	CF	CO	SU	LB	NY	LC	LH	PB	CR
4	37	44	21	47	0	45	60	46	0	39	0	0	42	45	56	38	52	43	0	62	63	65	0	54	67	22	58	26	50	61	47	0
5	34	26	22	23	0	36	47	40	0	27	0	0	25	26	33	27	46	55	0	56	55	46	0	38	58	35	41	23	46	63	40	0
6	53	42	41	17	0	26	32	55	0	36	0	0	18	15	35	26	44	77	0	45	44	41	0	52	56	34	43	58	49	64	38	0
7	44	38	57	30	0	38	40	29	0	45	0	0	35	31	42	32	43	72	0	57	62	54	0	33	37	38	40	59	60	61	35	0
8	59	52	60	28	0	39	37	34	0	30	0	0	29	24	57	26	40	71	0	58	59	48	0	35	56	55	57	61	75	72	49	0
11	54	52	53	35	0	38	35	41	0	53	0	0	41	42	46	14	28	56	0	62	59	53	0	46	47	26	42	69	76	79	55	0
12	57	56	49	23	0	25	29	65	0	66	0	0	22	18	21	16	35	72	0	60	53	52	0	43	42	39	25	74	37	43	20	0
13	66	72	40	22	0	36	27	51	0	67	0	0	27	19	35	20	27	53	0	47	41	56	0	48	46	48	38	55	30	25	18	0
14	35	47	21	71	0	77	70	64	0	63	0	0	56	49	59	47	21	40	0	38	34	39	0	65	55	55	33	59	43	44	38	0
15	29	36	27	64	0	65	77	81	0	52	0	0	56	50	68	42	3	21	0	19	11	14	0	58	39	31	29	45	38	36	35	0
18	33	42	26	50	0	51	72	63	0	61	0	0	62	42	57	24	38	31	0	43	32	27	0	63	56	47	19	50	40	41	38	0
19	30	35	43	39	0	42	49	67	0	38	0	0	55	32	45	26	53	55	0	57	51	43	0	41	70	59	30	61	49	40	47	0
20	59	53	37	33	0	35	43	54	0	29	0	0	41	35	30	18	32	48	0	39	45	31	0	46	71	57	38	69	55	43	46	0
21	28	39	24	36	0	40	37	38	0	53	0	0	45	40	39	31	27	49	0	42	39	32	0	40	55	37	35	75	53	38	37	0
22	36	41	40	28	0	22	53	57	0	44	0	0	35	24	38	39	37	32	0	38	24	26	0	48	51	49	20	80	56	40	35	0
25	45	52	53	26	0	32	30	48	0	61	0	0	24	19	33	28	24	30	0	17	23	18	0	36	68	72	36	53	31	36	38	0
26	39	44	40	22	0	27	31	59	0	55	0	0	46	41	37	35	48	49	0	57	64	47	0	38	89	46	44	54	47	45	37	0
27	52	46	55	34	0	37	42	60	0	54	0	0	48	53	46	43	53	55	0	61	65	46	0	31	67	40	48	62	59	46	41	0
28	22	18	41	35	0	38	33	54	0	28	0	0	43	40	34	31	50	37	0	70	68	57	0	18	71	42	35	63	55	44	42	0
29	41	34	22	32	0	37	50	69	0	38	0	0	45	43	46	30	61	33	0	78	74	73	0	16	64	14	34	75	52	34	33	0

DSI Data for May 1988

DAY	TR	ED	SP	SF	DM	JY	BP	CD	DX	CL	HO	UR	GC	SV	PL	CP	C	W	O	S	BO	SM	OJ	CF	CO	SU	LB	NY	LC	LH	PB	CR
2	23	30	32	24	0	35	27	46	0	9	0	0	14	20	16	33	67	41	0	74	69	59	0	25	58	19	31	56	45	41	42	29
3	47	41	57	19	0	28	29	31	0	28	0	0	12	13	24	47	50	29	0	52	40	36	0	34	67	49	28	61	72	60	37	38
4	34	42	44	23	0	35	28	37	0	13	0	0	26	30	38	70	76	45	0	54	46	55	0	41	52	31	24	60	53	69	30	37
5	57	58	21	15	0	30	24	42	0	29	0	0	35	41	45	46	39	26	0	55	58	54	0	63	54	47	23	64	58	90	61	39
6	45	47	14	34	0	37	31	22	0	38	0	0	23	39	50	61	34	36	0	59	65	76	0	73	66	44	17	51	70	77	46	43
9	42	38	17	37	0	40	52	31	0	35	0	0	47	65	73	77	32	50	0	73	64	65	0	36	55	58	24	68	69	75	41	72
10	41	32	18	33	0	39	50	32	0	36	0	0	54	71	84	78	43	67	0	79	77	76	0	52	59	73	23	70	61	52	42	89
11	52	53	19	30	0	44	47	69	0	38	0	0	51	60	72	50	15	42	0	58	53	64	0	53	45	79	33	67	65	82	69	64
12	59	61	26	32	0	36	54	62	0	31	0	0	44	51	69	61	14	35	0	47	38	46	0	33	31	70	32	71	72	84	81	48
13	65	62	41	15	0	21	42	44	0	35	0	0	43	54	56	50	42	61	0	72	59	66	0	25	63	88	42	75	64	73	71	70
16	50	52	35	10	0	16	28	27	0	56	0	0	57	55	63	47	62	74	0	75	69	76	0	29	51	70	20	89	66	57	63	81
17	17	22	21	9	0	10	25	33	0	66	0	0	60	48	64	44	41	79	0	83	70	78	0	32	59	72	14	76	62	45	46	68
18	25	37	18	29	0	31	34	14	0	35	0	0	73	59	77	36	62	81	0	78	68	70	0	36	72	63	29	58	65	70	66	69
19	38	44	33	19	0	19	22	26	0	50	0	0	57	62	56	41	58	75	0	72	55	63	0	48	69	64	49	65	50	52	47	73
20	43	45	34	17	0	18	27	42	0	31	0	0	58	65	64	39	63	68	0	60	62	57	0	50	70	71	30	69	52	61	55	66
23	42	43	27	31	0	45	48	33	0	30	0	0	79	64	75	34	50	52	0	24	22	25	0	46	61	49	31	42	34	53	56	50
24	50	52	49	30	0	59	47	32	0	24	0	0	59	60	66	23	73	82	0	65	58	67	0	29	80	42	53	64	21	40	43	72
25	67	55	48	16	0	40	45	34	0	19	0	0	35	41	43	21	79	48	0	46	37	45	0	54	76	34	42	41	26	47	45	44
26	45	42	40	27	0	39	36	50	0	36	0	0	33	42	61	23	38	34	0	33	30	34	0	31	41	35	60	48	44	63	58	43
27	43	43	31	15	0	18	20	47	0	32	0	0	19	21	55	22	48	40	0	41	32	42	0	50	33	39	70	52	39	71	62	46
31	67	54	71	14	0	19	16	72	0	44	0	0	32	38	78	42	56	51	0	82	69	85	0	68	45	37	74	75	55	86	69	60

DSI Data for June 1988

DAY	TR	ED	SP	SF	DM	JY	BP	CD	DX	CL	HO	UR	GC	SV	PL	CP	C	W	O	S	BO	SM	OJ	CF	CO	SU	LB	NY	LC	LH	PB	CR
1	80	77	82	30	0	18	14	63	0	48	0	0	47	61	86	57	45	43	0	71	54	65	0	60	34	83	52	51	46	65	75	62
2	57	45	48	35	0	26	29	61	0	53	0	0	72	74	89	71	67	60	0	72	58	74	0	76	37	53	42	55	57	66	63	77
3	89	70	67	29	0	32	30	54	0	55	0	0	77	77	63	75	82	79	0	87	76	89	0	73	19	77	68	42	44	45	50	85
6	74	72	59	42	0	39	32	55	0	31	0	0	52	75	66	57	89	93	0	90	87	91	0	86	30	78	80	77	76	79	67	81
7	36	51	40	72	0	55	73	58	0	37	0	0	41	46	42	71	83	64	0	75	62	77	0	85	38	50	60	57	70	68	55	52
8	77	69	66	53	0	42	48	62	0	19	0	0	40	38	45	63	60	58	0	65	57	59	0	66	22	52	63	45	43	27	31	48
9	58	56	57	55	0	64	60	79	0	14	0	0	47	47	42	46	74	73	0	71	68	70	0	67	35	72	44	61	30	24	19	63
10	64	63	49	26	0	44	35	74	0	25	0	0	28	31	24	58	75	69	0	66	56	68	0	52	33	57	50	53	37	40	24	45
13	73	71	48	24	0	43	37	68	0	21	0	0	33	50	36	55	70	44	0	59	48	57	0	51	56	38	27	59	23	35	21	42
14	72	72	70	13	0	15	20	80	0	45	0	0	42	51	30	32	93	65	0	81	59	74	0	29	52	43	24	67	22	23	18	55
15	56	53	45	23	0	24	31	69	0	41	0	0	38	57	46	48	99	83	0	94	82	93	0	50	68	42	18	92	20	17	21	72
16	38	47	36	35	0	39	38	67	0	46	0	0	28	44	41	40	94	48	0	82	71	80	0	56	22	49	23	52	37	50	45	52
17	24	28	35	29	0	32	25	70	0	31	0	0	46	65	54	52	92	60	0	85	77	84	0	57	39	74	15	63	21	34	20	64
20	50	34	30	21	0	16	23	84	0	33	0	0	28	45	39	34	93	88	0	94	89	92	0	42	22	68	31	72	38	30	29	82
21	43	40	38	46	0	33	48	66	0	35	0	0	31	53	52	72	90	70	0	91	87	96	0	46	34	71	35	57	39	45	50	73
22	67	76	75	10	0	9	12	45	0	50	0	0	24	29	28	77	85	61	0	76	86	82	0	27	54	82	38	55	35	42	33	56
23	66	58	62	30	0	23	26	67	0	48	0	0	14	12	19	43	54	45	0	52	53	41	0	16	46	42	39	32	24	26	20	40
24	57	51	46	12	0	10	13	78	0	25	0	0	13	16	14	27	76	72	0	64	70	63	0	17	53	54	28	37	50	43	18	59
27	44	32	29	30	0	33	24	59	0	26	0	0	34	39	33	42	91	80	0	82	85	84	0	30	21	86	45	68	60	62	41	78
28	57	55	43	28	0	25	45	50	0	34	0	0	20	23	27	39	44	32	0	37	41	35	0	43	54	69	54	24	75	48	40	42
29	46	37	34	32	0	31	35	31	0	15	0	0	23	16	22	30	23	26	0	19	35	16	0	27	56	65	66	14	61	50	42	24
30	59	40	44	53	0	42	46	40	0	15	0	0	30	33	32	31	73	56	0	64	65	51	0	45	77	81	79	23	46	47	41	54

DSI Data for July 1988

DAY	TR	ED	SP	SF	DM	JY	BP	CD	DX	CL	HO	UR	GC	SV	PL	CP	C	W	O	S	BO	SM	OJ	CF	CO	SU	LB	NY	LC	LH	PB	CR
1	50	41	38	33	0	30	34	32	0	17	0	0	43	42	48	35	72	76	0	58	73	59	0	47	51	89	74	30	54	20	14	60
5	62	50	63	30	0	35	39	40	0	48	0	0	46	50	47	28	54	26	0	27	42	28	0	35	75	43	34	18	73	37	20	34
6	44	35	37	51	0	47	50	64	0	55	0	0	40	48	52	39	60	63	0	57	59	56	0	50	73	68	39	37	56	43	31	74
7	49	36	45	38	0	53	52	56	0	57	0	0	47	60	66	53	34	37	0	24	35	21	0	57	65	54	62	25	59	56	60	36
8	26	18	24	21	0	25	27	51	0	38	0	0	35	56	48	30	31	32	0	18	36	20	0	60	69	78	79	29	60	42	41	27
11	47	40	46	32	0	34	28	59	0	30	0	0	19	31	23	21	32	34	0	27	24	25	0	62	76	49	60	32	68	37	34	20
12	24	19	9	55	0	61	62	38	0	49	0	0	46	43	37	12	65	63	0	64	58	63	0	59	67	70	53	31	52	60	45	57
13	30	23	34	32	0	36	38	59	0	31	0	0	53	70	48	29	72	62	0	65	73	69	0	77	73	78	46	24	30	39	52	63
14	41	33	35	46	0	42	45	60	0	54	0	0	56	78	36	57	66	35	0	60	55	53	0	61	50	64	11	38	49	68	76	55
15	54	48	55	34	0	36	39	64	0	56	0	0	59	67	33	38	57	40	0	58	48	44	0	50	26	62	10	34	65	78	77	54
18	25	31	25	40	0	49	47	44	0	71	0	0	45	48	34	32	20	31	0	22	17	21	0	33	43	45	29	30	80	61	54	16
19	40	47	32	67	0	68	71	85	0	57	0	0	66	69	65	68	37	40	0	20	22	17	0	44	48	71	27	42	57	46	48	59
20	38	46	43	65	0	69	74	66	0	55	0	0	67	79	66	82	42	47	0	21	19	18	0	49	63	39	30	57	58	37	50	53
21	33	37	31	69	0	73	85	70	0	75	0	0	52	60	45	52	58	61	0	39	32	47	0	56	38	17	65	63	82	67	69	51
22	49	52	16	61	0	70	79	57	0	68	0	0	50	44	59	51	54	57	0	33	31	38	0	47	35	48	52	75	71	72	66	45
25	75	67	42	38	0	37	41	30	0	43	0	0	10	18	16	27	34	42	0	26	23	25	0	55	36	43	23	56	76	50	47	20
26	66	51	45	34	0	40	35	47	0	52	0	0	19	17	18	20	32	37	0	28	22	26	0	18	30	11	29	50	45	34	30	21
27	27	22	19	67	0	73	66	62	0	68	0	0	48	45	43	37	35	58	0	50	36	39	0	13	35	30	26	54	68	49	25	27
28	40	34	53	38	0	41	43	55	0	66	0	0	29	21	15	19	22	51	0	32	25	27	0	25	42	24	42	22	64	28	24	8
29	55	47	61	27	0	29	34	48	0	59	0	0	44	47	50	38	72	73	0	76	68	67	0	40	39	56	23	64	71	42	30	59

DSI Data for August 1988

DAY	TR	ED	SP	SF	DM	JY	BP	CD	DX	CL	HO	UR	GC	SV	PL	CP	C	W	O	S	BO	SM	OJ	CF	CO	SU	LB	NY	LC	LH	PB	CR
1	64	57	68	33	0	45	41	54	0	52	0	0	35	44	29	24	78	74	0	82	76	88	0	19	21	44	22	66	36	63	58	70
2	80	71	74	37	0	40	42	66	0	18	0	0	15	17	12	10	56	53	0	50	44	51	0	9	27	53	17	32	24	39	27	45
3	63	54	77	43	0	52	56	65	0	31	0	0	30	39	35	44	53	70	0	64	52	69	0	41	48	47	46	30	38	45	56	50
4	69	56	58	31	0	45	52	48	0	32	0	0	39	43	46	53	61	65	0	67	55	68	0	47	56	54	42	48	47	36	30	59
5	45	27	37	22	0	25	29	43	0	54	0	0	28	37	53	64	80	74	0	86	68	87	0	44	41	55	34	36	70	69	51	66
8	48	36	60	19	0	21	35	32	0	67	0	0	16	18	20	19	33	45	0	47	43	46	0	29	57	28	25	19	53	44	36	42
9	25	20	26	16	0	19	21	22	0	56	0	0	31	32	29	21	25	52	0	51	39	48	0	46	24	36	20	50	48	55	41	46
10	31	32	17	38	0	34	39	13	0	66	0	0	27	33	58	32	47	70	0	67	61	69	0	52	19	56	29	53	82	79	58	49
11	42	35	53	52	0	55	58	49	0	61	0	0	44	50	52	56	57	68	0	69	53	72	0	45	28	37	36	51	60	66	57	53
12	53	48	40	50	0	43	67	37	0	45	0	0	26	29	34	38	24	41	0	30	29	33	0	48	17	10	42	9	55	58	54	19
15	39	43	32	41	0	37	53	46	0	57	0	0	54	45	48	42	50	69	0	66	49	73	0	36	13	51	44	35	49	57	42	54
16	60	55	54	23	0	26	34	29	0	46	0	0	27	25	32	31	22	47	0	48	23	52	0	46	22	26	61	20	33	44	25	18
17	49	47	36	18	0	20	23	17	0	37	0	0	43	46	50	43	26	62	0	61	38	67	0	53	16	35	45	40	52	56	45	30
18	44	48	43	48	0	47	54	38	0	42	0	0	47	49	64	73	32	58	0	52	46	62	0	70	39	52	53	41	59	81	75	45
19	46	37	35	31	0	38	43	36	0	55	0	0	56	47	71	68	19	61	0	35	21	44	0	73	33	54	48	29	56	67	58	27
22	26	27	15	42	0	44	37	38	0	64	0	0	59	65	78	77	10	36	0	22	11	25	0	71	45	47	23	22	17	38	46	8
23	30	32	21	13	0	16	18	36	0	46	0	0	57	56	75	64	25	53	0	18	15	21	0	32	31	54	17	19	35	37	48	14
24	38	33	37	48	0	41	46	25	0	44	0	0	64	63	74	65	59	73	0	49	50	48	0	60	55	65	33	34	54	50	53	59
25	41	42	40	75	0	46	51	10	0	24	0	0	63	57	72	56	32	78	0	43	41	43	0	47	20	38	25	32	71	77	79	42
26	31	26	25	71	0	44	39	19	0	33	0	0	58	42	65	66	23	69	0	38	31	25	0	30	19	30	45	36	74	73	66	45
29	71	57	58	52	0	39	28	23	0	29	0	0	45	41	62	63	30	56	0	35	39	33	0	25	34	36	65	67	63	40	39	32
30	62	60	63	53	0	32	45	48	0	47	0	0	40	43	44	49	50	80	0	56	52	55	0	33	43	51	64	65	36	27	33	57
31	58	51	54	38	0	28	34	38	0	41	0	0	50	52	63	65	62	87	0	68	54	69	0	37	16	50	60	66	31	15	10	55

DSI Data for September 1988

DAY	TR	ED	SP	SF	DM	JY	BP	CD	DX	CL	HO	UR	GC	SV	PL	CP	C	W	O	S	BO	SM	OJ	CF	CO	SU	LB	NY	LC	LH	PB	CR
1	50	53	55	59	0	37	44	52	0	24	0	0	44	50	53	51	58	65	0	60	54	53	0	29	17	62	41	43	30	25	27	38
2	73	68	70	75	0	58	63	51	0	35	0	0	47	54	46	42	46	74	0	57	65	61	0	30	36	69	72	56	61	39	35	59
6	67	66	61	64	0	47	62	53	0	14	0	0	24	27	29	58	75	79	0	82	63	85	0	78	18	57	50	74	27	10	12	48
7	48	52	59	71	0	65	79	40	0	42	0	0	37	46	50	47	54	66	0	56	40	70	0	83	19	36	35	60	59	37	32	45
8	42	40	43	48	0	51	55	37	0	38	0	0	50	59	64	61	60	67	0	65	45	75	0	68	39	44	25	59	28	20	18	52
9	70	69	80	39	0	30	38	33	0	11	0	0	21	32	37	63	36	38	0	42	29	47	0	60	26	35	32	62	13	22	20	19
12	43	52	51	65	0	54	64	45	0	37	0	0	35	39	40	66	38	56	0	31	19	34	0	57	32	36	55	41	24	30	29	18
13	50	55	53	28	0	41	43	79	0	52	0	0	51	54	39	70	40	68	0	43	33	45	0	22	46	59	47	66	54	49	48	60
14	61	53	54	22	0	27	40	75	0	66	0	0	45	48	46	72	55	67	0	50	52	63	0	25	42	64	53	85	50	69	62	67
15	47	39	40	33	0	34	32	69	0	54	0	0	42	51	43	55	26	44	0	32	14	38	0	16	27	65	34	35	39	50	59	17
16	54	45	50	42	0	26	46	77	0	18	0	0	17	20	24	48	10	32	0	15	12	23	0	34	13	22	31	20	28	53	73	5
19	28	44	29	45	0	46	37	68	0	39	0	0	30	34	29	33	19	33	0	16	15	13	0	22	35	17	50	17	21	42	43	25
20	37	42	43	40	0	30	39	66	0	44	0	0	26	25	18	45	23	48	0	23	22	24	0	58	38	25	70	24	56	61	68	34
21	46	45	47	28	0	25	32	85	0	57	0	0	22	28	26	21	25	46	0	17	18	27	0	52	44	34	42	37	39	58	66	26
22	33	35	39	24	0	22	25	65	0	75	0	0	45	49	58	66	48	64	0	46	42	44	0	31	36	38	17	42	53	63	71	47
23	28	40	50	37	0	36	34	46	0	33	0	0	10	32	22	61	24	45	0	27	17	25	0	44	16	29	34	29	55	64	60	24
26	31	34	44	32	0	37	38	60	0	35	0	0	23	30	29	62	11	30	0	10	12	13	0	48	12	16	43	15	79	86	75	9
27	35	36	38	40	0	35	54	67	0	29	0	0	39	42	46	81	48	56	0	44	46	37	0	63	20	36	45	21	80	51	40	42
28	34	45	46	39	0	58	67	68	0	22	0	0	48	50	57	58	40	47	0	36	34	39	0	69	21	30	33	37	63	45	35	38
29	59	52	79	23	0	42	53	55	0	17	0	0	43	31	60	82	34	22	0	21	28	25	0	77	18	64	41	55	64	58	53	35
30	78	67	77	51	0	54	59	71	0	11	0	0	17	19	34	75	50	39	0	30	38	43	0	60	26	69	61	45	66	62	57	52

DSI Data for October 1988

DAY	TR	ED	SP	SF	DM	JY	BP	CD	DX	CL	HO	UR	GC	SV	PL	CP	C	W	O	S	BO	SM	OJ	CF	CO	SU	LB	NY	LC	LH	PB	CR
3	60	46	47	63	0	74	73	82	0	20	0	0	49	53	66	61	63	61	0	49	34	55	0	33	41	50	64	74	62	39	41	36
4	61	35	50	57	0	64	71	90	0	26	0	0	45	55	69	64	81	69	0	68	61	82	0	16	40	59	57	63	66	55	28	60
5	43	23	44	46	0	59	56	63	0	24	0	0	59	62	74	66	64	65	0	41	30	58	0	20	52	75	50	55	54	53	33	42
6	46	27	39	37	0	44	45	71	0	20	0	0	60	66	72	80	76	78	0	47	48	59	0	36	54	62	61	56	63	50	30	52
7	79	76	80	45	0	61	65	69	0	42	0	0	55	63	56	73	57	70	0	14	24	25	0	19	70	58	82	57	66	44	23	24
10	40	36	48	76	0	78	84	73	0	56	0	0	81	83	75	82	62	60	0	31	30	42	0	47	71	40	74	69	55	30	22	50
11	55	67	49	74	0	80	87	68	0	38	0	0	35	38	33	84	63	79	0	43	44	57	0	45	51	48	75	74	43	36	29	51
12	35	45	25	84	0	87	82	57	0	60	0	0	50	52	62	71	67	82	0	36	47	56	0	15	60	76	58	59	71	44	36	40
13	44	46	43	75	0	76	73	72	0	57	0	0	48	51	55	59	69	76	0	62	60	73	0	28	64	80	66	78	56	49	42	75
14	51	54	45	69	0	73	67	78	0	66	0	0	65	64	76	79	58	60	0	54	63	75	0	26	65	46	57	60	36	40	37	64
17	64	62	53	67	0	71	68	70	0	63	0	0	59	61	77	58	74	76	0	66	62	79	0	48	74	75	62	53	60	33	17	70
18	67	58	56	72	0	69	77	85	0	30	0	0	49	47	59	74	46	40	0	41	46	55	0	45	82	54	53	37	39	52	33	56
19	52	47	46	61	0	57	66	77	0	62	0	0	44	39	56	80	40	46	0	42	45	58	0	50	55	57	42	49	32	51	20	53
20	48	46	57	75	0	78	83	74	0	50	0	0	35	46	53	91	28	25	0	23	22	52	0	54	60	58	55	51	22	28	39	27
21	52	43	52	79	0	77	66	79	0	36	0	0	27	21	43	62	26	27	0	19	17	23	0	63	72	77	46	62	47	38	57	41
24	45	46	44	47	0	50	56	64	0	30	0	0	23	18	41	64	40	48	0	39	40	46	0	57	79	76	61	75	56	45	66	52
25	42	48	45	34	0	44	39	58	0	29	0	0	19	22	50	52	25	31	0	30	24	29	0	75	52	43	56	57	45	37	58	26
26	39	42	43	73	0	75	71	54	0	44	0	0	41	34	65	40	45	43	0	41	42	45	0	64	53	72	40	46	31	16	39	58
27	70	71	40	52	0	48	67	51	0	47	0	0	38	32	54	59	46	42	0	47	48	44	0	56	34	61	30	45	22	23	28	33
28	71	68	45	56	0	67	76	44	0	65	0	0	64	56	75	77	49	40	0	59	50	48	0	39	68	55	32	60	23	26	21	62
31	75	70	48	32	0	35	29	17	0	38	0	0	61	59	76	79	58	59	0	67	56	63	0	24	52	78	47	57	45	56	29	66

DSI Data for November 1988

DAY	TR	ED	SP	SF	DM	JY	BP	CD	DX	CL	HO	UR	GC	SV	PL	CP	C	W	O	S	BO	SM	OJ	CF	CO	SU	LB	NY	LC	LH	PB	CR
1	58	67	55	49	0	60	51	20	0	35	0	0	52	53	75	64	60	54	0	62	31	50	0	42	66	43	42	45	32	54	36	63
2	41	32	47	80	0	83	74	55	0	54	0	0	81	79	86	83	72	65	0	67	59	75	0	64	85	87	29	76	44	70	58	84
3	67	60	64	59	0	56	55	48	0	51	0	0	62	54	60	43	45	47	0	58	42	59	0	46	50	47	25	63	19	34	30	49
4	26	17	36	45	0	47	50	31	0	70	0	0	69	68	72	46	44	42	0	56	21	64	0	35	71	40	23	62	54	61	45	58
7	30	23	34	60	0	64	69	32	0	62	0	0	74	67	73	34	51	61	0	57	33	68	0	65	73	41	25	52	55	56	53	59
8	36	34	41	42	0	48	52	49	0	46	0	0	58	64	57	39	56	63	0	69	40	70	0	54	65	30	24	43	45	57	38	66
9	31	30	27	76	0	77	83	48	0	72	0	0	79	78	81	58	47	59	0	62	39	55	0	71	75	62	22	29	28	36	27	61
10	40	36	35	80	0	66	68	62	0	67	0	0	45	56	64	25	18	37	0	24	15	32	0	83	48	46	39	50	43	33	36	20
11	21	18	14	75	0	76	75	60	0	56	0	0	54	53	62	31	16	40	0	15	23	29	0	78	64	32	48	39	21	27	22	28
14	39	46	45	42	0	38	47	33	0	75	0	0	63	50	59	34	48	44	0	39	32	43	0	50	56	58	49	53	40	41	45	46
15	52	45	43	46	0	42	49	28	0	47	0	0	55	43	41	18	24	32	0	25	16	23	0	48	29	44	35	40	68	53	47	35
16	17	19	18	78	0	82	79	43	0	32	0	0	53	26	50	22	33	36	0	29	24	37	0	56	52	42	38	39	72	62	40	25
17	25	21	24	66	0	64	65	48	0	23	0	0	32	20	28	41	19	24	0	27	18	26	0	38	50	24	71	25	37	20	19	13
18	27	24	39	48	0	60	52	37	0	44	0	0	23	19	25	42	38	41	0	34	28	38	0	33	39	45	74	14	25	21	22	24
21	42	38	33	50	0	59	53	75	0	39	0	0	28	30	36	24	58	52	0	60	54	62	0	59	77	49	55	32	31	30	18	51
22	41	30	54	57	0	65	68	86	0	62	0	0	33	32	47	66	63	61	0	69	43	59	0	42	65	68	57	35	46	34	29	48
23	59	45	62	58	0	56	60	68	0	57	0	0	42	37	51	80	48	55	0	56	35	52	0	32	53	77	62	36	76	43	44	60
25	26	21	30	65	0	66	69	84	0	80	0	0	62	58	72	92	63	79	0	67	38	54	0	35	78	85	70	49	77	41	20	62
28	61	54	60	34	0	37	45	65	0	58	0	0	36	37	50	67	26	38	0	27	16	29	0	12	32	75	53	52	63	54	59	44
29	63	62	71	37	0	42	36	64	0	47	0	0	28	21	38	60	42	74	0	46	31	38	0	37	43	76	55	50	48	52	55	46
30	58	60	66	41	0	59	74	62	0	64	0	0	55	52	73	68	57	76	0	63	54	56	0	39	24	67	29	61	45	59	65	78

DSI Data for December 1988

DAY	TR	ED	SP	SF	DM	JY	BP	CD	DX	CL	HO	UR	GC	SV	PL	CP	C	W	O	S	BO	SM	OJ	CF	CO	SU	LB	NY	LC	LH	PB	CR
1	69	63	43	34	0	45	46	66	0	68	0	0	42	35	62	76	21	47	0	38	57	36	0	65	41	84	54	77	61	70	75	72
2	40	37	34	66	0	70	73	67	0	75	0	0	78	59	89	55	59	65	0	71	69	57	0	48	46	78	50	80	9	51	64	83
5	48	42	63	41	0	44	62	69	0	64	0	0	57	46	71	64	19	34	0	55	53	45	0	52	63	77	66	86	17	79	78	60
6	71	66	64	25	0	40	50	53	0	58	0	0	52	39	77	70	56	67	0	65	78	63	0	55	34	54	60	66	24	63	49	71
7	69	60	56	17	0	19	29	30	0	63	0	0	44	33	70	79	48	59	0	68	71	69	0	57	48	72	44	75	40	52	41	68
8	54	56	47	24	0	25	41	39	0	45	0	0	30	26	48	76	69	83	0	70	79	66	0	59	22	54	63	72	15	31	28	64
9	61	48	57	18	0	20	32	41	0	69	0	0	36	40	47	63	70	59	0	66	75	67	0	68	30	79	67	76	60	69	47	72
12	59	40	38	19	0	18	37	25	0	57	0	0	28	34	32	45	77	62	0	56	73	51	0	79	21	72	76	80	66	81	70	67
13	62	31	56	13	0	11	18	29	0	53	0	0	22	36	39	26	70	63	0	45	51	37	0	80	17	67	58	31	52	75	64	48
14	32	17	28	40	0	37	34	30	0	66	0	0	59	56	76	44	75	48	0	60	53	65	0	86	31	63	67	50	54	62	51	75
15	37	28	39	16	0	14	17	25	0	43	0	0	20	28	21	38	79	71	0	65	56	63	0	87	29	33	53	42	70	67	46	47
16	40	26	45	18	0	15	12	26	0	67	0	0	41	35	16	25	80	73	0	69	63	75	0	84	48	43	50	52	78	83	62	76
19	68	46	71	8	0	9	19	62	0	45	0	0	39	36	19	69	83	81	0	87	69	78	0	80	43	36	55	68	77	77	58	84
20	73	52	59	30	0	26	23	61	0	57	0	0	38	35	48	71	58	58	0	58	52	52	0	77	72	68	79	68	77	64	57	86
21	63	50	63	32	0	32	35	62	0	55	0	0	42	41	46	61	76	81	0	86	74	85	0	76	68	71	57	67	82	67	42	76
22	67	58	78	28	0	24	28	62	0	72	0	0	46	44	50	56	72	65	0	68	75	63	0	46	42	57	55	72	85	78	46	52
23	75	55	76	27	0	32	38	73	0	68	0	0	67	68	57	86	74	75	0	74	71	57	0	37	78	67	85	67	83	83	45	86
27	38	25	58	14	0	30	38	60	0	76	0	0	33	46	45	57	76	64	0	80	76	76	0	32	62	57	65	38	65	68	55	55
28	29	14	29	26	0	30	35	81	0	63	0	0	16	23	9	48	63	46	0	44	42	52	0	77	47	54	56	41	55	50	14	33
29	64	41	65	22	0	26	37	70	0	62	0	0	30	28	29	63	60	57	0	54	45	64	0	92	64	56	67	54	55	39	31	52
30	64	39	78	64	0	64	67	77	0	69	0	0	39	37	57	42	74	70	0	79	50	77	0	82	61	63	85	58	54	44	26	70

DSI Data for January 1989

DAY	TR	ED	SP	SF	DM	JY	BP	CD	DX	CL	HO	UR	GC	SV	PL	CP	C	W	O	S	BO	SM	OJ	CF	CO	SU	LB	NY	LC	LH	PB	CR
3	27	17	30	38	0	52	62	64	0	69	0	0	37	39	54	52	48	48	0	48	30	66	0	92	85	27	27	26	69	48	36	29
4	19	16	74	47	0	57	61	72	0	48	0	0	25	25	32	70	65	70	0	83	50	82	0	57	50	46	25	19	50	58	58	67
5	26	17	58	13	0	17	22	68	0	71	0	0	25	22	40	68	34	71	0	68	50	61	0	61	27	19	76	71	59	82	87	82
6	57	32	71	26	0	26	30	48	0	73	0	0	32	39	52	46	79	68	0	63	52	73	0	61	19	48	63	67	64	78	68	59
9	60	33	70	32	0	45	34	35	0	69	0	0	30	32	55	23	64	59	0	47	49	42	0	12	28	36	67	70	74	53	31	54
10	47	38	56	33	0	40	36	31	0	60	0	0	22	23	42	21	53	45	0	38	40	43	0	46	25	28	65	59	55	44	32	34
11	45	29	60	31	0	37	46	40	0	64	0	0	29	28	34	26	41	35	0	30	29	37	0	32	21	33	74	67	63	28	34	42
12	72	61	73	22	0	29	35	64	0	65	0	0	18	21	37	42	58	52	0	44	36	51	0	54	45	50	72	70	69	33	39	49
13	84	70	87	10	0	16	9	42	0	72	0	0	12	16	17	66	61	50	0	62	30	57	0	48	30	34	81	85	64	25	26	37
16	73	71	75	24	0	21	25	49	0	85	0	0	24	30	33	82	19	20	0	15	13	20	0	51	29	59	76	72	40	13	22	14
17	65	47	62	35	0	33	43	48	0	72	0	0	44	46	53	83	11	45	0	19	25	14	0	64	23	29	52	75	56	31	27	35
18	68	60	57	20	0	17	18	62	0	79	0	0	33	38	57	63	26	42	0	32	43	34	0	61	42	41	69	76	24	10	11	53
19	53	56	50	48	0	42	43	87	0	49	0	0	58	57	55	67	17	56	0	20	31	19	0	55	62	30	51	44	21	26	23	52
20	50	55	46	65	0	56	66	63	0	47	0	0	81	85	83	72	29	58	0	26	33	21	0	62	93	36	34	35	16	25	28	57
23	56	72	51	57	0	45	55	70	0	44	0	0	67	79	75	80	42	76	0	32	27	38	0	35	75	32	26	37	14	15	13	45
24	72	78	67	28	0	25	33	81	0	56	0	0	40	58	62	61	45	38	0	35	32	51	0	14	64	7	29	42	34	20	16	36
25	43	52	50	44	0	33	46	53	0	72	0	0	59	77	78	40	26	36	0	25	12	25	0	30	51	32	10	26	45	39	44	28
26	61	50	69	35	0	34	41	62	0	40	0	0	32	39	53	31	59	65	0	63	45	66	0	50	57	24	33	53	41	36	40	52
27	70	56	75	33	0	27	34	73	0	53	0	0	29	35	37	42	48	38	0	40	34	43	0	24	71	44	52	82	59	38	35	36
30	64	57	79	45	0	35	39	80	0	38	0	0	28	24	46	21	47	51	0	52	48	49	0	65	44	43	36	57	78	55	33	47
31	49	40	78	25	0	24	28	56	0	32	0	0	31	26	37	27	69	63	0	70	59	67	0	32	48	83	65	64	79	72	50	68

DSI Data for February 1989

DAY	TR	ED	SP	SF	DM	JY	BP	CD	DX	CL	HO	UR	GC	SV	PL	CP	C	W	O	S	BO	SM	OJ	CF	CO	SU	LB	NY	LC	LH	PB	CR
1	44	46	59	30	0	37	36	40	0	69	0	0	34	32	55	10	46	28	0	56	54	50	0	25	52	63	36	75	80	63	51	55
2	48	33	57	29	0	31	27	36	0	62	0	0	30	26	42	14	54	30	0	55	62	53	0	43	72	69	50	62	71	49	36	38
3	43	19	52	34	0	40	26	65	0	51	0	0	33	27	43	17	50	56	0	63	75	58	0	54	65	57	71	59	88	69	50	62
6	32	25	39	50	0	48	40	69	0	47	0	0	68	62	66	18	29	30	0	43	42	36	0	57	88	73	44	70	63	37	28	24
7	68	50	79	32	0	33	25	64	0	67	0	0	52	48	65	39	40	32	0	42	38	34	0	80	63	70	58	51	72	32	33	46
8	57	35	70	41	0	40	42	53	0	50	0	0	56	55	67	54	17	34	0	23	24	27	0	51	35	74	75	52	54	39	28	32
9	23	34	38	62	0	64	60	61	0	42	0	0	47	45	50	35	26	20	0	27	29	24	0	62	56	73	40	15	24	35	38	19
10	16	13	36	32	0	35	37	59	0	40	0	0	17	16	31	23	39	43	0	22	40	26	0	32	55	76	42	25	23	44	47	27
13	29	17	24	49	0	53	50	34	0	64	0	0	27	39	42	20	25	31	0	13	38	12	0	37	52	60	39	18	40	48	41	20
14	21	23	34	67	0	74	73	68	0	45	0	0	36	44	46	22	50	26	0	48	60	52	0	28	92	74	48	30	32	53	45	51
15	33	28	42	70	0	67	74	77	0	71	0	0	43	46	69	35	44	27	0	24	53	40	0	55	67	58	69	27	20	43	34	48
16	34	24	46	75	0	71	57	23	0	72	0	0	31	50	67	39	51	24	0	27	55	32	0	48	65	80	33	20	39	52	37	29
17	37	29	57	69	0	66	75	22	0	77	0	0	30	67	70	20	54	25	0	55	64	45	0	52	61	82	42	17	62	38	36	60
21	41	25	34	54	0	39	36	19	0	76	0	0	59	68	55	65	52	34	0	56	76	47	0	25	44	60	46	79	81	84	72	66
22	32	21	33	65	0	61	35	17	0	73	0	0	53	66	54	70	54	36	0	57	75	52	0	18	64	61	50	65	72	74	49	70
23	29	17	37	63	0	67	60	41	0	72	0	0	61	65	56	69	58	49	0	59	74	53	0	44	66	52	37	68	60	76	57	75
24	31	26	18	59	0	53	50	22	0	71	0	0	56	69	64	56	59	67	0	68	75	65	0	32	79	51	19	57	58	73	44	53
27	50	41	35	53	0	46	38	10	0	72	0	0	55	51	50	63	56	55	0	65	73	62	0	43	38	70	23	80	61	82	59	64
28	53	36	32	55	0	44	33	28	0	71	0	0	46	47	49	65	66	72	0	79	80	73	0	47	34	67	16	76	60	83	60	65

DSI Data for March 1989

DAY	TR	ED	SP	SF	DM	JY	BP	CD	DX	CL	HO	UR	GC	SV	PL	CP	C	W	O	S	BO	SM	OJ	CF	CO	SU	LB	NY	LC	LH	PB	CR
1	39	28	30	51	0	48	38	29	0	69	0	0	49	50	50	64	61	63	0	63	71	59	0	42	50	58	22	70	57	77	56	63
2	47	35	31	41	0	37	29	29	0	70	0	0	40	43	43	66	64	62	0	65	71	61	0	46	41	54	20	70	59	75	57	63
3	52	37	36	34	0	33	25	31	0	68	0	0	39	37	39	73	68	61	0	64	70	60	0	54	31	52	21	70	56	71	55	62
6	56	41	42	27	0	28	24	39	0	66	0	0	37	35	41	73	70	62	0	65	68	63	0	61	28	79	24	65	53	67	57	61
7	59	45	45	20	0	24	21	39	0	62	0	0	41	36	45	74	69	59	0	61	64	59	0	65	28	45	29	62	47	63	56	63
8	67	49	49	19	0	23	23	34	0	61	0	0	45	38	50	69	66	53	0	63	62	60	0	69	29	49	36	63	43	62	53	61
9	65	48	49	21	0	27	27	31	0	54	0	0	54	43	61	62	65	59	0	64	61	63	0	71	33	56	38	65	33	58	47	59
10	60	42	46	20	0	24	25	32	0	50	0	0	57	50	67	57	59	62	0	59	60	63	0	71	31	58	37	68	36	58	50	62
13	51	33	49	20	0	22	21	29	0	50	0	0	61	58	66	52	59	65	0	59	59	61	0	67	29	62	36	70	40	56	44	65
14	47	28	50	22	0	23	24	34	0	55	0	0	60	62	65	45	63	70	0	64	63	67	0	61	30	65	38	71	41	52	41	63
15	42	27	56	19	0	20	25	38	0	59	0	0	59	69	59	45	66	74	0	68	69	72	0	62	35	61	35	70	46	49	44	64
16	38	23	61	19	0	17	24	41	0	65	0	0	53	69	52	39	65	72	0	68	67	69	0	62	41	63	38	68	46	48	46	61
17	35	23	60	19	0	17	25	40	0	75	0	0	51	67	48	34	67	69	0	76	69	71	0	63	46	64	41	68	44	43	48	64
20	34	22	48	23	0	23	31	40	0	73	0	0	49	63	47	32	69	59	0	78	71	74	0	65	51	64	43	67	43	40	53	63
21	29	22	44	21	0	24	34	42	0	76	0	0	46	60	43	40	67	50	0	75	67	70	0	65	54	64	42	67	48	39	57	62
22	31	23	34	29	0	31	42	52	0	75	0	0	47	59	47	31	61	43	0	74	64	70	0	57	54	59	44	67	48	40	55	59
23	32	27	25	31	0	36	45	57	0	74	0	0	46	53	43	34	54	35	0	72	63	69	0	48	48	44	42	66	53	42	56	54
27	39	31	29	31	0	36	46	60	0	70	0	0	38	46	38	38	45	26	0	60	55	59	0	37	45	37	49	62	52	43	49	41
28	44	38	37	24	0	30	38	57	0	70	0	0	29	36	31	43	35	27	0	47	42	46	0	30	43	30	55	63	45	44	48	29
29	49	44	41	24	0	27	32	53	0	62	0	0	24	28	26	42	27	27	0	37	32	37	0	28	43	30	61	62	45	42	45	23
30	50	45	46	19	0	23	26	44	0	61	0	0	21	22	21	39	21	24	0	25	22	24	0	26	39	34	63	57	42	34	42	18
31	53	51	55	19	0	24	21	37	0	57	0	0	24	24	27	34	22	23	0	18	16	17	0	28	42	46	65	56	42	30	41	18

DSI Data for April 1989

DAY	TR	ED	SP	SF	DM	JY	BP	CD	DX	CL	HO	UR	GC	SV	PL	CP	C	W	O	S	BO	SM	OJ	CF	CO	SU	LB	NY	LC	LH	PB	CR
3	56	58	59	51	0	57	52	65	0	39	0	0	33	29	32	14	9	30	0	13	19	14	0	44	38	75	69	77	19	17	18	12
4	72	79	53	55	0	56	63	82	0	51	0	0	35	26	15	18	29	22	0	25	26	23	0	52	24	68	71	78	27	28	14	30
5	67	62	60	48	0	50	44	59	0	27	0	0	20	25	21	17	35	32	0	34	29	28	0	64	5	42	20	70	26	27	25	14
6	51	46	45	53	0	49	47	44	0	21	0	0	23	25	16	30	36	31	0	32	27	29	0	65	19	65	24	54	29	18	19	20
7	53	50	73	34	0	32	31	35	0	28	0	0	17	20	14	28	23	13	0	15	20	22	0	79	25	67	36	61	32	25	20	19
10	46	59	68	29	0	33	37	58	0	72	0	0	60	62	47	74	31	34	0	50	42	51	0	86	30	31	35	76	43	38	22	47
11	47	48	65	19	0	25	26	46	0	59	0	0	43	55	36	64	27	39	0	48	43	38	0	73	45	37	20	82	25	23	13	28
12	32	46	54	25	0	27	28	51	0	64	0	0	70	75	61	89	50	53	0	59	52	57	0	60	18	42	21	65	20	39	26	52
13	25	40	42	43	0	46	50	67	0	33	0	0	62	69	76	44	45	58	0	50	31	42	0	61	25	43	24	75	23	55	32	56
14	73	76	78	50	0	54	69	89	0	53	0	0	27	29	55	68	63	79	0	70	57	77	0	76	26	35	71	64	30	57	38	69
17	55	51	54	63	0	53	72	65	0	67	0	0	24	25	50	43	80	74	0	77	73	79	0	66	57	52	56	69	46	68	53	71
18	77	75	71	78	0	60	63	72	0	54	0	0	8	15	34	40	51	55	0	53	48	52	0	50	65	56	25	73	44	67	39	56
19	72	78	76	64	0	53	50	54	0	70	0	0	16	17	35	36	39	66	0	35	49	43	0	86	50	82	34	68	14	29	15	42
20	44	47	64	70	0	65	53	88	0	68	0	0	42	36	60	29	45	43	0	46	35	51	0	72	63	67	23	34	25	37	7	48
21	54	48	62	53	0	48	46	51	0	66	0	0	41	38	59	41	63	65	0	74	70	73	0	78	36	72	16	69	41	46	55	72
24	59	57	79	33	0	47	44	46	0	58	0	0	56	49	64	55	34	58	0	31	28	29	0	60	39	53	45	57	30	45	42	54
25	68	73	56	20	0	39	31	34	0	75	0	0	48	47	52	61	18	59	0	16	27	19	0	58	46	54	47	60	22	61	57	35
26	65	80	54	12	0	38	13	24	0	60	0	0	32	37	58	69	38	67	0	29	48	28	0	34	26	46	10	38	30	56	63	24
27	77	86	73	16	0	29	21	35	0	38	0	0	17	25	43	45	37	35	0	11	14	16	0	32	12	39	48	32	42	77	52	17
28	70	62	64	10	0	17	14	56	0	27	0	0	9	11	21	40	42	63	0	15	23	18	0	14	28	26	50	25	46	60	37	16

DSI Data for May 1989

DAY	TR	ED	SP	SF	DM	JY	BP	CD	DX	CL	HO	UR	GC	SV	PL	CP	C	W	O	S	BO	SM	OJ	CF	CO	SU	LB	NY	LC	LH	PB	CR
1	37	32	34	13	0	16	14	45	0	43	0	0	24	25	21	20	73	85	0	61	66	63	0	17	29	53	48	32	54	70	42	56
2	53	54	46	23	0	15	26	84	0	21	0	0	16	14	33	13	55	78	0	42	62	39	0	36	52	50	69	53	55	72	40	47
3	48	56	52	20	0	18	15	65	0	38	0	0	25	26	25	12	74	84	0	73	76	60	0	64	50	46	62	75	63	71	29	62
4	47	48	54	28	0	34	20	66	0	50	0	0	17	25	40	33	64	65	0	62	68	63	0	47	18	49	70	86	77	72	38	67
5	54	65	55	19	0	17	14	57	0	22	0	0	18	24	34	15	75	74	0	76	73	71	0	44	35	58	56	66	72	70	39	65
8	43	50	31	18	0	22	15	58	0	20	0	0	27	26	39	8	71	75	0	65	82	62	0	60	9	52	33	84	65	74	50	34
9	24	33	25	39	0	35	29	36	0	34	0	0	52	50	48	27	55	62	0	63	69	43	0	76	28	51	40	57	83	81	77	55
10	19	40	32	43	0	38	36	37	0	35	0	0	33	42	44	41	60	46	0	52	61	39	0	27	25	54	63	78	69	84	80	56
11	30	66	50	21	0	19	17	56	0	50	0	0	59	53	65	37	39	48	0	40	49	26	0	29	27	85	70	82	62	63	64	48
12	80	89	86	6	0	8	9	39	0	58	0	0	17	15	30	29	44	47	0	43	32	30	0	43	59	70	84	90	68	87	88	54
15	66	62	70	13	0	14	7	28	0	64	0	0	14	10	22	15	46	26	0	19	9	12	0	28	42	40	73	62	51	74	57	20
16	69	55	54	16	0	15	20	37	0	73	0	0	21	13	21	11	22	24	0	10	8	9	0	64	19	55	42	58	35	37	41	12
17	84	75	82	4	0	7	5	26	0	35	0	0	16	8	13	24	15	29	0	11	18	10	0	50	59	53	45	63	20	45	58	28
18	72	61	79	26	0	32	25	23	0	44	0	0	11	14	9	15	41	34	0	40	35	38	0	89	60	45	43	79	12	39	42	43
19	70	60	76	27	0	30	28	42	0	40	0	0	10	9	16	28	33	31	0	29	37	33	0	75	82	41	66	59	26	65	64	33
22	75	72	78	21	0	17	24	15	0	37	0	0	13	16	17	10	12	10	0	14	13	10	0	78	66	8	61	44	14	62	46	9
23	67	64	55	28	0	24	22	33	0	50	0	0	23	27	15	8	21	25	0	26	29	27	0	69	70	7	72	56	32	59	54	13
24	68	62	48	23	0	16	19	17	0	72	0	0	26	33	30	23	18	34	0	31	30	35	0	47	58	11	65	69	10	44	35	22
25	54	50	55	46	0	34	42	19	0	68	0	0	51	49	56	25	44	35	0	37	34	40	0	65	76	19	60	52	8	23	18	32
26	62	61	68	45	0	43	40	39	0	54	0	0	33	40	34	32	20	29	0	45	31	46	0	60	57	18	69	68	21	20	25	15
30	41	43	29	44	0	25	22	30	0	75	0	0	40	42	38	55	17	19	0	39	27	45	0	64	18	37	46	80	30	14	10	13
31	55	52	51	60	0	36	37	32	0	59	0	0	21	17	29	43	26	15	0	33	18	32	0	33	11	10	45	64	35	33	28	18

DSI Data for June 1989

DAY	TR	ED	SP	SF	DM	JY	BP	CD	DX	CL	HO	UR	GC	SV	PL	CP	C	W	O	S	BO	SM	OJ	CF	CO	SU	LB	NY	LC	LH	PB	CR
1	59	53	63	70	0	35	33	34	0	60	0	0	37	29	38	28	32	25	0	40	15	39	0	32	12	62	43	65	57	37	40	32
2	75	69	83	84	0	67	74	50	0	73	0	0	58	50	42	56	39	21	0	32	25	38	0	43	30	42	68	61	28	26	25	48
5	64	70	42	38	0	42	32	44	0	65	0	0	45	41	40	19	53	43	0	55	39	54	0	29	25	46	77	23	56	67	62	50
6	43	46	44	59	0	50	41	56	0	52	0	0	67	65	63	30	37	31	0	52	50	38	0	33	32	44	71	28	53	45	32	39
7	65	68	64	57	0	48	55	67	0	27	0	0	63	64	54	42	31	22	0	40	38	32	0	21	33	70	62	24	66	53	50	36
8	73	69	60	53	0	32	46	57	0	40	0	0	62	65	52	60	28	27	0	54	43	42	0	41	56	75	47	27	52	36	54	61
9	85	78	64	22	0	15	14	38	0	46	0	0	16	17	10	33	23	42	0	26	19	21	0	40	43	66	52	39	72	20	29	17
12	61	55	48	35	0	21	15	37	0	11	0	0	36	35	30	27	22	54	0	9	12	10	0	26	57	79	65	64	75	49	67	18
13	49	47	50	32	0	23	27	42	0	21	0	0	33	28	22	29	35	62	0	43	37	39	0	8	48	77	40	72	66	34	55	30
14	57	52	61	23	0	16	14	36	0	50	0	0	35	31	37	53	64	68	0	79	62	56	0	32	35	83	36	80	71	25	46	49
15	29	19	30	65	0	57	64	55	0	56	0	0	58	52	51	46	60	53	0	77	54	70	0	33	37	89	50	69	78	59	65	58
16	33	26	32	58	0	46	44	52	0	20	0	0	40	43	54	42	74	70	0	73	53	72	0	22	34	80	62	73	84	76	68	55
19	27	25	40	72	0	55	58	39	0	48	0	0	59	60	68	77	85	72	0	87	58	83	0	17	24	63	60	52	86	82	69	80
20	53	48	46	41	0	32	37	38	0	54	0	0	32	35	46	55	69	61	0	68	49	72	0	36	31	70	56	29	57	53	52	59
21	47	36	42	84	0	68	66	75	0	50	0	0	69	62	70	52	68	79	0	64	46	65	0	13	26	88	55	71	48	60	37	61
22	40	35	53	78	0	85	62	77	0	51	0	0	64	46	55	44	56	65	0	50	29	54	0	24	57	85	67	70	56	57	45	50
23	63	56	72	77	0	76	73	56	0	54	0	0	79	59	71	42	70	63	0	62	40	64	0	32	75	78	72	54	50	61	46	67
26	70	69	54	54	0	56	42	77	0	79	0	0	58	38	70	13	42	62	0	37	19	42	0	8	63	63	37	68	84	79	72	64
27	76	75	74	44	0	43	52	66	0	70	0	0	75	58	78	38	56	72	0	64	38	64	0	17	86	73	35	52	76	70	57	65
28	50	54	38	52	0	36	61	50	0	42	0	0	63	36	52	21	72	80	0	73	44	71	0	33	43	44	33	57	76	67	75	62
29	74	77	36	65	0	33	47	69	0	69	0	0	46	11	33	20	68	62	0	48	20	45	0	22	61	77	22	60	84	50	58	42
30	83	76	21	86	0	40	65	65	0	69	0	0	34	24	33	4	82	56	0	78	45	69	0	52	57	88	29	71	54	47	57	65

DSI Data for July 1989

DAY	TR	ED	SP	SF	DM	JY	BP	CD	DX	CL	HO	UR	GC	SV	PL	CP	C	W	O	S	BO	SM	OJ	CF	CO	SU	LB	NY	LC	LH	PB	CR
3	58	69	26	77	0	69	68	80	35	69	0	0	69	45	60	4	94	58	0	86	56	69	40	18	77	83	5	85	41	16	13	41
5	42	61	42	85	0	85	88	87	17	72	0	0	89	75	76	34	89	67	0	93	85	93	47	30	60	40	40	81	59	7	7	83
6	57	59	46	61	0	57	57	54	39	36	0	0	75	68	76	24	67	62	0	55	53	57	45	17	45	32	50	56	64	35	40	50
7	84	88	79	75	0	66	66	72	25	66	0	0	44	30	60	52	48	60	0	44	42	53	41	9	61	38	61	52	34	46	52	40
10	57	58	75	84	0	60	79	65	28	45	0	0	65	53	41	44	38	38	0	29	37	34	63	18	54	26	61	40	38	61	60	40
11	48	50	62	40	0	32	36	43	59	52	0	0	46	51	40	58	34	25	0	29	25	30	50	33	47	29	52	52	64	30	24	45
12	42	55	64	61	0	57	60	68	40	34	0	0	30	25	48	64	37	14	0	20	21	18	63	21	36	28	44	81	65	33	26	36
13	53	51	64	44	0	56	41	43	60	70	0	0	30	29	54	56	40	46	0	46	44	40	68	34	58	62	85	91	81	50	44	57
14	31	39	50	19	0	23	28	41	79	42	0	0	14	35	56	69	39	51	0	48	46	46	42	52	86	64	61	80	60	71	57	63
17	24	40	65	60	0	48	66	60	40	61	0	0	42	48	62	59	3	14	0	3	10	7	20	40	79	70	47	83	74	69	38	43
18	23	27	53	56	0	51	62	52	37	51	0	0	39	51	50	75	23	40	0	29	36	30	25	33	70	73	52	84	67	55	29	45
19	46	48	85	18	0	18	35	57	64	44	0	0	17	33	10	75	51	58	0	54	51	58	9	33	57	90	33	78	62	68	46	56
20	75	71	58	64	0	54	73	60	30	50	0	0	41	43	30	58	42	66	0	41	27	39	13	33	64	78	66	73	67	74	60	60
21	37	40	56	50	0	21	44	64	54	24	0	0	45	46	43	53	43	53	0	36	37	37	30	26	48	67	79	57	56	62	37	38
24	40	37	32	74	0	35	80	56	26	10	0	0	60	62	61	78	20	33	0	12	16	20	66	16	24	40	77	34	32	67	40	24
25	56	46	37	64	0	44	74	60	25	22	0	0	67	72	53	71	13	30	0	12	13	13	54	24	61	43	60	65	28	51	25	28
26	60	55	51	77	0	62	78	72	24	14	0	0	71	65	57	53	13	33	0	16	13	20	54	24	53	56	50	84	51	39	22	30
27	89	92	84	50	0	53	46	54	54	11	0	0	51	53	53	50	35	42	0	37	28	39	47	25	45	60	52	79	37	57	30	47
28	86	89	78	64	0	64	50	51	40	10	0	0	17	16	21	25	16	30	0	12	13	16	54	22	44	76	40	65	39	44	31	3
31	84	87	76	80	0	86	83	78	7	46	0	0	58	59	58	60	15	18	0	12	12	15	40	11	37	70	69	55	54	41	17	25

DSI Data for August 1989

DAY	TR	ED	SP	SF	DM	JY	BP	CD	DX	CL	HO	UR	GC	SV	PL	CP	C	W	O	S	BO	SM	OJ	CF	CO	SU	LB	NY	LC	LH	PB	CR
1	84	87	76	83	0	80	77	86	18	16	0	0	45	53	58	54	31	40	0	30	25	31	41	35	31	45	48	55	38	20	13	35
2	60	65	61	54	0	58	58	50	40	35	0	0	26	48	50	64	31	53	0	27	28	15	29	34	75	68	36	66	78	62	41	48
3	45	50	56	33	0	50	34	71	53	30	0	0	41	59	58	50	25	50	0	18	18	18	34	46	65	68	25	60	78	75	36	37
4	18	22	44	26	0	26	20	37	70	46	0	0	20	48	41	66	36	65	0	38	36	36	26	52	72	61	45	56	80	76	48	52
7	33	31	77	22	0	41	33	75	55	35	0	0	19	25	23	46	51	63	0	54	53	53	32	44	53	39	54	26	56	56	48	37
8	45	46	70	51	0	66	48	82	42	50	0	0	30	35	34	41	43	62	0	32	29	25	29	48	62	18	39	50	73	68	48	37
9	15	16	41	53	0	62	55	82	52	50	0	0	30	38	34	37	43	62	0	45	41	37	39	46	55	37	30	57	58	43	20	35
10	38	36	60	41	0	48	46	74	56	68	0	0	41	36	39	53	74	83	0	65	70	64	60	19	53	32	27	48	65	39	34	62
11	9	13	33	10	0	20	10	42	88	53	0	0	43	51	35	72	70	80	0	65	70	67	36	20	33	53	41	57	63	44	35	84
14	12	12	32	13	0	23	16	32	81	66	0	0	54	59	53	90	48	53	0	18	19	22	50	19	32	25	43	25	38	53	44	26
15	29	23	30	35	0	37	37	37	58	75	0	0	66	67	64	79	77	77	0	51	50	63	66	30	10	20	36	22	40	43	39	69
16	50	41	48	37	0	35	42	50	65	70	0	0	50	48	51	82	56	63	0	33	24	37	65	36	15	30	19	48	32	64	71	54
17	20	24	25	30	0	26	30	36	73	50	0	0	62	64	57	81	64	57	0	39	35	50	45	29	16	35	33	42	53	66	70	65
18	48	38	56	44	0	40	48	54	50	56	0	0	60	57	60	60	51	44	0	33	23	40	38	33	16	33	19	44	61	76	84	50
21	35	21	26	55	0	55	52	72	37	77	0	0	63	60	66	63	70	40	0	40	50	75	33	37	26	20	29	44	25	50	31	55
22	14	10	25	61	0	61	57	64	40	83	0	0	60	61	57	68	71	47	0	57	71	80	50	50	36	33	43	70	40	50	52	61
23	52	50	52	23	0	29	22	37	71	64	0	0	52	50	50	66	55	55	0	55	70	70	46	66	33	60	20	70	47	52	55	58
24	47	37	61	40	0	33	18	57	75	60	0	0	35	41	31	81	44	55	0	33	55	55	58	23	31	38	14	73	52	64	33	46
25	41	41	64	31	0	25	31	53	71	43	0	0	17	22	25	81	55	44	0	44	55	61	46	46	12	33	28	56	64	43	40	43
28	22	12	61	31	0	26	35	62	69	81	0	0	27	15	29	64	31	26	0	21	42	36	46	71	31	31	42	50	22	38	35	18
29	42	38	57	52	0	58	61	50	35	70	0	0	42	40	41	61	30	30	0	30	40	40	57	80	38	14	33	56	42	61	58	29
30	55	52	60	38	0	33	47	47	46	77	0	0	40	38	42	36	38	38	0	47	38	47	53	81	47	23	31	35	30	52	55	22
31	25	21	40	22	0	22	31	17	62	72	0	0	35	23	22	36	61	42	0	57	57	61	60	70	36	38	50	16	20	50	68	44

DSI Data for September 1989

DAY	TR	ED	SP	SF	DM	JY	BP	CD	DX	CL	HO	UR	GC	SV	PL	CP	C	W	O	S	BO	SM	OJ	CF	CO	SU	LB	NY	LC	LH	PB	CR
1	60	42	66	7	0	15	21	7	83	76	0	0	33	25	28	57	31	37	0	37	31	50	50	83	30	25	45	25	13	33	76	38
5	45	38	68	44	0	44	30	42	53	77	0	0	45	42	45	45	28	61	0	38	47	42	57	43	35	28	41	21	23	19	55	22
6	57	27	42	44	0	38	50	12	56	72	0	0	52	50	66	38	35	65	0	35	65	50	57	56	35	25	35	25	36	31	55	33
7	76	65	52	36	0	36	25	11	70	78	0	0	47	54	65	45	54	68	0	40	63	54	28	43	21	42	73	11	38	33	65	68
8	65	50	40	26	0	31	26	16	64	78	0	0	40	38	47	42	61	71	0	47	66	61	42	62	22	45	73	33	30	35	63	63
11	52	52	36	29	0	29	33	23	66	88	0	0	42	45	55	61	71	66	0	57	76	76	50	76	35	40	64	37	26	26	72	83
12	45	50	36	40	0	40	38	40	61	57	0	0	45	43	47	61	56	56	0	47	65	65	50	29	50	78	68	36	38	42	75	75
13	38	47	22	47	0	41	52	35	40	64	0	0	27	21	37	70	15	15	0	26	31	42	30	7	17	89	61	50	27	41	58	29
14	33	47	9	42	0	31	45	40	31	52	0	0	52	50	68	75	34	30	0	26	21	26	26	22	42	59	50	55	61	61	89	57
15	35	50	33	68	0	63	60	31	17	57	0	0	66	61	68	75	27	18	0	27	36	31	13	25	25	65	75	63	65	75	73	52
18	40	45	36	70	0	60	61	47	11	65	0	0	59	56	61	85	25	25	0	20	29	33	47	27	19	78	66	52	45	61	57	50
19	36	45	40	65	0	50	47	60	23	60	0	0	45	43	52	71	29	29	0	25	41	29	29	27	42	69	66	68	40	59	47	30
20	30	36	45	78	0	78	78	52	11	73	0	0	75	71	78	57	27	27	0	31	63	40	31	41	31	66	52	44	35	70	73	57
21	14	16	40	66	0	55	63	55	37	66	0	0	70	71	63	42	50	40	0	59	68	31	31	56	47	76	55	21	25	60	47	72
22	23	15	33	63	0	50	50	50	41	31	0	0	76	77	70	50	26	26	0	34	56	17	35	35	36	68	44	35	42	71	65	65
25	19	21	24	67	0	63	75	80	12	68	0	0	62	59	68	20	35	17	0	39	65	26	58	56	37	59	19	53	29	62	50	68
26	32	30	23	75	0	70	80	67	33	45	0	0	59	65	85	19	33	33	0	33	58	29	56	67	55	57	35	26	73	64	57	65
27	36	25	43	65	0	62	62	67	32	50	0	0	52	55	67	29	35	61	0	39	52	30	53	65	55	59	53	30	59	55	43	65
28	45	35	45	68	0	74	65	63	38	82	0	0	52	50	65	35	48	73	0	41	64	36	31	53	20	45	63	42	71	76	60	80
29	27	24	55	90	0	90	81	68	17	76	0	0	70	67	79	60	57	73	0	45	59	27	20	33	35	64	63	35	52	57	55	80

DSI Data for October 1989

DAY	TR	ED	SP	SF	DM	JY	BP	CD	DX	CL	HO	UR	GC	SV	PL	CP	C	W	O	S	BO	SM	OJ	CF	CO	SU	LB	NY	LC	LH	PB	CR
2	48	42	80	44	0	56	58	44	50	74	0	0	55	52	74	68	91	64	0	73	64	68	43	20	28	48	47	67	45	80	74	95
3	60	44	84	53	0	35	35	50	71	76	0	0	67	53	71	63	86	76	0	57	55	71	31	19	18	50	50	63	47	74	50	88
4	30	24	74	76	0	59	67	72	38	82	0	0	63	70	83	68	62	52	0	57	52	67	36	13	35	80	47	44	47	53	39	59
5	68	50	86	42	0	42	55	60	67	53	0	0	43	41	53	79	92	83	0	57	52	74	47	17	35	52	50	58	52	62	50	74
6	91	85	81	53	0	47	55	65	53	42	0	0	38	36	45	70	54	52	0	29	30	43	31	11	37	30	63	63	52	62	50	32
9	82	73	80	50	0	50	33	56	46	29	0	0	44	41	44	73	50	53	0	24	24	41	18	14	40	41	83	57	69	76	63	31
10	71	68	58	33	0	28	21	50	38	61	0	0	14	14	25	47	30	45	0	18	27	32	29	6	30	29	53	33	55	65	47	21
11	38	42	33	32	0	32	15	47	56	68	0	0	38	41	42	60	35	43	0	22	22	30	27	28	20	30	69	50	76	76	60	32
12	67	63	35	37	0	37	35	47	44	63	0	0	40	33	35	60	27	50	0	23	23	32	43	29	21	45	63	63	67	71	55	42
13	57	58	20	74	0	68	60	68	11	79	0	0	43	45	42	42	22	35	0	17	22	17	27	17	26	74	38	58	81	86	80	60
16	58	59	58	65	0	59	67	44	27	65	0	0	53	45	44	47	33	43	0	38	29	33	29	38	24	71	25	41	32	16	44	29
17	68	72	40	61	0	67	56	44	19	58	0	0	71	50	40	26	64	55	0	55	36	45	20	29	44	55	40	33	65	80	84	50
18	57	61	35	72	0	72	67	44	13	61	0	0	67	43	39	28	73	55	0	59	61	59	20	39	37	68	31	39	75	65	58	63
19	71	72	57	63	0	47	32	26	41	55	0	0	50	32	35	40	78	57	0	61	70	65	27	41	32	73	13	21	76	71	55	63
20	63	65	39	44	0	38	29	31	43	12	0	0	47	21	33	12	60	50	0	55	71	75	31	40	31	68	14	33	72	67	71	59
23	73	68	19	63	0	53	58	62	29	45	0	0	68	43	48	10	52	48	0	43	52	61	20	44	75	52	41	42	76	76	45	40
24	60	65	32	53	0	59	56	41	33	39	0	0	80	57	68	26	43	33	0	52	43	48	17	60	39	43	14	25	68	63	56	53
25	60	63	30	47	0	53	63	39	38	32	0	0	40	38	26	26	77	32	0	50	55	55	40	47	33	52	27	47	55	60	47	53
26	48	52	27	45	0	40	38	25	50	24	0	0	61	48	57	14	71	33	0	58	64	54	35	22	20	52	29	63	50	45	43	38
27	35	35	26	88	0	82	50	42	18	39	0	0	85	75	83	39	52	24	0	43	59	52	25	25	17	71	27	35	32	26	22	39
30	52	59	30	50	0	50	42	39	38	37	0	0	52	38	63	16	55	23	0	50	61	36	36	47	22	64	53	67	30	30	47	42
31	57	55	55	45	0	45	38	50	44	62	0	0	48	43	52	38	33	13	0	38	52	33	50	50	24	48	41	75	59	59	71	52

DSI Data for November 1989

DAY	TR	ED	SP	SF	DM	JY	BP	CD	DX	CL	HO	UR	GC	SV	PL	CP	C	W	O	S	BO	SM	OJ	CF	CO	SU	LB	NY	LC	LH	PB	CR
1	60	44	37	50	0	44	47	50	41	72	0	0	58	48	58	42	24	24	0	29	36	29	64	35	17	65	20	56	45	60	68	63
2	67	53	15	63	0	42	30	50	39	53	0	0	76	62	85	15	50	45	0	50	61	55	60	53	37	81	47	53	43	62	65	95
3	45	16	10	53	0	42	37	45	47	58	0	0	71	52	60	35	45	64	0	68	70	55	44	42	30	67	44	45	62	62	75	80
6	27	15	5	47	0	37	40	60	33	35	0	0	81	64	67	20	27	45	0	52	52	43	40	42	14	55	29	33	52	57	55	50
7	76	68	42	72	0	56	58	60	24	56	0	0	90	74	84	37	38	57	0	48	52	38	53	47	28	95	71	67	50	70	63	84
8	57	45	42	55	0	42	58	63	33	37	0	0	95	67	85	60	32	32	0	41	41	32	47	72	65	82	59	56	71	52	60	85
9	64	47	30	37	0	42	40	68	53	55	0	0	76	68	86	55	23	32	0	45	52	41	47	65	47	91	81	56	76	52	55	75
10	62	58	37	21	0	21	32	58	61	67	0	0	60	43	70	21	48	57	0	67	76	48	33	56	50	86	63	32	60	60	58	79
13	55	44	50	17	0	28	37	61	73	44	0	0	76	52	85	53	50	32	0	77	77	59	57	71	33	57	73	6	60	75	79	78
14	43	40	23	60	0	55	71	45	33	37	0	0	82	87	81	48	54	25	0	71	72	67	67	79	20	67	67	29	32	45	38	57
15	68	68	52	42	0	26	30	29	44	43	0	0	68	91	67	45	61	48	0	57	57	70	53	32	15	65	67	53	57	67	55	75
16	57	56	40	39	0	39	37	56	53	63	0	0	71	86	75	53	59	64	0	77	64	73	43	41	22	59	67	35	45	45	32	74
17	40	47	53	53	0	47	50	38	33	59	0	0	95	90	89	28	48	57	0	57	48	67	54	25	12	76	64	38	44	74	56	89
20	45	53	33	35	0	29	39	53	44	78	0	0	85	86	84	11	48	67	0	57	38	57	86	31	24	57	71	13	63	42	39	78
21	32	48	38	75	0	80	55	75	6	63	0	0	86	87	86	30	35	48	0	39	26	43	50	24	37	52	81	28	81	71	55	67
22	57	58	40	72	0	44	21	50	35	42	0	0	81	57	68	21	50	50	0	68	59	68	73	19	22	27	88	39	80	80	58	74
24	58	69	59	69	0	44	41	65	20	71	0	0	83	74	72	53	47	58	0	47	32	47	64	29	25	41	69	63	89	83	71	82
27	39	40	50	75	0	55	33	60	17	60	0	0	57	58	55	52	29	54	0	29	21	54	65	33	15	38	71	16	59	50	48	52
28	50	50	59	85	0	60	48	65	11	29	0	0	65	67	59	57	33	46	0	33	17	58	69	32	30	46	65	10	59	50	43	52
29	38	33	36	57	0	71	36	57	32	41	0	0	57	54	57	43	33	50	0	29	29	33	81	37	29	13	56	30	32	18	10	33
30	64	68	70	63	0	63	50	62	37	68	0	0	90	73	62	40	55	59	0	41	36	45	69	44	50	24	72	47	19	29	10	43

DSI Data for December 1989

DAY	TR	ED	SP	SF	DM	JY	BP	CD	DX	CL	HO	UR	GC	SV	PL	CP	C	W	O	S	BO	SM	OJ	CF	CO	SU	LB	NY	LC	LH	PB	CR
1	65	62	67	55	0	50	33	52	48	86	0	0	82	57	68	24	26	57	0	35	39	30	75	47	29	27	59	37	45	41	14	38
4	65	50	43	37	0	26	26	50	53	68	0	0	43	38	15	20	23	41	0	23	32	27	80	28	30	5	50	16	55	25	10	32
5	57	53	33	68	0	47	53	79	18	53	0	0	48	36	30	15	39	39	0	48	48	39	65	47	50	32	59	28	52	71	25	42
6	53	47	47	65	0	35	50	83	13	71	0	0	53	40	33	22	43	48	0	43	38	38	62	38	33	40	73	25	47	58	28	47
7	50	26	50	63	0	26	55	60	28	56	0	0	74	70	63	37	57	52	0	43	48	43	73	39	15	33	72	22	43	38	15	32
8	57	39	43	32	0	16	32	55	41	79	0	0	67	59	40	20	39	65	0	57	65	39	80	41	35	27	88	22	19	14	10	26
11	45	48	32	65	0	40	71	60	17	67	0	0	74	71	50	19	38	63	0	46	52	50	78	40	50	22	71	50	64	32	19	55
12	43	32	70	76	0	43	77	48	14	68	0	0	75	56	61	9	32	52	0	36	40	36	84	38	64	46	74	41	64	30	18	57
13	40	26	70	72	0	39	63	68	31	61	0	0	35	33	11	47	52	74	0	61	61	57	88	78	53	43	75	58	70	55	53	61
14	59	42	52	58	0	32	55	60	39	50	0	0	57	45	30	60	43	70	0	65	61	65	69	47	20	35	63	42	86	57	40	55
15	57	40	50	78	0	39	84	80	17	72	0	0	90	59	50	63	45	59	0	50	55	55	69	78	26	36	76	47	80	25	21	53
18	58	44	32	82	0	59	83	72	7	88	0	0	58	50	33	50	48	57	0	48	62	57	73	38	17	29	79	47	79	58	50	56
19	41	33	14	45	0	45	52	57	50	70	0	0	50	43	24	57	35	61	0	43	61	57	95	35	33	27	89	30	77	59	24	50
20	55	53	35	61	0	44	74	58	31	67	0	0	62	50	50	58	43	55	0	50	59	59	82	56	53	9	75	39	65	50	11	32
21	43	50	65	61	0	50	89	53	31	79	0	0	52	41	40	63	45	64	0	45	32	36	88	44	42	27	75	67	80	60	26	58
22	22	24	56	75	0	81	88	76	7	81	0	0	63	60	61	75	40	50	0	35	40	40	81	56	29	37	60	69	44	44	35	56
26	25	27	33	50	0	80	82	33	22	82	0	0	31	50	33	73	23	23	0	31	31	17	70	80	45	15	70	83	92	50	36	73
27	27	20	43	79	0	57	71	80	7	57	0	0	20	19	14	36	40	13	0	13	13	20	57	15	8	50	62	64	50	50	38	43
28	37	39	44	24	0	29	39	63	63	65	0	0	39	32	33	50	68	63	0	63	47	63	75	47	22	47	50	61	68	58	53	65
29	33	27	58	40	0	60	42	54	33	80	0	0	50	54	33	67	46	25	0	33	25	33	80	20	33	46	50	25	23	15	25	42

DSI Data for January 1990

DAY	TR	ED	SP	SF	DM	JY	BP	CD	DX	CL	HO	UR	GC	SV	PL	CP	C	W	O	S	BO	SM	OJ	CF	CO	SU	LB	NY	LC	LH	PB	CR
2	26	28	72	25	0	6	41	53	57	88	0	0	53	40	28	71	35	30	0	15	20	30	81	40	53	40	27	44	72	33	29	65
3	25	20	53	28	0	22	61	44	53	89	0	0	20	14	16	72	48	48	0	48	38	52	65	47	22	67	38	65	63	42	33	79
4	44	41	67	75	0	56	88	41	21	56	0	0	78	63	53	93	40	55	0	45	45	40	53	60	53	84	71	38	78	83	71	88
5	26	22	58	53	0	41	67	39	40	71	0	0	79	55	56	88	33	48	0	43	43	52	73	44	56	75	87	29	47	79	67	88
8	10	15	67	79	0	47	85	44	6	32	0	0	62	64	40	84	39	48	0	48	65	43	76	56	40	68	65	32	45	76	60	74
9	25	32	37	67	0	44	74	44	31	28	0	0	58	50	32	67	48	38	0	43	71	24	81	71	58	74	81	44	55	55	63	78
10	25	39	21	67	0	28	79	80	24	83	0	0	84	65	53	61	33	24	0	43	57	24	71	59	68	90	59	26	75	65	68	83
11	28	24	47	75	0	44	76	76	27	63	0	0	88	56	56	63	47	26	0	53	74	37	67	60	94	67	73	53	83	72	76	94
12	17	25	12	75	0	38	76	82	20	56	0	0	71	61	59	69	58	21	0	37	58	26	87	33	47	67	75	59	61	44	53	69
15	17	29	22	44	0	25	59	28	53	44	0	0	78	53	53	24	75	30	0	35	50	25	53	27	59	68	75	47	72	61	65	63
16	19	15	48	32	0	32	35	15	71	63	0	0	57	27	30	42	61	4	0	9	30	4	56	33	50	59	82	53	71	43	55	37
17	27	19	36	60	0	40	33	24	37	26	0	0	64	48	52	37	57	26	0	25	46	21	74	56	85	50	90	60	82	59	71	75
18	29	11	35	28	0	17	26	11	81	53	0	0	45	19	32	35	67	18	0	27	48	19	41	38	50	55	78	44	81	48	60	67
19	52	55	52	42	0	26	35	24	47	74	0	0	57	23	25	21	45	13	0	26	35	17	63	50	40	50	67	58	90	62	55	47
22	45	42	16	22	0	11	21	15	82	33	0	0	47	40	37	28	29	24	0	29	24	19	82	63	67	70	71	56	65	65	79	50
23	41	38	45	60	0	45	67	38	50	40	0	0	82	70	52	30	46	25	0	38	42	33	67	35	67	61	63	58	64	50	52	45
24	38	30	43	53	0	42	70	24	53	42	0	0	76	55	70	30	39	26	0	35	39	30	53	53	60	68	78	37	67	52	55	47
25	18	14	23	80	0	75	86	9	33	80	0	0	73	39	71	40	21	8	0	21	17	13	71	78	62	83	68	40	77	68	67	40
26	13	18	26	52	0	57	82	48	30	67	0	0	83	58	68	48	40	20	0	20	24	12	60	70	73	67	62	27	65	52	41	48
29	10	11	30	83	0	61	95	35	12	83	0	0	65	38	79	21	27	5	0	18	18	14	65	47	63	62	78	37	55	25	21	50
30	19	15	19	32	0	26	40	43	65	42	0	0	52	33	70	30	30	17	0	9	26	9	69	47	74	50	56	63	81	43	35	37
31	55	48	64	45	0	50	62	38	41	65	0	0	50	17	38	55	29	17	0	33	42	29	67	61	45	35	72	70	50	18	24	30

DSI Data for February 1990

DAY	TR	ED	SP	SF	DM	JY	BP	CD	DX	CL	HO	UR	GC	SV	PL	CP	C	W	O	S	BO	SM	OJ	CF	CO	SU	LB	NY	LC	LH	PB	CR
1	50	50	52	68	0	37	85	33	18	58	0	0	57	45	63	42	22	9	0	26	43	13	41	65	47	45	94	79	48	10	10	32
2	47	39	50	53	0	24	56	26	38	71	0	0	56	47	61	59	25	35	0	35	60	30	38	50	39	42	82	78	63	11	17	35
5	25	21	45	84	0	58	75	28	18	16	0	0	65	55	79	37	24	33	0	24	38	24	29	47	55	50	82	84	80	50	60	42
6	11	22	32	78	0	50	84	24	19	33	0	0	47	32	53	22	30	10	0	45	70	45	25	44	39	37	75	61	63	32	47	28
7	43	40	43	50	0	40	57	14	47	25	0	0	57	38	45	65	59	50	0	59	64	55	56	63	29	57	68	67	71	52	48	65
8	58	56	47	44	0	44	53	22	50	33	0	0	47	22	33	53	35	30	0	25	45	20	50	63	41	58	65	71	63	47	32	39
9	71	65	57	40	0	45	80	20	42	45	0	0	33	33	48	85	41	50	0	68	82	55	33	72	55	71	83	70	48	29	29	70
12	47	50	37	33	0	50	68	32	38	44	0	0	53	47	53	56	55	40	0	40	65	35	19	56	39	63	88	50	68	47	37	61
13	62	65	40	21	0	42	60	30	61	47	0	0	35	33	55	58	59	45	0	55	68	36	76	72	35	45	83	85	62	38	30	79
14	30	42	42	50	0	50	63	21	63	56	0	0	42	40	53	83	76	38	0	62	81	43	60	63	59	35	81	83	60	55	37	72
15	23	33	67	15	0	35	43	55	83	75	0	0	24	27	43	80	65	22	0	74	70	57	56	44	60	41	95	80	64	41	43	75
16	32	44	44	47	0	59	72	37	67	65	0	0	56	58	78	88	53	25	0	40	55	40	60	63	53	37	65	75	63	47	44	59
20	10	16	25	72	0	33	89	37	31	72	0	0	65	52	89	72	50	14	0	45	50	23	63	75	67	24	47	56	45	50	53	50
21	32	19	27	75	0	45	85	67	21	55	0	0	27	26	48	70	79	46	0	63	71	29	79	79	81	35	47	76	23	45	33	65
22	43	35	38	58	0	32	68	62	29	63	0	0	38	27	45	70	83	65	0	61	78	39	47	71	63	27	72	84	24	48	45	84
23	38	40	38	42	0	16	50	38	39	37	0	0	33	14	45	75	70	65	0	35	78	22	28	61	55	36	32	75	19	62	60	63
26	64	70	64	35	0	24	24	50	72	79	0	0	36	30	33	55	54	50	0	8	46	17	22	61	52	43	16	70	32	64	29	45
27	75	78	67	33	0	22	39	61	73	35	0	0	35	24	21	47	50	23	0	23	55	23	19	50	67	24	19	88	30	60	32	44
28	52	64	57	24	0	14	36	57	80	30	0	0	26	22	18	86	72	40	0	60	88	44	37	84	81	25	26	85	36	68	57	67

DAY	TR	ED	SP	SF	DM	JY	BP	CD	DX	CL	HO	UR	GC	SV	PL	CP	C	W	O	S	BO	SM	OJ	CF	CO	SU	LB	NY	LC	LH	PB	CR
1	48	55	70	10	0	14	9	70	79	40	0	0	43	43	32	82	56	24	0	56	64	44	42	84	76	33	26	40	50	64	43	52
2	60	79	79	17	0	22	21	61	81	71	0	0	37	35	26	89	67	24	0	62	76	33	31	88	78	40	24	59	55	65	32	78
5	22	41	29	56	0	63	35	75	36	60	0	0	41	28	35	88	63	16	0	58	79	42	50	71	56	67	53	94	50	39	12	75
6	47	44	53	35	0	35	44	72	60	50	0	0	58	55	53	59	57	38	0	81	62	76	53	67	65	60	67	71	42	47	17	71
7	52	50	43	16	0	32	25	80	71	44	0	0	33	36	25	74	39	35	0	70	52	57	59	59	55	68	44	74	57	76	55	68
8	52	45	57	21	0	37	35	81	59	33	0	0	33	36	35	74	39	30	0	78	65	57	59	65	70	91	39	83	62	81	65	84
9	36	29	59	20	0	35	14	45	74	37	0	0	36	39	24	50	54	42	0	88	79	71	32	37	50	83	53	76	82	77	43	70
12	44	35	61	13	0	19	18	63	80	31	0	0	28	26	24	69	35	35	0	55	50	55	40	20	40	58	53	50	72	67	59	69
13	18	12	33	50	0	56	59	76	47	63	0	0	44	42	41	35	35	30	0	50	45	60	60	47	53	63	25	56	72	67	59	81
14	50	33	50	36	0	43	27	75	36	43	0	0	50	65	80	64	22	22	0	28	33	17	57	50	50	53	33	53	44	38	27	64
15	56	25	65	60	0	53	56	24	50	87	0	0	47	56	63	69	68	32	0	63	68	58	57	43	29	78	53	47	47	76	69	71
16	88	56	65	67	0	53	63	18	13	40	0	0	56	53	50	73	61	33	0	44	61	44	60	13	27	88	47	50	53	65	56	87
19	71	50	65	53	0	32	35	38	53	42	0	0	52	59	47	58	83	70	0	83	87	78	58	16	21	50	30	55	81	81	70	79
20	86	58	67	21	0	11	20	33	61	42	0	0	19	27	20	50	65	43	0	78	70	83	35	33	5	36	44	53	29	45	20	68
21	57	45	62	21	0	21	15	57	72	58	0	0	43	41	40	79	52	57	0	74	52	83	41	12	28	41	47	53	29	52	45	47
22	50	47	20	41	0	24	28	53	53	72	0	0	55	57	47	67	59	50	0	73	59	73	63	41	65	33	29	61	63	68	53	71
23	63	63	37	28	0	22	22	68	72	72	0	0	32	30	39	59	48	29	0	48	24	52	39	39	71	40	41	56	58	58	39	61
26	89	74	53	33	0	28	44	53	65	83	0	0	21	30	22	35	71	52	0	67	57	76	50	18	88	40	63	76	63	68	56	65
27	62	63	67	26	0	16	40	57	58	70	0	0	24	27	25	37	52	39	0	43	48	57	39	17	68	27	42	68	52	48	35	42
28	67	70	52	32	0	11	45	67	58	37	0	0	19	18	20	70	43	26	0	26	30	35	53	47	79	36	47	75	81	81	84	61
29	40	32	11	72	0	50	84	90	18	56	0	0	47	40	32	72	57	24	0	48	38	48	76	24	68	58	53	83	70	58	42	65
30	40	37	37	61	0	33	68	85	24	61	0	0	32	25	39	78	67	33	0	62	52	57	82	53	83	55	53	83	80	65	53	82

DSI Data for April 1990

DAY	TR	ED	SP	SF	DM	JY	BP	CD	DX	CL	HO	UR	GC	SV	PL	CP	C	W	O	S	BO	SM	OJ	CF	CO	SU	LB	NY	LC	LH	PB	CR
2	55	47	26	33	0	28	37	78	47	78	0	0	32	30	26	56	86	62	0	48	33	52	71	29	29	30	39	89	75	85	84	76
3	58	56	67	41	0	41	39	68	35	67	0	0	53	47	41	82	70	65	0	55	50	40	69	38	71	21	44	53	53	58	61	76
4	71	63	65	42	0	42	65	57	39	21	0	0	60	75	58	63	82	86	0	68	64	59	72	67	74	10	63	84	57	76	70	84
5	70	85	58	47	0	58	63	33	44	16	0	0	37	55	37	42	76	71	0	71	81	71	50	61	56	30	50	44	60	60	68	68
6	52	70	40	63	0	53	60	62	32	26	0	0	65	71	50	50	55	45	0	59	64	68	44	37	47	33	42	56	76	71	60	63
9	48	60	71	63	0	26	58	68	33	42	0	0	33	55	42	37	39	39	0	52	30	61	39	44	42	41	61	47	86	86	70	39
10	58	72	58	76	0	47	76	71	19	35	0	0	47	45	50	24	81	38	0	71	43	67	44	63	76	55	25	82	89	95	83	81
11	48	65	62	68	0	37	75	48	33	42	0	0	43	59	65	16	39	35	0	52	35	35	59	39	58	59	33	58	71	76	80	78
12	60	74	85	67	0	50	68	58	29	33	0	0	45	38	47	39	43	29	0	38	57	29	59	53	65	62	37	61	75	65	74	59
16	32	56	42	29	47	18	39	11	56	71	67	73	53	40	61	22	70	50	87	60	65	50	33	67	31	45	19	41	53	63	56	75
17	32	56	47	71	53	18	65	33	27	47	50	62	47	50	44	29	86	48	89	76	86	62	38	63	31	25	19	53	58	74	78	81
18	20	26	35	79	67	56	74	56	18	28	33	40	50	62	63	39	73	45	79	68	68	64	35	41	50	48	28	39	65	80	74	67
19	22	28	33	35	27	53	59	53	63	65	58	75	61	68	65	31	75	50	82	80	80	85	13	25	60	32	40	44	44	83	76	88
20	25	31	25	27	27	53	47	31	47	53	46	54	50	65	53	21	83	56	69	83	83	67	33	60	57	41	20	67	56	81	87	73
23	17	28	24	35	18	41	41	47	50	71	57	71	71	72	71	35	68	47	76	74	74	63	33	60	36	29	27	75	72	83	82	88
24	53	47	47	39	44	44	41	74	47	61	47	53	42	55	50	65	38	24	76	43	52	43	18	53	38	55	53	65	37	53	44	61
25	65	55	65	74	58	63	56	63	33	26	31	44	25	38	37	72	73	55	79	73	73	68	56	28	18	62	47	56	30	65	53	74
26	30	30	60	79	63	53	39	47	33	32	19	38	35	38	42	56	68	55	79	86	77	86	39	44	41	52	59	67	45	65	58	79
27	33	45	33	63	47	42	47	30	26	39	25	47	40	38	37	53	65	61	76	74	70	74	39	33	39	50	56	79	57	52	50	74
30	40	35	45	74	47	63	68	45	32	42	29	47	25	24	26	44	55	59	80	55	50	64	26	32	44	67	44	53	55	70	79	61

DSI Data for May 1990

DAY	TR	ED	SP	SF	DM	JY	BP	CD	DX	CL	HO	UR	GC	SV	PL	CP	C	W	O	S	BO	SM	OJ	CF	CO	SU	LB	NY	LC	LH	PB	CR
1	21	25	29	58	42	53	53	40	37	56	47	71	65	67	74	83	59	50	65	55	55	68	42	42	78	57	68	32	60	80	79	82
2	48	40	52	47	35	42	50	45	39	47	41	41	52	68	70	63	65	78	81	74	70	78	28	28	68	55	94	67	76	86	80	78
3	64	52	55	60	57	60	48	43	42	35	39	44	59	61	67	55	58	63	55	46	50	54	37	53	55	35	80	55	77	64	57	65
4	82	86	45	75	71	70	76	50	32	40	28	28	50	61	71	40	63	71	55	46	50	46	26	53	50	22	71	45	91	68	62	53
7	63	67	58	72	79	78	89	50	35	44	25	56	47	60	56	33	71	76	70	71	86	67	41	47	71	35	81	65	68	74	67	69
8	71	80	57	74	80	68	80	33	42	47	28	50	43	45	50	53	74	52	64	70	74	65	58	47	35	27	58	65	62	48	45	67
9	40	58	50	72	79	72	68	20	28	78	65	82	40	33	47	67	73	59	62	68	73	64	78	33	47	29	67	67	55	40	32	65
10	60	80	70	68	70	63	50	21	39	58	53	71	50	62	61	72	73	59	50	59	64	68	61	50	72	19	65	78	60	45	37	61
11	86	85	90	53	50	79	58	20	33	37	41	53	52	50	55	58	57	48	48	61	61	57	61	22	58	32	67	58	48	43	35	58
14	76	65	86	89	70	84	68	15	17	79	76	88	43	64	68	50	43	52	33	52	65	39	44	24	84	41	76	67	52	29	30	44
15	60	67	58	47	56	67	47	20	35	72	75	56	63	60	79	47	43	43	25	38	48	24	47	59	61	40	59	65	65	40	32	41
16	58	59	56	47	56	71	41	22	50	59	56	75	50	53	72	53	20	35	21	35	40	25	44	69	71	37	53	71	89	74	61	25
17	65	63	68	39	47	56	56	45	56	61	71	71	42	45	78	44	67	57	45	71	76	48	44	67	74	20	61	74	85	90	84	59
18	47	41	56	44	47	69	56	24	53	63	67	73	63	47	93	40	33	44	24	39	44	28	47	63	69	24	73	80	82	82	69	53
21	63	61	63	18	39	53	33	39	63	47	44	50	58	65	72	41	29	33	16	24	38	24	50	75	76	15	71	82	84	74	56	56
22	58	67	74	35	50	76	61	26	50	53	44	50	89	90	94	59	33	33	26	33	33	24	75	63	76	40	59	76	74	79	61	69
23	53	63	35	40	25	60	56	44	57	40	36	50	24	44	47	33	47	33	35	42	42	37	50	43	40	50	53	93	47	24	25	46
24	56	65	44	31	18	50	53	41	67	50	47	67	50	63	69	20	60	37	33	60	50	50	64	53	53	37	53	63	28	39	12	57
25	53	44	41	40	31	73	50	38	57	60	54	62	59	67	73	27	79	37	53	68	58	63	64	43	40	50	67	60	41	47	31	69
29	63	53	50	43	40	50	53	19	46	50	38	69	44	47	64	31	50	39	31	33	39	33	62	46	20	53	69	79	63	69	73	71
30	61	53	61	50	29	69	71	47	47	44	29	71	33	42	50	19	30	15	11	30	40	25	67	53	44	26	60	50	61	44	35	33
31	63	56	50	40	25	47	31	53	71	53	43	50	35	56	50	27	26	32	29	37	37	37	50	43	27	17	67	33	53	24	13	20

DSI Data for June 1990

DAY	TR	ED	SP	SF	DM	JY	BP	CD	DX	CL	HO	UR	GC	SV	PL	CP	C	W	O	S	BO	SM	OJ	CF	CO	SU	LB	NY	LC	LH	PB	CR
1	94	81	69	19	19	38	20	44	73	50	53	67	31	31	38	20	53	53	56	53	53	47	40	25	19	13	71	53	56	20	19	44
4	63	60	75	21	33	36	20	44	62	29	31	31	19	24	29	15	17	33	31	22	22	17	46	31	20	24	77	57	75	31	20	23
5	60	43	53	54	36	38	36	40	46	23	23	31	40	44	64	31	59	35	44	47	41	35	23	38	43	13	64	46	73	47	43	38
6	47	50	47	20	25	33	40	56	73	47	36	43	24	22	25	27	53	42	61	37	37	21	33	53	56	28	80	80	71	24	19	50
7	53	50	53	40	50	60	67	59	73	53	47	53	24	22	38	27	74	68	67	58	74	42	40	60	63	28	56	31	71	29	38	47
8	39	44	33	25	29	38	47	53	73	31	20	40	28	16	44	27	62	43	53	57	76	43	33	33	41	16	67	31	84	16	33	47
11	35	28	37	33	42	22	42	40	67	33	28	56	42	35	44	28	86	57	57	62	86	62	28	29	17	25	72	32	75	40	53	72
12	40	40	58	37	30	37	79	50	61	63	59	71	37	35	35	18	81	62	55	48	48	48	39	28	39	25	67	44	50	15	37	47
13	80	74	47	78	53	39	79	45	22	56	76	65	16	15	32	11	57	48	33	57	52	52	44	26	47	25	84	63	80	35	47	56
14	61	53	35	56	53	38	47	33	38	75	69	81	18	17	18	18	37	53	32	32	21	21	31	25	24	22	82	53	56	22	18	38
15	33	16	55	68	60	47	70	20	28	47	56	67	25	19	32	26	23	23	19	27	23	14	11	22	35	19	74	32	52	29	30	21
18	22	18	12	81	71	53	81	41	7	44	36	75	24	22	24	69	58	26	28	58	42	53	20	27	41	11	93	50	78	39	18	50
19	10	11	5	78	68	56	56	37	22	44	44	61	16	20	11	22	48	38	38	52	43	29	22	17	32	35	63	68	70	50	32	33
20	14	8	8	83	62	83	85	50	17	58	67	75	46	43	46	31	73	60	53	60	47	40	42	17	46	43	85	54	36	29	31	50
21	42	42	56	61	58	50	67	37	28	78	76	82	44	47	47	29	55	55	55	75	70	65	28	22	28	32	78	39	58	26	17	33
22	45	53	32	83	63	72	84	45	11	89	78	78	47	30	42	21	38	43	29	43	48	48	39	22	37	55	68	79	30	40	16	28
25	8	9	25	60	27	30	50	58	45	60	70	80	45	38	55	55	54	54	50	69	54	62	45	30	27	31	64	64	54	62	8	55
26	32	28	15	82	67	53	78	74	22	50	61	72	58	55	67	37	57	43	40	62	67	62	24	39	42	33	72	67	21	63	28	47
27	55	63	53	44	47	61	74	89	29	28	24	35	40	38	47	53	59	57	50	68	55	59	24	18	42	19	56	50	50	55	58	61
28	38	52	57	35	38	60	76	82	42	65	63	42	41	22	43	70	83	70	82	75	58	67	68	15	48	43	70	75	36	45	38	70
29	60	53	26	61	63	78	74	85	6	56	56	67	79	70	74	72	71	43	57	90	81	81	67	24	42	40	74	58	35	40	21	67

DSI Data for July 1990

DAY	TR	ED	SP	SF	DM	JY	BP	CD	DX	CL	HO	UR	GC	SV	PL	CP	C	W	O	S	BO	SM	OJ	CF	CO	SU	LB	NY	LC	LH	PB	CR
2	50	33	41	88	94	82	94	72	6	35	35	47	65	89	71	47	84	68	63	95	89	95	71	53	88	72	47	71	56	67	53	88
3	50	56	38	80	75	63	88	59	14	53	57	64	65	65	63	36	68	53	71	79	68	79	79	50	88	67	47	80	53	47	19	60
5	45	42	16	56	47	56	58	42	35	22	24	35	55	48	58	56	41	36	50	45	32	45	59	41	44	43	44	61	60	70	26	39
6	37	33	56	67	56	53	67	50	25	31	31	31	58	55	63	75	24	24	25	43	43	43	79	25	65	40	47	44	79	47	17	24
9	33	29	53	71	59	63	53	76	33	44	33	47	28	26	25	44	35	25	28	45	30	40	40	20	41	16	56	31	78	39	12	31
10	16	11	44	78	72	82	82	47	12	76	65	82	33	26	33	35	35	30	30	50	45	50	65	63	22	39	39	22	68	37	33	35
11	37	33	44	56	50	59	76	50	38	71	67	67	22	21	22	82	35	25	26	30	15	25	56	44	22	21	50	24	74	32	33	41
12	41	35	69	73	75	75	69	67	20	93	87	87	47	33	27	73	26	33	24	37	32	32	79	29	47	39	53	53	94	47	50	47
13	69	80	71	40	40	64	53	53	46	71	77	77	69	59	60	54	33	39	35	50	39	33	75	23	50	53	29	64	75	50	27	43
16	37	44	67	22	22	47	50	39	63	88	88	88	53	35	17	53	10	10	10	10	14	5	73	33	61	25	29	41	83	79	44	29
17	39	41	24	65	61	76	94	76	19	65	69	63	35	17	19	38	16	32	22	26	32	16	44	31	31	11	27	50	67	72	35	29
18	31	33	27	40	33	64	60	63	62	57	69	62	60	44	50	43	18	24	25	29	29	24	46	46	36	13	29	36	81	50	33	29
19	25	38	33	64	63	73	73	73	21	73	71	71	44	29	40	46	17	17	13	22	22	17	71	57	36	47	50	14	50	25	20	20
20	41	44	50	63	69	40	81	65	29	67	64	64	41	22	33	47	16	26	22	22	21	21	47	43	43	50	47	7	65	47	31	21
23	24	38	6	88	81	73	88	71	13	93	93	93	76	56	56	33	58	53	56	53	47	53	47	40	44	22	25	31	53	24	25	53
24	18	25	13	88	81	53	69	56	14	87	79	79	31	35	27	57	33	50	59	28	28	17	29	50	53	24	47	60	88	53	56	33
25	53	50	64	57	64	23	43	79	42	23	25	33	53	25	38	67	47	41	63	41	65	35	58	58	69	31	69	23	80	87	93	83
26	47	44	31	63	69	40	75	50	33	40	40	47	38	35	40	80	61	47	65	61	56	56	57	67	69	41	69	53	76	71	63	73
27	75	73	18	73	73	70	91	75	20	50	50	60	25	31	36	91	29	36	46	36	57	36	30	60	82	31	45	36	92	75	64	30
30	94	94	31	88	94	87	88	75	14	60	57	57	12	17	27	27	32	16	35	37	53	32	21	36	33	33	64	14	88	76	56	47
31	63	79	33	93	93	93	93	71	8	93	85	85	25	18	43	85	33	22	71	72	78	44	62	85	36	24	69	21	81	81	80	71

DSI Data for August 1990

DAY	TR	ED	SP	SF	DM	JY	BP	CD	DX	CL	HO	UR	GC	SV	PL	CP	C	W	O	S	BO	SM	OJ	CF	CO	SU	LB	NY	LC	LH	PB	CR
1	76	80	38	63	69	73	63	47	27	93	93	87	76	33	81	87	11	5	32	32	47	16	47	87	25	17	63	25	53	47	38	40
2	35	50	13	50	56	40	63	65	27	67	67	73	59	28	50	53	16	32	28	37	42	26	67	47	19	17	47	31	12	24	19	47
3	27	71	21	79	71	54	86	85	25	69	67	67	57	40	54	46	19	19	25	44	38	25	67	42	14	13	23	38	40	27	71	58
6	15	58	17	98	92	45	98	83	10	82	80	80	85	71	91	56	47	20	46	57	47	57	50	73	8	46	18	55	62	62	83	70
7	20	50	21	43	43	38	57	67	31	69	69	69	50	33	43	57	44	25	31	50	56	44	46	54	36	27	29	50	80	40	64	69
8	8	33	33	58	62	45	58	75	27	55	70	60	62	43	55	82	40	40	14	33	33	33	70	60	25	29	18	45	85	31	42	55
9	54	69	25	45	42	50	50	75	55	73	73	73	85	43	75	75	27	60	29	67	73	60	80	64	42	29	36	27	62	23	42	50
10	36	38	38	77	69	25	77	57	25	67	58	58	85	71	85	54	27	27	33	87	87	87	58	58	54	36	31	31	50	43	31	83
13	33	43	29	86	71	46	86	80	23	85	85	92	93	93	93	57	6	13	19	44	56	38	77	77	36	33	36	29	67	47	43	46
14	50	45	64	91	91	70	82	82	11	70	67	78	64	67	50	45	23	23	38	69	62	69	89	67	27	58	50	10	42	33	64	56
15	54	42	58	75	75	73	83	75	10	82	80	90	58	62	55	75	36	43	62	64	57	57	80	70	27	69	64	18	38	23	33	64
16	17	10	9	73	82	70	91	64	22	80	89	89	83	77	80	50	36	36	36	57	36	57	78	56	60	54	60	30	42	42	27	78
17	27	9	20	90	73	40	70	82	11	90	89	89	60	64	78	44	67	50	67	75	33	75	22	67	67	91	44	44	9	36	40	56
20	38	27	47	40	33	50	40	53	62	69	69	69	50	41	43	43	50	39	56	72	56	72	15	62	64	50	43	57	25	56	60	64
21	33	21	21	79	64	54	79	80	23	77	77	77	64	67	71	54	35	24	41	76	65	71	23	62	50	44	43	64	40	33	43	29
22	29	31	23	62	46	38	77	77	25	83	75	83	64	60	69	33	44	25	47	63	69	63	8	58	50	40	31	75	50	7	23	50
23	20	29	14	79	57	54	71	73	31	62	69	62	67	50	64	15	47	29	47	82	71	71	46	69	86	63	50	62	27	27	14	62
24	27	29	36	54	57	46	64	57	42	62	67	58	60	56	54	17	59	41	63	82	76	76	42	83	85	81	67	77	7	27	29	64
27	76	75	75	44	69	73	63	44	36	7	7	7	18	22	20	43	21	21	22	42	42	42	79	71	60	56	60	80	53	47	75	27
28	40	33	43	29	27	43	57	33	38	57	57	50	20	19	29	15	29	18	18	35	35	53	57	50	29	27	62	36	7	7	7	21
29	79	77	85	33	23	67	54	31	64	17	18	27	36	33	50	25	19	13	27	25	19	25	27	55	42	29	75	50	29	43	23	17
30	60	57	43	23	21	54	36	43	58	62	50	58	40	31	54	15	18	12	24	29	29	29	25	83	57	33	77	62	36	21	21	38
31	80	79	71	8	14	46	14	15	85	42	50	42	20	19	31	15	24	12	29	29	29	12	33	67	64	20	77	38	36	21	14	23

DSI Data for September 1990

DAY	TR	ED	SP	SF	DM	JY	BP	CD	DX	CL	HO	UR	GC	SV	PL	CP	C	W	O	S	BO	SM	OJ	CF	CO	SU	LB	NY	LC	LH	PB	CR
4	53	64	36	43	43	62	50	50	58	77	75	67	64	36	54	38	25	25	56	56	63	63	8	58	69	54	67	69	80	73	50	69
5	47	73	64	86	80	86	71	71	15	64	62	54	57	40	46	36	50	56	73	69	69	63	31	83	23	46	73	85	73	67	64	77
6	53	57	21	57	73	71	71	46	23	86	77	77	71	57	50	50	44	50	69	63	50	63	31	54	62	79	62	62	60	40	43	86
7	69	67	67	29	33	79	33	27	69	36	31	38	33	44	38	57	29	24	24	41	24	35	8	31	20	20	54	64	75	56	47	36
10	60	43	50	7	29	85	7	14	75	43	54	38	13	13	8	42	39	61	50	67	56	61	25	42	46	53	67	31	75	81	53	46
11	44	20	33	13	20	71	40	40	69	60	64	64	50	38	40	62	47	58	53	84	47	79	31	46	40	69	54	21	82	76	56	64
12	63	67	47	33	27	93	53	36	58	57	46	54	53	53	47	54	24	41	40	65	29	65	23	8	50	27	43	62	63	56	60	71
13	60	64	38	79	71	92	71	43	25	69	75	67	50	47	54	17	13	19	20	31	25	44	25	8	69	29	54	62	40	33	43	31
14	44	53	20	73	73	71	79	40	31	71	77	62	63	63	57	46	22	33	38	50	33	56	15	38	71	20	57	57	63	75	73	57
17	38	50	73	87	86	86	88	60	7	64	50	64	81	59	60	43	22	39	28	22	33	33	43	57	80	50	33	33	69	81	80	57
18	53	56	44	63	63	53	69	50	43	60	50	43	47	47	47	13	32	37	32	42	42	42	43	15	47	35	27	60	65	59	63	47
19	64	46	58	38	43	67	42	77	50	50	55	36	29	33	36	17	12	6	13	12	29	18	27	64	38	21	33	75	75	50	40	33
20	40	43	14	29	29	62	50	50	75	62	58	58	67	40	31	8	28	22	24	28	28	22	25	33	29	33	15	77	63	75	60	38
21	20	14	36	36	43	85	36	80	46	85	85	85	40	38	21	31	44	39	22	22	28	22	38	62	43	20	14	36	44	63	47	38
24	13	7	13	80	67	50	80	69	7	93	86	86	81	76	67	36	63	53	32	42	37	47	36	29	60	56	13	7	18	41	25	64
25	35	25	50	38	44	73	40	53	36	60	57	50	65	44	38	13	32	53	32	47	47	47	50	36	38	47	33	53	18	24	6	40
26	27	21	14	57	57	69	64	42	27	85	67	67	80	31	21	15	41	72	50	33	44	44	73	25	15	27	75	77	6	13	7	54
27	33	40	7	57	53	43	71	27	29	79	85	77	67	38	21	46	41	56	44	56	44	50	31	38	57	20	31	46	31	6	27	71
28	79	54	46	46	31	25	62	38	45	58	45	36	50	20	15	25	41	41	60	35	35	35	36	18	46	29	42	25	33	40	43	67

DSI Data for October 1990

DAY	TR	ED	SP	SF	DM	JY	BP	CD	DX	CL	HO	UR	GC	SV	PL	CP	C	W	O	S	BO	SM	OJ	CF	CO	SU	LB	NY	LC	LH	PB	CR
1	93	86	92	62	64	85	77	38	17	15	17	8	7	7	8	17	12	12	19	18	6	18	25	8	8	23	50	17	60	73	86	23
2	63	69	47	73	75	73	80	57	14	13	20	20	25	24	40	21	33	28	41	22	17	22	57	64	73	31	50	50	56	63	73	53
3	45	40	36	73	70	70	70	70	10	70	70	60	75	42	30	60	50	50	45	58	36	50	50	22	50	25	20	40	73	82	82	50
4	71	69	38	85	85	83	77	79	18	50	36	27	29	13	15	17	59	47	53	41	29	41	36	18	50	15	27	36	67	67	69	50
5	54	50	33	33	50	55	67	31	40	82	60	70	46	31	58	45	47	53	50	53	33	67	50	10	45	46	45	64	38	62	58	64
8	54	42	25	58	83	82	75	69	9	82	64	64	54	57	42	27	87	87	79	87	67	80	55	36	42	38	55	83	8	23	25	70
9	20	14	7	64	71	54	43	36	42	85	75	75	27	25	46	17	61	56	63	67	39	72	17	42	21	40	46	54	38	38	27	67
10	33	21	14	57	73	62	64	64	31	62	67	50	33	25	21	46	78	61	53	50	39	61	33	33	38	33	8	46	13	13	27	54
11	19	27	7	87	93	86	87	73	8	86	77	77	60	25	20	14	56	50	59	50	39	50	15	31	57	21	21	64	6	18	31	29
12	53	43	36	43	50	62	43	64	46	46	42	33	33	31	43	15	29	24	31	41	24	53	8	42	54	27	25	38	27	53	50	31
15	64	50	53	36	38	86	36	31	54	23	17	17	27	19	29	62	6	24	38	12	12	12	33	50	15	13	31	54	33	60	57	31
16	54	33	17	83	83	91	83	58	10	55	50	50	15	21	25	27	13	19	27	13	19	13	40	30	27	23	8	64	21	7	25	18
17	50	23	38	46	38	50	31	38	45	17	18	18	50	53	62	25	35	53	60	47	41	41	9	36	38	36	50	64	20	20	57	42
18	73	29	64	79	79	77	79	50	42	31	15	15	53	50	46	50	33	56	56	39	56	33	8	25	31	50	38	50	50	38	53	54
19	85	33	50	50	50	55	42	38	45	27	27	18	58	62	58	91	40	40	57	47	47	47	27	27	58	25	58	67	50	29	38	64
22	85	46	58	17	33	45	27	33	60	18	20	10	38	29	33	73	31	50	53	38	25	31	30	60	36	58	64	91	29	29	33	36
23	67	50	36	36	50	31	43	60	50	46	50	42	67	50	54	92	56	50	59	39	44	39	42	42	31	47	42	69	69	56	64	77
24	69	67	45	67	69	55	82	62	33	64	64	55	54	36	50	73	63	56	63	38	31	38	36	55	75	38	27	67	57	36	31	73
25	67	64	43	36	36	38	14	60	54	69	69	69	47	31	29	54	47	47	56	35	35	24	23	38	64	20	54	71	67	33	36	62
26	71	64	31	62	57	62	62	54	50	54	50	50	29	27	23	33	25	25	31	13	19	13	17	50	83	15	42	54	79	21	31	31
29	38	46	17	33	38	33	33	62	75	58	58	58	50	46	50	27	27	33	33	20	20	20	25	42	67	25	33	75	29	7	8	50
30	36	46	23	62	69	50	85	62	27	50	45	45	62	77	67	42	38	50	50	44	50	44	27	36	15	33	33	83	53	20	14	67
31	62	67	33	42	50	27	50	50	50	36	30	30	54	57	64	45	38	40	62	50	50	50	30	30	42	33	27	82	64	36	31	55

DSI Data for November 1990

DAY	TR	ED	SP	SF	DM	JY	BP	CD	DX	CL	HO	UR	GC	SV	PL	CP	C	W	O	S	BO	SM	OJ	CF	CO	SU	LB	NY	LC	LH	PB	CR
1	79	69	38	92	85	33	62	46	36	42	36	27	71	93	67	17	53	41	67	76	59	59	36	36	33	50	36	67	40	40	43	82
2	79	69	62	92	92	92	85	36	8	33	33	25	43	53	31	62	41	71	65	59	41	65	17	25	23	29	31	54	33	53	64	50
5	94	73	60	87	73	79	87	56	21	29	29	36	60	56	47	29	22	33	28	11	11	17	21	7	20	27	20	13	41	35	63	29
6	88	60	67	53	53	43	53	47	46	54	50	42	81	71	64	54	28	39	35	11	11	17	46	31	53	60	43	21	69	69	73	64
7	40	14	7	64	64	46	64	21	42	77	75	75	67	56	46	42	44	56	56	39	39	44	50	25	54	33	15	38	63	56	73	69
8	62	38	33	50	46	38	67	27	58	67	64	55	69	54	55	20	44	56	53	19	19	25	36	45	64	38	45	36	36	21	42	50
9	93	85	69	54	54	67	62	43	50	25	25	17	21	20	23	58	47	41	35	12	12	12	17	17	31	71	38	31	73	40	50	38
12	87	79	64	64	86	85	57	57	17	38	42	33	27	19	15	33	39	44	19	17	6	17	42	33	42	57	42	38	81	75	80	31
13	81	67	67	60	47	43	73	44	29	64	64	57	56	35	47	57	42	32	32	32	26	32	29	29	43	50	36	60	71	65	63	36
14	94	73	81	67	80	57	67	53	31	29	38	23	25	25	20	29	21	5	11	11	11	11	31	38	50	44	29	57	71	59	56	31
15	56	53	40	47	47	43	60	60	54	50	46	31	38	25	43	50	21	21	33	37	37	32	7	7	79	27	21	64	53	65	44	21
16	86	46	50	85	85	67	77	38	18	25	36	27	21	21	54	75	24	25	47	53	47	53	9	9	83	67	15	67	80	53	69	55
19	65	44	69	63	63	67	69	69	36	67	64	57	59	28	40	47	42	32	41	42	32	42	29	64	73	29	25	60	65	35	56	60
20	71	44	31	63	63	38	31	60	43	20	29	21	29	17	27	40	26	11	24	21	21	21	36	21	53	18	7	53	47	24	38	27
21	63	40	20	33	47	71	80	63	36	71	69	62	50	31	20	7	37	32	29	58	37	47	33	38	60	47	27	79	69	38	40	57
23	60	43	43	36	36	62	64	50	58	85	67	58	71	50	77	54	31	19	27	56	50	63	36	25	85	43	57	54	60	33	29	62
26	69	33	27	33	33	43	60	67	46	79	69	62	63	41	57	64	16	21	24	37	21	26	15	69	53	73	27	57	69	7	13	43
27	57	15	43	50	62	69	64	36	15	46	31	31	43	29	29	14	20	13	13	47	53	60	17	54	57	57	38	50	57	36	43	31
28	71	38	85	38	54	42	54	33	45	58	55	45	50	40	75	17	29	24	20	35	53	35	27	18	75	54	23	58	43	7	15	33
29	47	21	36	43	43	38	50	50	67	62	54	50	80	31	77	14	44	28	31	61	67	39	17	42	62	43	14	15	38	19	27	54
30	94	59	82	59	65	50	59	29	33	25	31	25	28	47	41	19	70	42	39	45	40	42	27	20	59	28	31	50	22	22	24	38

DSI Data for December 1990

DAY	TR	ED	SP	SF	DM	JY	BP	CD	DX	CL	HO	UR	GC	SV	PL	CP	C	W	O	S	BO	SM	OJ	CF	CO	SU	LB	NY	LC	LH	PB	CR
3	75	47	80	14	20	7	20	27	92	57	46	43	25	35	29	36	63	47	65	63	68	67	15	50	31	20	36	38	29	12	25	64
4	73	57	71	43	36	38	43	40	54	54	54	46	27	38	36	46	50	33	53	50	44	61	31	46	36	33	64	50	19	6	7	46
5	88	73	67	40	40	27	20	40	64	21	29	21	13	25	33	36	41	35	53	41	47	47	43	79	60	73	47	36	44	38	27	43
6	50	43	46	38	43	31	38	71	54	23	23	23	23	29	31	58	50	56	63	69	63	75	8	69	69	38	8	42	67	13	14	46
7	80	71	50	71	71	54	64	53	23	31	23	15	7	6	7	15	33	50	24	44	56	44	14	36	33	25	47	60	56	25	33	38
10	76	63	69	31	38	13	38	41	60	47	47	40	53	33	50	47	60	55	47	45	65	50	7	40	63	53	63	69	72	56	53	60
11	78	71	41	35	35	13	24	17	50	6	13	6	22	32	35	25	62	43	45	38	57	38	31	69	53	61	53	47	63	37	33	38
12	93	80	75	53	50	40	60	40	38	14	21	14	25	29	27	57	63	37	22	47	37	42	36	57	27	44	47	60	65	41	31	29
13	50	27	47	20	33	7	29	60	57	50	50	43	44	41	33	29	32	26	22	16	26	21	29	57	40	38	60	71	35	6	6	36
14	31	13	38	31	19	13	13	50	67	53	67	47	47	11	19	20	55	35	32	30	30	45	27	33	44	35	38	69	61	39	29	53
17	59	53	33	40	27	33	20	67	71	47	50	36	47	22	27	67	65	40	32	60	55	50	14	43	20	35	63	50	67	33	13	60
18	81	67	60	47	47	7	40	75	54	64	62	54	38	18	27	50	37	21	18	16	21	32	54	38	14	38	53	57	65	12	13	31
19	31	53	47	40	60	7	27	38	54	57	71	64	73	63	67	62	33	28	22	17	17	28	54	38	29	33	60	79	59	47	47	64
20	43	50	62	23	21	23	15	43	85	31	31	31	57	93	85	75	6	6	7	6	13	6	54	15	38	50	38	92	57	36	31	54
21	47	38	63	19	19	20	19	44	71	40	47	33	50	35	47	71	21	26	17	11	16	16	57	21	53	41	40	67	53	29	38	40
26	45	70	78	20	22	13	40	43	88	50	50	50	56	36	33	57	55	55	40	50	45	50	50	13	13	70	44	67	80	40	44	38
27	69	69	42	27	25	9	33	31	64	55	45	55	38	29	17	42	29	36	23	21	21	14	78	55	36	54	82	82	69	15	8	18
28	40	60	40	70	70	78	90	45	44	78	67	67	60	55	60	90	27	18	36	9	18	18	75	22	30	10	90	70	45	36	30	56

PART IIIB

Weekly Average DSI History 1987-1991*

The following listing is a weekly version of the daily DSI data presented earlier. The weekly figure is a simple average of the daily figures for the given week.

*Data updates either in printout form and/or computer disk can be obtained from my office. For price and additional details, contact MBH, P.O. Box 353, Winnetka, IL, 60093.

DSI Weekly Average Report

DATE	TR	ED	SP	SF	DM	JY	BP	CD	DX	CL	HO	UR	GC	SV	PL	CP	C	W	O	S	BO	SM	OJ	CF	CO	SU	LB	NY	LC	LH	PB	CR
870410	53	0	66	57	0	61	68	65	0	37	0	0	30	45	43	23	78	47	0	82	73	80	0	66	52	54	18	43	65	81	77	0
870416	52	0	64	44	0	44	51	44	0	36	0	0	38	41	45	26	76	53	0	72	49	60	0	68	65	59	33	84	47	55	67	0
870424	36	0	47	52	0	52	65	47	0	44	0	0	57	65	66	41	74	44	0	82	65	77	0	76	68	65	38	67	56	67	68	0
870501	62	0	75	41	0	40	59	37	0	52	0	0	43	45	42	31	75	53	0	82	72	77	0	61	55	64	57	74	67	68	62	0
870508	53	0	62	49	0	51	57	43	0	58	0	0	53	54	54	70	83	84	0	90	87	86	0	50	73	58	60	70	83	75	72	0
870515	46	0	55	51	0	48	50	38	0	71	0	0	53	59	53	63	75	63	0	79	80	79	0	62	53	80	65	88	51	57	52	0
870522	55	0	47	32	0	31	36	41	0	44	0	0	31	30	35	38	64	48	0	63	61	58	0	60	53	66	43	76	48	62	45	0
870529	61	0	64	26	0	31	32	46	0	49	0	0	32	35	32	38	66	40	0	61	50	61	0	38	31	44	46	70	71	75	70	0
870605	52	0	60	40	0	43	45	39	0	67	0	0	49	48	45	64	70	42	0	75	81	82	0	26	28	33	55	55	62	76	80	0
870612	61	0	71	47	0	42	57	60	0	60	0	0	50	52	58	60	61	39	0	74	56	79	0	46	56	37	59	67	66	66	70	0
870619	64	0	58	37	0	36	42	56	0	73	0	0	38	37	43	46	72	61	0	73	64	65	0	18	71	57	58	61	67	71	69	0
870626	50	0	53	37	0	29	41	62	0	44	0	0	33	34	33	52	56	53	0	51	52	53	0	35	84	51	43	48	63	40	39	0
870702	38	0	36	49	0	30	47	58	0	57	0	0	49	56	56	75	48	57	0	40	49	38	0	41	65	50	29	66	45	50	48	0
870710	46	0	51	36	0	35	62	66	0	66	0	0	45	61	55	62	41	64	0	56	52	51	0	35	63	63	48	62	64	66	72	0
870717	44	0	50	43	0	40	55	60	0	65	0	0	52	54	51	41	32	60	0	39	42	46	0	60	55	36	32	60	35	38	41	0
870724	28	0	37	44	0	44	45	40	0	48	0	0	59	59	61	60	55	53	0	60	60	65	0	58	42	34	25	66	38	56	70	0
870731	53	0	68	49	0	51	41	50	0	42	0	0	53	55	62	48	60	71	0	65	70	64	0	41	34	48	35	63	61	64	65	0
870807	45	0	52	28	0	33	34	63	0	37	0	0	60	58	61	49	34	63	0	42	46	42	0	70	36	49	52	52	66	55	65	0
870814	69	0	77	36	0	42	54	44	0	23	0	0	41	40	48	51	51	80	0	51	42	65	0	47	39	49	50	57	50	58	56	0
870821	48	0	58	64	0	64	72	50	0	19	0	0	48	51	46	40	60	75	0	63	61	49	0	40	42	41	68	66	46	63	56	0
870828	42	0	50	45	0	46	49	69	0	37	0	0	44	41	50	42	61	73	0	59	55	57	0	81	59	26	36	48	61	55	49	0
870904	40	0	45	55	0	59	64	66	0	33	0	0	52	50	55	47	50	63	0	57	46	60	0	78	43	49	35	28	67	70	46	0
870911	45	0	52	41	0	42	47	41	0	34	0	0	45	46	36	70	78	74	0	78	56	80	0	57	29	65	36	35	61	43	34	0

870918	36	0	40	39	0	52	63	55	0	44	0	0	35	34	32	59	69	72	0	71	54	69	0	39	32	57	31	48	34	42	39	0
870925	42	0	54	31	0	37	56	57	0	54	0	0	54	49	45	50	52	57	0	49	67	43	0	46	50	55	21	47	58	39	49	0
871002	41	0	73	22	0	24	30	70	0	63	0	0	35	34	37	34	66	55	0	71	68	66	0	65	32	69	44	34	29	48	36	0
871009	27	0	31	65	0	59	66	61	0	45	0	0	51	42	42	63	63	66	0	63	58	55	0	77	31	68	28	35	44	67	62	0
871016	37	0	35	51	0	53	58	69	0	51	0	0	48	48	49	76	68	70	0	70	68	65	0	74	23	71	42	34	44	41	34	0
871023	57	0	28	46	0	40	51	44	0	47	0	0	54	43	36	35	36	46	0	41	37	53	0	51	42	57	38	22	27	33	33	0
871030	61	0	34	61	0	54	61	34	0	39	0	0	39	22	21	27	34	35	0	47	34	56	0	38	40	55	40	44	33	36	34	0
871106	60	0	31	62	0	62	64	30	0	21	0	0	24	18	16	64	38	39	0	45	46	52	0	54	30	36	51	59	50	42	44	0
871113	43	0	22	46	0	48	49	46	0	31	0	0	30	31	28	51	54	50	0	79	61	76	0	46	54	56	51	48	59	56	58	0
871120	57	0	37	50	0	47	52	60	0	33	0	0	40	37	36	55	64	62	0	67	45	67	0	58	36	56	45	48	67	56	42	0
871127	33	0	44	58	0	55	69	71	0	43	0	0	55	51	59	69	69	66	0	68	68	67	0	44	54	61	77	57	63	75	70	0
871204	60	41	23	40	0	44	42	44	0	43	0	0	41	35	37	39	48	65	0	48	45	46	0	24	50	58	55	38	41	39	36	0
871211	26	27	53	50	0	57	55	62	0	28	0	0	53	40	43	60	48	47	0	53	59	52	0	30	31	62	59	47	60	60	58	0
871218	63	60	63	50	0	51	49	52	0	19	0	0	36	35	31	54	47	60	0	54	73	43	0	45	40	79	77	48	68	63	50	0
871224	72	69	72	53	0	57	48	51	0	41	0	0	28	35	34	75	66	67	0	75	68	71	0	51	37	72	65	74	38	50	34	0
871231	95	88	80	42	0	47	37	43	0	46	0	0	26	31	33	73	76	67	0	83	74	79	0	59	18	85	83	81	42	47	38	0
880108	56	47	61	30	0	30	29	64	0	50	0	0	48	57	50	29	70	71	0	72	79	57	0	52	69	66	52	39	74	79	68	0
880115	49	50	41	33	0	36	37	58	0	41	0	0	30	35	33	34	71	65	0	60	64	46	0	36	47	56	51	42	68	68	66	0
880122	69	61	49	44	0	48	43	63	0	49	0	0	46	48	49	39	63	47	0	54	66	36	0	62	69	63	46	40	70	71	68	0
880129	69	61	63	30	0	35	29	62	0	39	0	0	20	21	21	29	56	53	0	35	42	28	0	61	18	57	71	39	45	45	38	0
880205	52	48	30	40	0	39	39	67	0	55	0	0	35	37	39	40	55	64	0	47	45	53	0	76	32	45	65	54	70	66	47	0
880212	44	45	41	32	0	32	28	60	0	47	0	0	43	40	49	54	70	64	0	72	65	64	0	65	41	44	74	43	56	52	51	0
880219	44	43	52	41	0	42	38	49	0	32	0	0	46	42	43	49	52	50	0	59	55	55	0	48	34	63	60	65	54	34	30	0
880226	40	39	40	44	0	50	62	47	0	29	0	0	30	29	30	32	39	34	0	49	37	45	0	45	35	33	31	49	54	41	34	0
880304	42	29	38	32	0	44	58	69	0	45	0	0	48	52	65	66	54	30	0	53	46	62	0	24	38	63	54	61	42	35	38	0
880311	34	35	43	69	0	68	74	58	0	52	0	0	39	43	62	56	47	31	0	39	36	49	0	34	52	65	29	53	61	49	46	0
880318	43	52	41	34	0	44	45	60	0	65	0	0	44	40	58	47	50	49	0	60	50	68	0	29	41	58	53	68	68	65	59	0
880325	52	52	26	42	0	61	59	68	0	59	0	0	52	57	57	61	56	40	0	69	50	69	0	38	63	63	49	62	63	59	58	0

DSI Weekly Average Report

DATE	TR	ED	SP	SF	DM	JY	BP	CD	DX	CL	HO	UR	GC	SV	PL	CP	C	W	O	S	BO	SM	OJ	CF	CO	SU	LB	NY	LC	LH	PB	CR
880331	44	44	33	56	0	61	62	62	0	54	0	0	47	51	57	55	62	39	0	59	57	56	0	54	49	61	49	63	62	54	49	0
880408	45	40	40	29	0	36	43	40	0	35	0	0	29	28	44	29	45	63	0	55	56	50	0	42	54	36	47	45	56	64	41	0
880415	48	52	38	43	0	48	47	60	0	60	0	0	40	35	45	27	22	48	0	45	39	42	0	52	45	39	33	60	44	45	33	0
880422	37	42	34	37	0	38	50	55	0	45	0	0	47	34	41	27	37	43	0	43	38	31	0	47	60	49	28	67	50	40	40	0
880429	39	38	42	29	0	34	37	58	0	47	0	0	41	39	39	33	47	40	0	56	58	48	0	27	71	42	39	61	48	41	38	0
880506	41	43	33	23	0	33	27	35	0	23	0	0	22	28	34	51	53	35	0	58	55	56	0	47	59	38	24	58	59	67	43	37
880513	51	49	24	29	0	36	49	47	0	35	0	0	47	60	70	63	29	51	0	65	58	63	0	39	50	73	30	70	66	73	60	68
880520	34	40	28	16	0	18	27	28	0	47	0	0	61	57	64	41	57	75	0	73	64	68	0	39	64	68	28	71	59	57	55	71
880527	49	47	39	23	0	40	39	39	0	28	0	0	45	45	60	24	57	51	0	41	35	42	0	42	58	39	51	49	32	54	52	51
880603	73	61	67	27	0	23	22	62	0	50	0	0	57	62	79	61	62	58	0	78	64	78	0	69	33	62	59	55	50	65	64	71
880610	61	62	54	49	0	48	49	65	0	25	0	0	41	47	43	59	76	71	0	73	66	73	0	71	31	61	59	58	51	47	39	57
880617	52	54	46	24	0	30	30	70	0	36	0	0	37	53	41	45	89	60	0	80	67	77	0	48	47	49	21	66	24	31	25	57
880624	56	51	50	23	0	18	24	68	0	38	0	0	22	31	30	50	79	67	0	75	77	74	0	29	41	63	34	50	37	37	30	62
880701	51	41	37	35	0	32	36	42	0	21	0	0	30	30	32	35	60	54	0	52	59	49	0	38	51	78	63	31	59	45	35	51
880708	45	34	42	35	0	40	42	52	0	49	0	0	42	53	53	37	44	39	0	31	43	31	0	50	70	60	53	27	62	44	38	42
880715	39	32	35	39	0	41	42	56	0	44	0	0	46	57	35	31	58	46	0	54	51	50	0	61	58	64	36	31	52	56	56	49
880722	37	42	29	60	0	65	71	64	0	65	0	0	56	60	53	57	42	47	0	27	24	28	0	45	45	44	40	53	69	56	57	44
880729	52	44	44	40	0	44	43	48	0	57	0	0	30	29	28	28	39	52	0	42	34	36	0	30	36	32	28	49	64	40	31	27
880805	64	53	62	33	0	41	44	55	0	37	0	0	29	36	35	39	65	67	0	69	59	72	0	32	38	50	32	42	43	50	44	58
880812	39	34	39	35	0	34	44	30	0	59	0	0	28	32	38	33	37	55	0	52	45	53	0	44	29	33	30	36	59	60	49	41
880819	47	46	40	32	0	33	41	33	0	47	0	0	45	42	53	51	29	59	0	52	35	59	0	55	24	43	50	33	49	61	49	34
880826	33	32	27	49	0	38	38	25	0	42	0	0	60	56	72	65	29	61	0	34	29	32	0	48	34	46	28	28	50	55	58	33
880902	62	57	60	55	0	38	42	42	0	35	0	0	45	48	53	54	49	72	0	55	52	54	0	30	29	53	60	59	44	29	28	48
880909	56	56	60	55	0	48	58	40	0	26	0	0	33	41	45	57	56	62	0	61	44	69	0	72	25	43	35	63	31	22	20	41

880916	51	48	49	38	0	36	45	69	0	45	0	0	38	42	38	62	33	53	0	34	26	40	0	30	32	49	44	49	39	50	54	33
880923	34	41	41	34	0	31	33	66	0	49	0	0	26	33	30	45	27	47	0	25	22	26	0	41	33	28	42	29	44	57	61	31
880930	47	46	56	37	0	45	54	64	0	22	0	0	34	34	45	71	36	38	0	28	31	31	0	63	19	43	44	34	70	60	52	35
881007	57	41	52	49	0	60	62	75	0	26	0	0	53	59	67	68	68	68	0	43	39	55	0	24	51	60	62	61	62	48	31	42
881014	45	49	42	75	0	78	78	69	0	55	0	0	55	57	60	75	63	71	0	45	48	60	0	32	62	58	66	68	52	39	33	56
881021	56	51	52	70	0	70	72	77	0	48	0	0	42	42	57	73	42	42	0	38	38	53	0	52	68	64	51	50	40	40	33	49
881028	53	55	43	52	0	56	61	54	0	43	0	0	37	32	57	58	41	40	0	43	40	42	0	58	57	61	43	56	35	29	42	46
881104	53	49	50	53	0	56	51	34	0	49	0	0	65	62	73	63	55	53	0	62	41	62	0	42	64	59	33	60	38	55	39	64
881111	31	28	30	66	0	66	69	50	0	60	0	0	62	63	67	37	37	52	0	45	30	50	0	70	65	42	31	42	38	41	35	46
881118	32	31	33	56	0	57	58	37	0	44	0	0	45	31	40	31	32	35	0	30	23	33	0	45	45	42	53	34	48	39	34	28
881125	42	33	44	57	0	61	62	78	0	59	0	0	41	39	51	65	58	61	0	63	42	56	0	42	68	69	61	38	57	37	27	55
881202	58	55	54	42	0	50	54	64	0	62	0	0	47	40	62	65	41	60	0	49	45	43	0	40	37	76	48	64	45	57	63	64
881209	60	54	57	25	0	29	42	46	0	59	0	0	43	36	62	70	52	60	0	64	71	62	0	58	39	67	60	75	31	58	48	67
881216	46	28	41	21	0	19	23	27	0	57	0	0	34	37	36	35	76	63	0	59	59	58	0	83	29	55	60	51	64	73	58	62
881223	69	52	69	25	0	24	28	64	0	59	0	0	46	44	44	68	72	72	0	74	68	67	0	63	60	59	66	68	80	73	49	76
881230	48	29	57	31	0	37	44	72	0	67	0	0	29	33	35	52	68	59	0	64	53	67	0	70	58	57	68	47	57	50	31	52
890106	32	20	58	31	0	38	43	63	0	65	0	0	29	31	44	59	56	64	0	65	45	70	0	67	45	35	47	45	60	66	62	59
890113	61	46	69	25	0	33	32	42	0	66	0	0	22	24	37	35	55	48	0	44	36	46	0	38	29	36	71	70	65	36	32	43
890120	61	57	58	38	0	33	39	61	0	66	0	0	48	51	56	73	20	44	0	22	29	21	0	58	49	39	56	60	31	21	22	42
890127	60	61	62	39	0	32	41	67	0	53	0	0	45	57	61	50	44	50	0	39	30	44	0	30	63	27	30	48	38	29	29	39
890203	49	39	65	32	0	33	31	55	0	50	0	0	31	27	44	17	53	45	0	59	59	55	0	43	56	63	51	63	79	61	44	54
890210	39	31	52	43	0	44	40	61	0	49	0	0	48	45	55	33	30	31	0	31	34	29	0	56	59	73	51	42	47	37	34	29
890217	30	24	40	66	0	66	65	44	0	65	0	0	33	49	58	27	44	26	0	33	54	36	0	44	67	70	46	22	38	46	38	41
890224	33	22	30	60	0	55	45	24	0	73	0	0	57	67	57	65	55	46	0	60	75	54	0	29	63	56	38	67	67	76	55	66
890303	48	35	32	46	0	41	32	25	0	70	0	0	45	45	46	66	63	62	0	67	73	63	0	46	38	60	20	73	58	77	57	63
890310	61	45	46	21	0	25	24	35	0	58	0	0	46	40	52	67	65	59	0	62	63	61	0	67	29	57	32	64	42	61	52	61
890317	42	26	55	19	0	19	23	36	0	60	0	0	56	65	58	43	64	70	0	67	65	68	0	63	36	63	37	69	43	49	44	63

DSI Weekly Average Report

DATE	TR	ED	SP	SF	DM	JY	BP	CD	DX	CL	HO	UR	GC	SV	PL	CP	C	W	O	S	BO	SM	OJ	CF	CO	SU	LB	NY	LC	LH	PB	CR
890323	31	23	37	26	0	28	38	47	0	74	0	0	47	58	45	34	62	46	0	74	66	70	0	58	51	57	42	66	48	40	55	59
890331	47	41	41	23	0	28	32	50	0	64	0	0	27	31	28	39	30	25	0	37	33	36	0	29	42	35	58	60	45	38	45	25
890407	59	59	58	48	0	48	47	57	0	33	0	0	25	25	19	21	26	25	0	23	24	23	0	60	22	63	44	68	26	23	19	19
890414	44	53	61	33	0	37	42	62	0	56	0	0	52	58	55	67	43	52	0	55	45	53	0	71	28	37	34	72	28	42	26	50
890421	60	59	65	65	0	55	56	66	0	65	0	0	26	26	47	37	55	60	0	57	55	59	0	70	54	65	30	62	34	49	33	57
890428	67	71	65	18	0	34	24	39	0	51	0	0	32	33	47	54	33	56	0	20	28	22	0	39	30	43	40	42	34	59	50	29
890505	47	51	48	20	0	20	17	63	0	34	0	0	20	22	30	18	68	77	0	62	69	59	0	41	36	51	61	62	64	71	37	59
890512	39	55	44	25	0	24	21	45	0	39	0	0	37	37	45	28	53	55	0	52	58	40	0	47	29	62	58	78	69	77	71	49
890519	72	62	72	17	0	19	17	31	0	51	0	0	14	10	16	18	31	28	0	21	21	20	0	61	52	46	53	64	28	52	52	27
890526	65	61	60	32	0	26	29	24	0	56	0	0	29	33	30	19	23	26	0	30	27	31	0	63	65	12	65	57	17	41	35	18
890602	57	54	56	64	0	40	41	36	0	66	0	0	39	34	36	45	28	20	0	36	21	38	0	43	17	37	50	67	37	27	25	27
890609	66	66	54	45	0	37	37	52	0	46	0	0	50	50	43	36	34	33	0	45	37	37	0	32	37	60	61	28	59	44	45	40
890616	45	39	44	42	0	32	32	44	0	31	0	0	40	37	38	39	51	61	0	56	43	49	0	24	42	81	50	71	74	48	60	42
890623	46	40	50	70	0	63	59	57	0	51	0	0	60	52	62	54	69	68	0	66	44	67	0	24	42	76	62	55	59	62	49	63
890630	70	70	44	60	0	41	53	65	0	65	0	0	55	33	53	19	64	66	0	60	33	58	0	26	62	69	31	61	74	62	63	59
890707	60	69	48	74	0	69	69	73	29	60	0	0	69	54	68	28	74	61	0	69	59	68	43	18	60	48	39	68	49	26	28	53
890714	46	50	63	49	0	45	48	52	53	48	0	0	37	38	47	58	37	34	0	34	34	33	57	31	56	41	60	68	61	49	42	48
890721	41	45	63	49	0	38	56	58	45	46	0	0	36	44	39	64	32	46	0	32	32	34	19	33	63	75	55	75	65	65	42	48
890728	66	63	56	65	0	51	65	58	33	13	0	0	53	53	49	55	19	33	0	17	16	21	55	22	45	55	55	65	37	51	29	26
890804	58	62	62	55	0	60	54	64	37	34	0	0	38	53	53	58	27	45	0	25	23	23	34	35	56	62	44	58	65	54	31	39
890811	28	28	56	35	0	47	38	71	58	51	0	0	32	37	33	49	56	70	0	52	52	49	39	35	51	35	38	47	63	50	37	51
890818	31	27	38	31	0	32	34	41	65	63	0	0	58	59	57	78	59	58	0	34	30	42	52	29	17	28	30	36	44	60	61	52
890825	37	31	45	42	0	40	36	56	58	65	0	0	45	46	45	71	59	48	0	45	60	68	46	44	27	36	26	62	45	51	42	52
890901	40	33	56	30	0	30	39	36	59	75	0	0	35	28	32	50	38	34	0	38	41	46	53	77	36	26	40	36	25	46	58	30

890908	60	45	50	37	0	37	32	20	60	76	0	0	46	46	55	42	44	66	0	40	60	51	46	51	28	35	55	22	31	29	59	46
890915	40	49	27	45	0	40	45	33	43	63	0	0	46	44	55	68	40	37	0	36	45	48	33	31	33	66	63	48	43	49	73	59
890922	28	31	38	68	0	58	59	52	24	59	0	0	65	63	64	61	31	29	0	33	51	30	34	37	35	71	56	44	37	64	57	54
890929	31	27	38	73	0	71	72	69	26	64	0	0	59	59	72	32	41	51	0	39	59	29	43	54	40	56	46	37	56	62	53	71
891006	59	49	81	53	0	47	54	58	55	65	0	0	53	50	65	69	77	65	0	54	50	64	37	16	30	52	51	59	48	66	52	69
891013	63	60	45	45	0	43	32	53	39	60	0	0	35	34	37	56	32	45	0	20	23	30	28	18	27	43	61	52	69	74	61	37
891020	63	65	45	61	0	56	50	37	28	50	0	0	57	38	38	30	61	52	0	53	53	55	25	37	33	67	24	33	64	59	62	52
891027	55	56	26	59	0	57	53	41	33	35	0	0	66	52	56	23	59	34	0	49	54	54	27	39	36	54	27	42	56	54	42	44
891103	56	45	29	52	0	44	38	46	41	56	0	0	61	48	63	29	41	33	0	47	56	41	50	45	26	65	41	59	47	54	65	66
891110	57	46	31	46	0	39	45	61	40	50	0	0	80	63	78	38	33	44	0	50	54	40	44	56	40	81	60	48	61	58	58	74
891117	52	51	43	42	0	39	45	45	47	49	0	0	78	81	79	45	54	45	0	67	63	67	54	49	20	64	67	32	47	61	52	74
891124	48	57	42	62	0	49	39	60	26	63	0	0	83	76	77	28	45	55	0	52	38	53	68	25	27	44	77	35	78	69	55	75
891201	51	50	56	67	0	59	40	59	29	56	0	0	70	61	60	43	35	53	0	33	28	44	71	38	30	29	64	28	42	37	25	43
891208	56	43	43	53	0	30	43	65	30	65	0	0	57	48	36	22	40	49	0	42	46	37	72	38	32	27	68	22	43	41	17	35
891215	48	37	54	69	0	38	70	63	23	63	0	0	66	52	40	39	42	63	0	51	53	52	77	56	42	36	71	47	72	39	30	56
891222	43	40	40	64	0	55	77	63	25	77	0	0	57	48	41	60	42	57	0	44	50	49	83	45	34	25	75	50	69	54	29	50
891229	30	28	44	48	0	56	58	57	31	71	0	0	35	38	28	56	44	31	0	35	29	33	70	40	27	39	58	58	58	43	38	55
900105	30	27	62	45	0	31	64	44	42	76	0	0	57	43	38	81	39	45	0	37	36	43	68	47	46	66	55	44	65	59	50	80
900112	21	27	36	72	0	40	78	65	21	52	0	0	72	59	48	68	45	31	0	44	65	30	76	55	61	73	70	42	63	62	64	79
900119	28	25	38	41	0	28	37	20	57	52	0	0	60	34	38	31	61	18	0	24	41	17	57	40	56	56	78	52	79	54	61	57
900126	31	28	30	53	0	46	65	26	49	52	0	0	72	52	59	35	35	20	0	28	29	21	66	59	65	69	68	43	67	57	58	46
900202	36	32	43	56	0	39	67	35	34	63	0	0	56	36	62	41	26	16	0	24	37	19	56	54	53	46	76	65	59	21	21	36
900209	41	40	44	59	0	47	69	21	35	30	0	0	49	36	51	52	37	34	0	44	59	39	38	57	43	54	74	70	65	42	43	48
900216	38	46	46	33	0	47	61	35	62	57	0	0	42	41	56	73	61	34	0	54	67	42	54	59	49	44	82	74	63	45	38	69
900223	30	27	32	61	0	31	73	51	30	56	0	0	40	29	56	71	70	47	0	51	69	28	54	71	66	30	49	72	27	51	47	65
900302	59	69	67	23	0	19	25	59	77	51	0	0	35	30	26	71	59	32	0	41	65	32	30	73	70	33	22	68	40	64	38	57
900309	41	41	48	29	0	40	30	70	60	44	0	0	40	38	34	69	50	32	0	75	67	60	50	59	59	73	51	79	58	64	38	73

DSI Weekly Average Report

DATE	TR	ED	SP	SF	DM	JY	BP	CD	DX	CL	HO	UR	GC	SV	PL	CP	C	W	O	S	BO	SM	OJ	CF	CO	SU	LB	NY	LC	LH	PB	CR
900316	51	32	54	45	0	44	44	51	45	52	0	0	45	48	51	62	44	30	0	48	51	46	54	34	39	68	42	51	57	62	54	74
900323	65	52	50	32	0	22	24	49	62	57	0	0	40	42	38	62	61	49	0	71	58	73	47	28	38	40	38	55	52	60	45	65
900330	59	55	44	44	0	27	56	70	44	61	0	0	28	28	27	58	58	34	0	49	45	54	60	31	77	43	51	77	69	64	54	63
900406	61	64	51	45	0	44	52	59	39	41	0	0	49	55	42	58	73	65	0	60	58	58	61	46	55	24	47	65	64	70	68	73
900412	53	67	69	68	0	40	69	61	28	38	0	0	42	49	51	29	50	35	0	53	41	48	50	49	60	54	39	62	80	80	76	64
900420	26	39	36	48	44	39	56	36	42	52	50	60	52	57	57	28	77	49	81	73	76	65	30	51	45	38	25	48	55	76	74	76
900427	39	41	45	58	46	48	44	52	37	45	35	50	42	48	47	56	62	48	77	70	69	66	37	43	34	49	48	68	48	63	57	75
900504	51	47	45	62	50	57	59	44	36	44	36	46	50	56	61	57	60	64	67	55	55	62	31	41	59	47	71	50	71	73	71	67
900511	64	74	65	67	71	72	69	28	35	52	42	62	46	50	53	56	69	58	58	65	71	64	59	39	56	28	67	66	58	50	43	64
900518	61	59	64	53	55	69	53	25	42	66	69	72	52	53	78	46	41	46	29	47	54	32	45	56	71	32	64	71	74	63	55	44
900525	56	60	51	32	32	62	50	37	58	50	45	55	56	65	71	36	49	34	32	45	44	39	60	55	57	38	60	74	54	52	37	59
900601	70	60	57	38	28	51	43	40	59	49	40	64	35	44	50	24	39	34	31	38	42	35	54	41	27	27	66	53	58	39	35	42
900608	52	49	52	32	34	41	42	50	65	36	31	39	27	25	40	25	53	44	51	44	50	31	35	43	44	21	68	49	74	29	30	41
900615	49	42	46	54	47	36	63	37	43	54	57	68	27	24	32	20	56	48	39	45	46	39	30	26	32	23	75	44	62	28	37	46
900622	26	26	22	77	64	62	74	42	17	62	60	74	35	32	34	34	54	44	40	57	50	47	30	21	36	35	77	58	54	36	22	38
900629	38	41	35	56	48	56	70	77	28	51	54	59	52	44	57	57	64	53	55	72	63	66	45	25	40	33	67	62	39	53	30	60
900706	45	41	37	72	68	63	76	55	20	35	36	44	60	64	63	53	54	45	52	65	58	65	72	42	71	55	46	64	62	57	28	52
900713	39	37	56	63	59	68	66	58	29	71	65	72	39	33	33	57	32	30	28	42	32	36	63	35	36	33	45	38	77	41	31	39
900720	34	40	40	50	49	60	71	63	38	70	72	69	46	29	31	45	15	21	18	21	23	16	56	42	41	29	36	29	69	54	32	25
900727	43	46	26	73	73	51	73	66	24	58	57	62	44	36	39	65	45	45	57	43	50	39	44	55	63	29	51	40	77	62	60	54
900803	59	74	27	74	76	69	78	68	20	76	73	73	45	27	51	59	22	18	38	44	51	28	52	59	25	20	53	25	54	51	52	52
900810	26	49	26	64	61	40	68	71	29	69	70	68	73	52	69	64	37	34	30	58	59	56	60	61	33	33	26	41	67	39	52	65

900817	36	29	36	83	78	59	82	76	15	81	82	87	71	72	71	54	33	33	44	61	48	59	69	67	43	61	50	26	39	36	41	60
900824	29	27	28	62	51	48	66	68	36	70	71	69	61	54	60	32	47	31	50	75	67	70	26	66	67	55	46	67	29	30	33	53
900831	67	64	63	27	30	56	44	33	56	37	36	36	26	24	36	22	22	15	24	32	30	32	44	65	50	33	70	53	32	27	28	25
900907	55	65	47	53	57	74	56	48	41	65	61	59	56	44	47	45	37	38	55	57	51	56	19	56	43	49	64	70	72	59	51	67
900914	54	49	37	41	44	82	50	34	51	60	63	57	45	42	41	44	29	42	40	59	38	61	23	28	55	39	55	46	64	64	57	53
900921	43	41	45	50	52	70	57	63	44	64	59	57	52	43	39	22	27	28	23	25	32	27	35	46	47	31	24	56	63	65	58	42
900928	37	29	26	55	50	52	63	45	28	75	68	63	68	41	32	27	43	55	43	42	41	44	45	29	43	35	38	41	21	24	21	59
901005	65	62	49	65	68	73	74	55	19	46	40	37	36	23	30	32	40	38	41	38	24	39	43	24	45	28	38	41	58	69	73	48
901012	35	29	17	61	74	69	62	61	27	72	65	59	41	32	34	23	62	55	57	59	41	63	25	36	42	31	31	57	18	29	32	50
901019	65	33	44	58	57	71	54	43	39	30	25	23	40	41	44	51	25	38	47	31	35	29	23	33	33	29	37	59	34	30	46	41
901026	71	58	42	43	49	46	45	53	49	50	50	45	47	34	37	65	44	45	52	32	30	29	29	49	57	35	45	70	60	35	39	55
901102	58	59	34	64	66	47	63	51	39	43	40	37	56	65	55	38	39	47	55	49	44	47	27	33	36	34	32	72	43	31	32	60
901109	75	54	47	61	58	54	66	38	43	50	48	45	59	51	47	40	37	45	41	18	18	23	34	25	44	45	32	27	56	44	60	50
901116	80	63	60	64	69	59	66	50	29	41	45	34	33	25	35	48	29	25	28	30	25	29	23	23	59	49	28	57	71	63	62	34
901123	64	42	40	48	52	59	61	60	43	60	57	49	52	31	41	37	34	23	30	44	35	43	33	37	67	34	29	61	60	32	40	51
901130	67	33	54	44	51	48	57	43	41	54	48	42	52	37	55	25	35	25	25	45	46	40	20	40	61	51	26	46	45	18	24	39
901207	73	58	62	41	42	31	37	46	57	37	35	29	19	26	27	38	47	44	51	53	55	58	22	56	45	37	40	45	43	18	21	47
901214	65	50	54	34	35	17	32	41	54	34	39	30	38	29	32	35	54	39	33	35	43	39	26	51	45	46	52	63	59	35	30	43
901221	52	52	53	33	34	18	24	53	67	47	52	43	53	46	50	65	32	24	19	22	24	26	46	31	30	39	50	69	60	31	28	49
901228	51	66	53	39	39	33	54	39	65	61	54	57	51	40	36	63	37	36	33	26	28	27	67	30	26	44	72	73	64	30	27	37
901207	73	58	62	41	42	31	37	46	57	37	35	29	19	26	27	38	47	44	51	53	55	58	22	56	45	37	40	45	43	18	21	47
901214	65	50	54	34	35	17	32	41	54	34	39	30	38	29	32	35	54	39	33	35	43	39	26	51	45	46	52	63	59	35	30	43
901221	52	52	53	33	34	18	24	53	67	47	52	43	53	46	50	65	32	24	19	22	24	26	46	31	30	39	50	69	60	31	28	49
901228	51	66	53	39	39	33	54	39	65	61	54	57	51	40	36	63	37	36	33	26	28	27	67	30	26	44	72	73	64	30	27	37

PART IV

Selected Price versus DSI Charts

The charts which follow are self-explanatory. They should be familiar to you from preceding chapters. They are included to assist you in your understanding and application of DSI. (Up-to-date charts are available from MBH, P.O. Box 353, Winnetka, IL 60093.)

Swiss Franc—March 1989

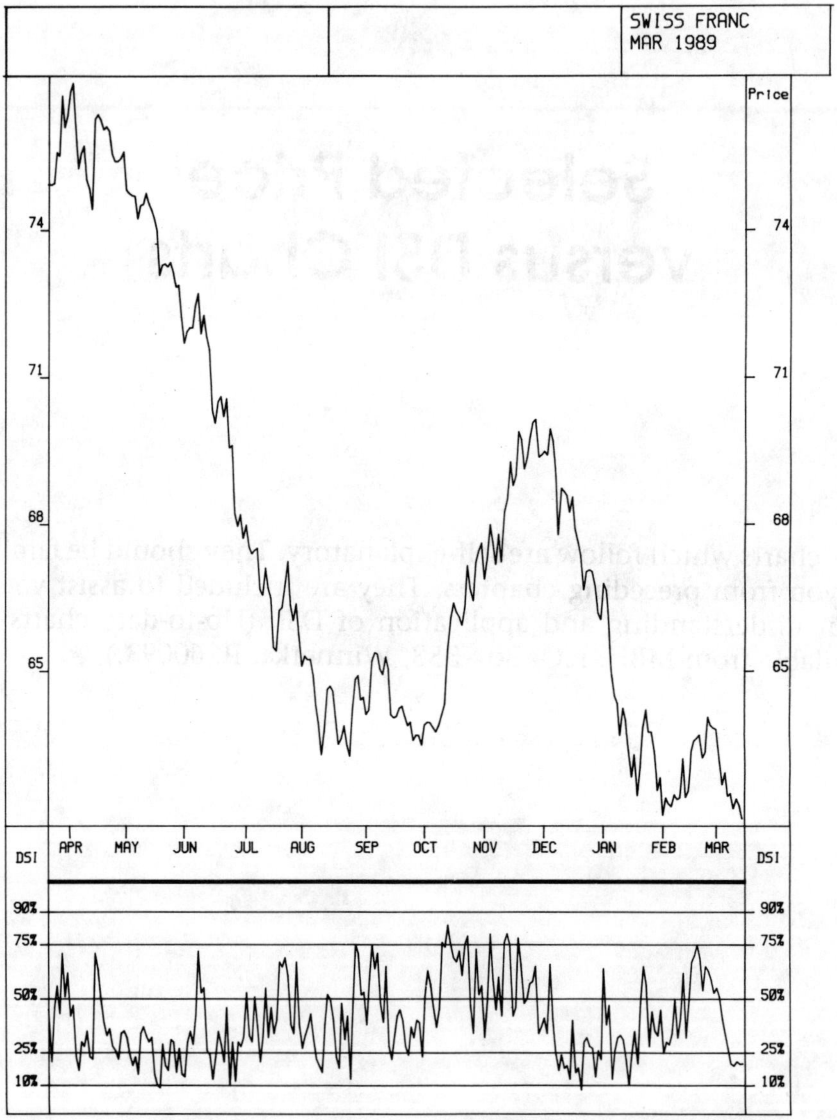

Soybeans—May 1990

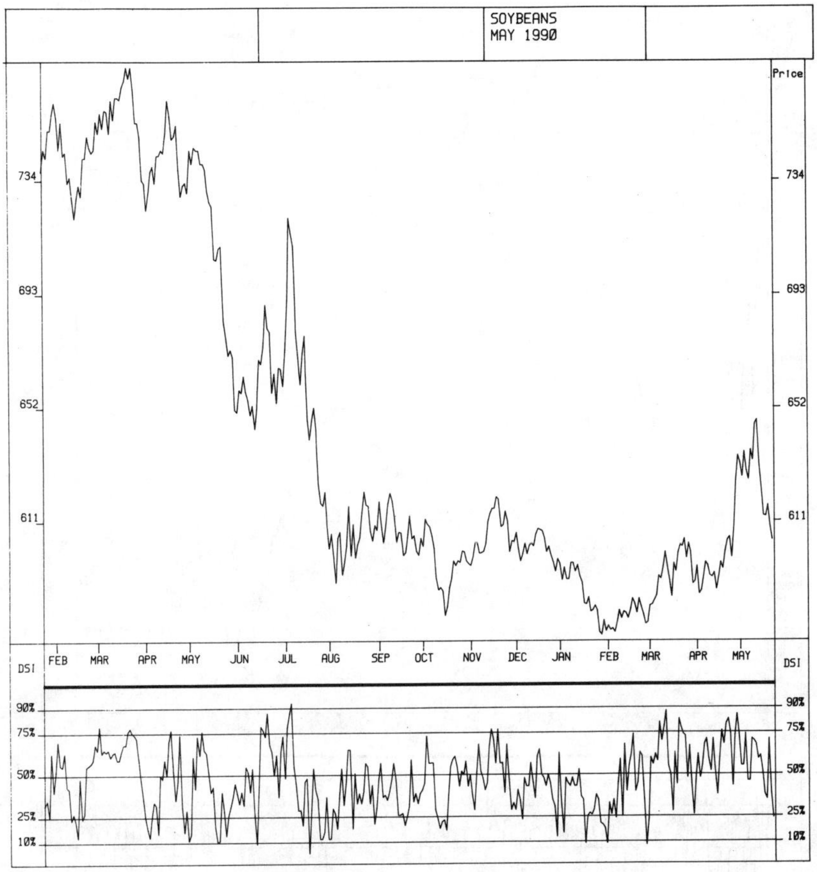

Soy Meal—September 1989

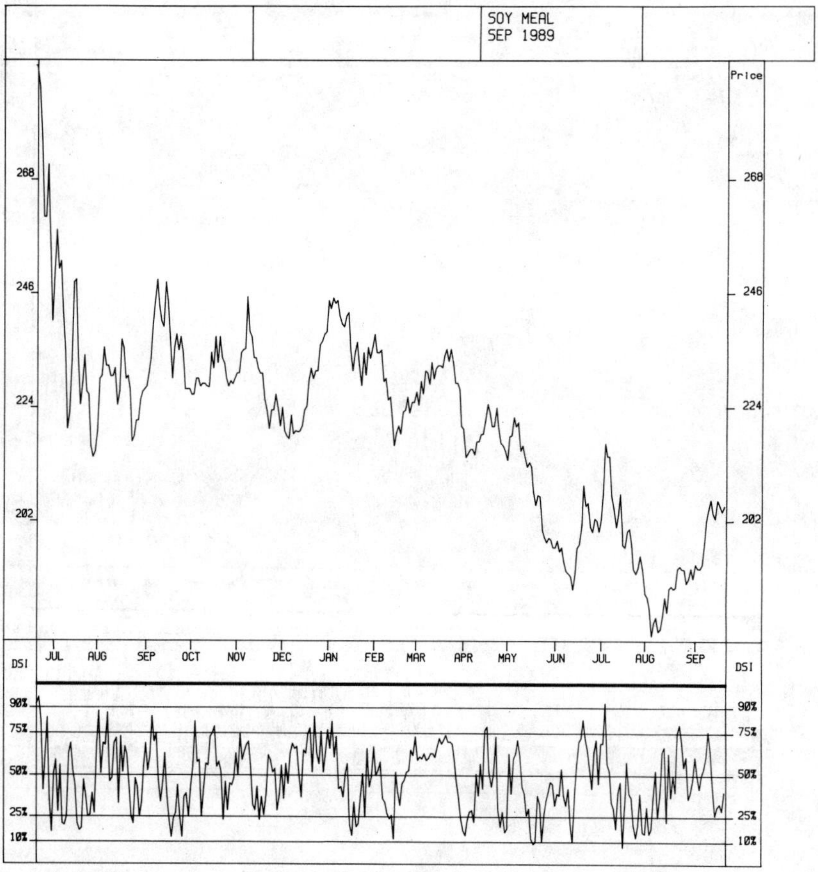

S&P Index—March 1989

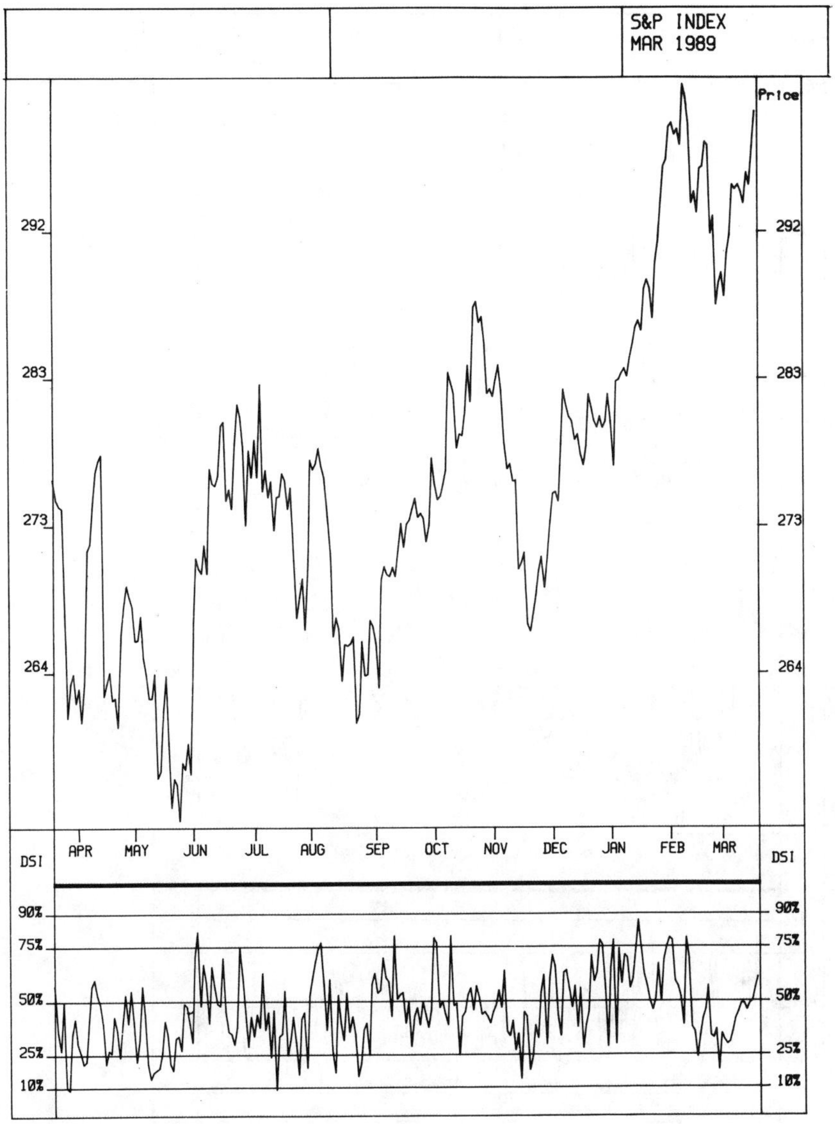

S&P Index—March 1990

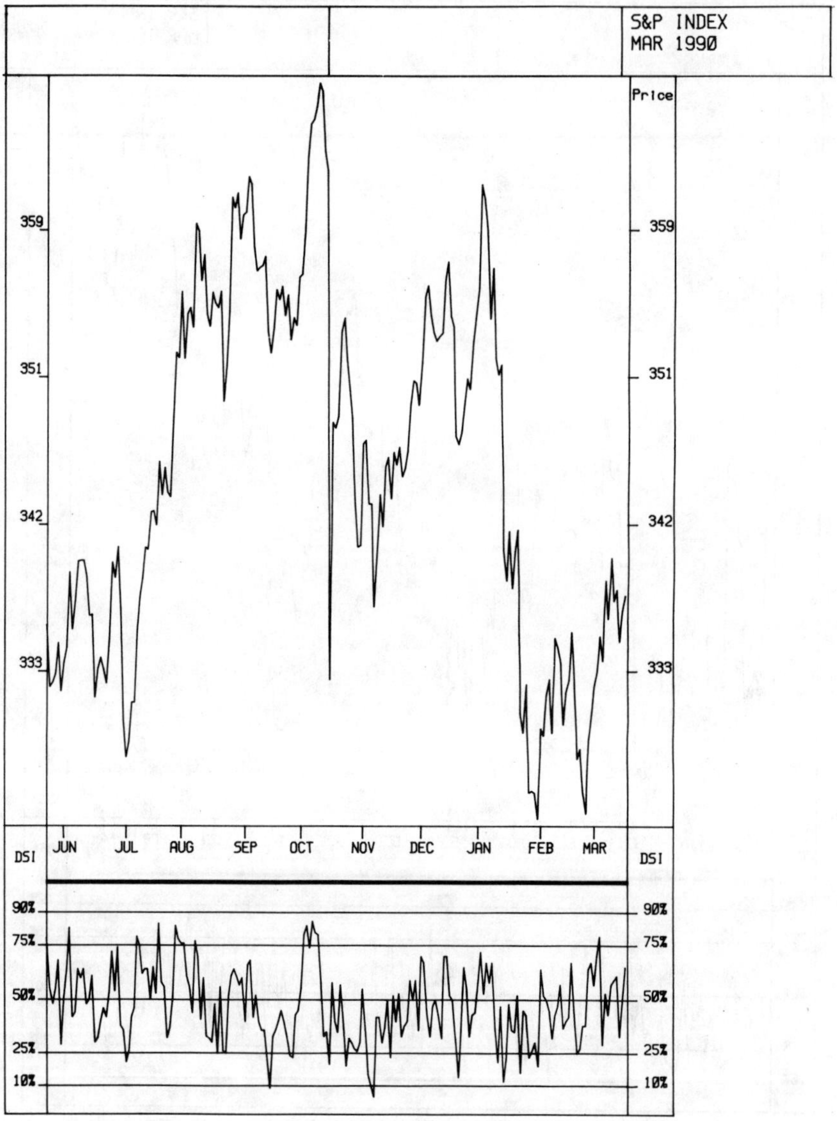

Sugar—May 1989

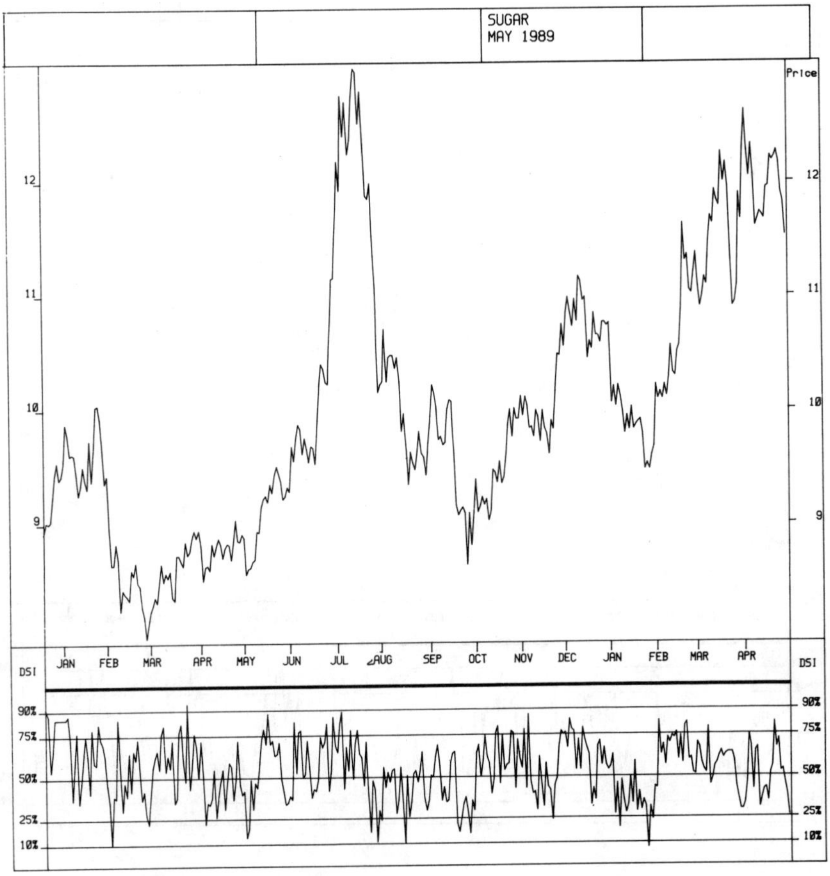

Sugar—May 1990

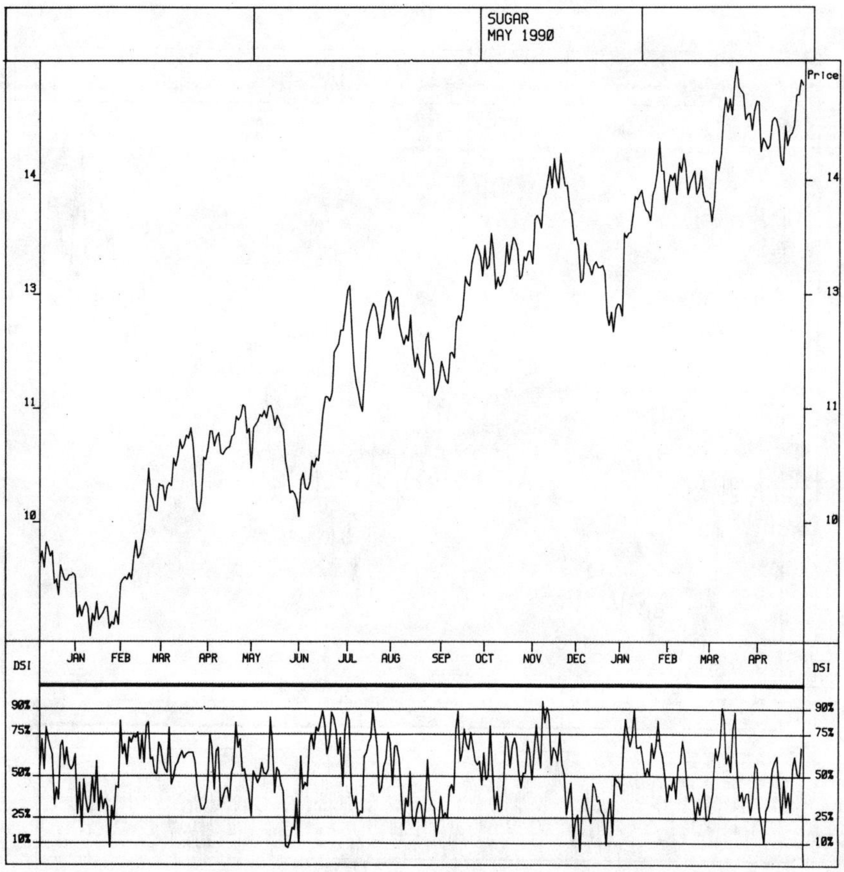

Wheat—July 1989

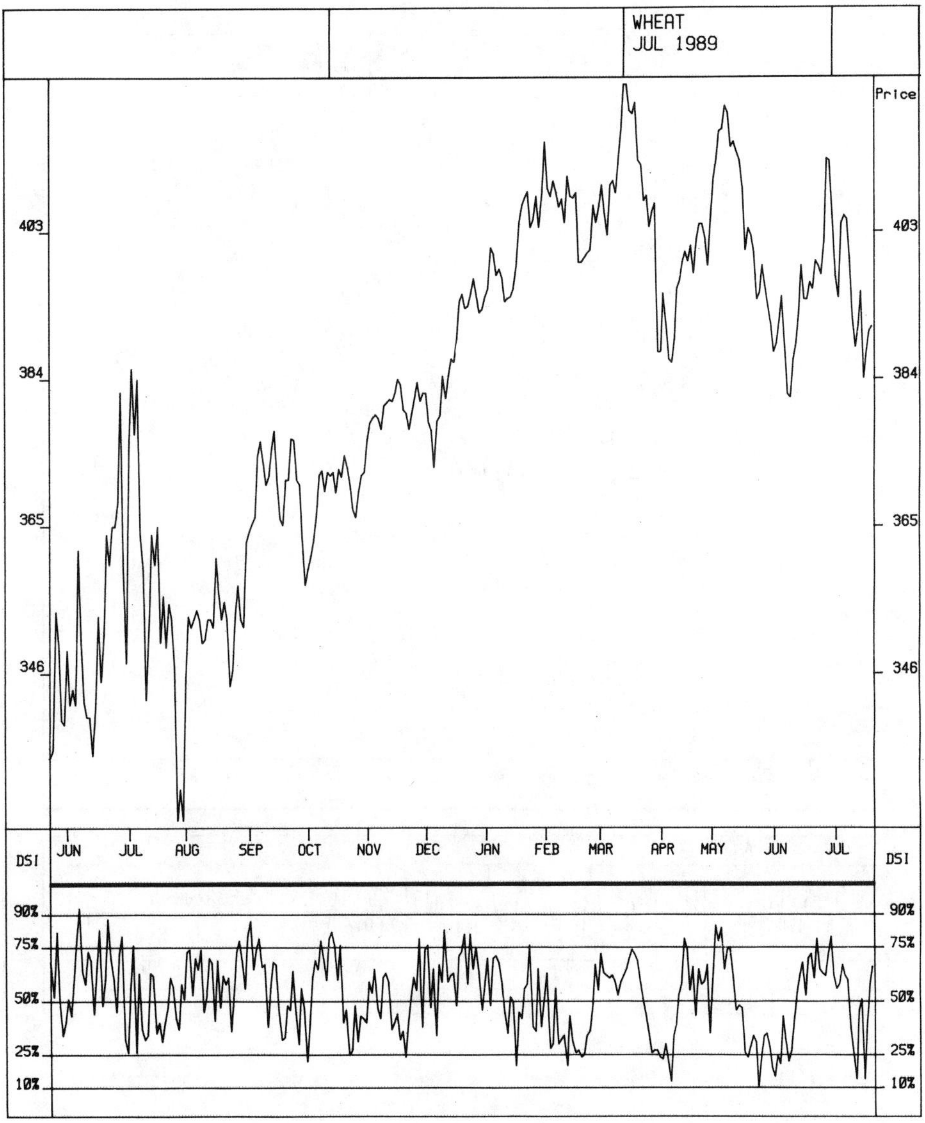

Corn—July 1989

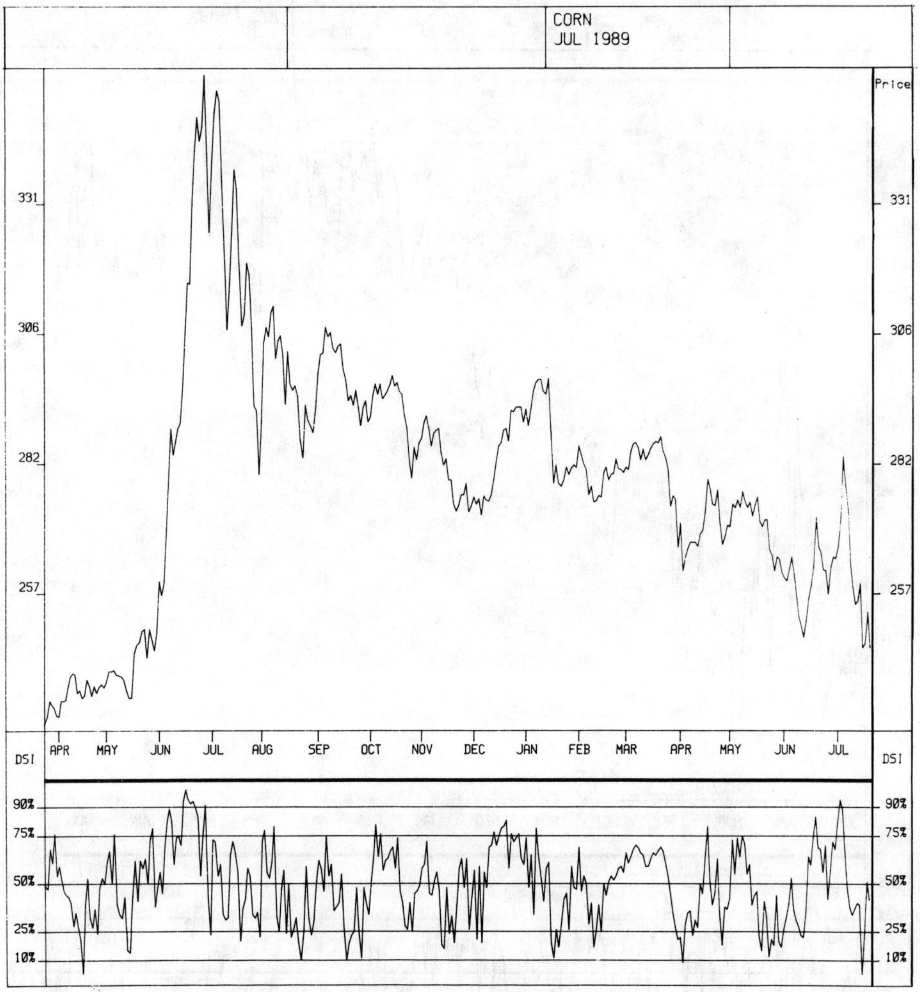

Soy Oil—January 1990

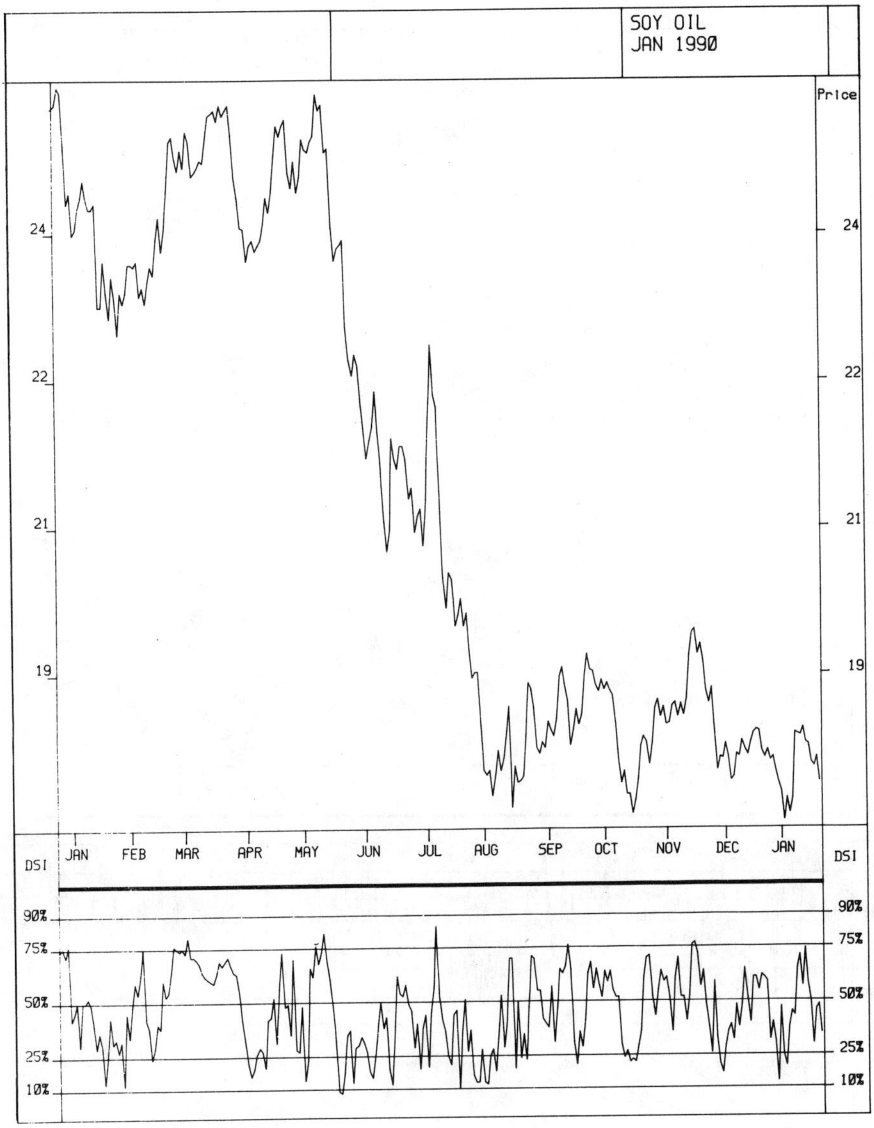

Coffee—March 1990

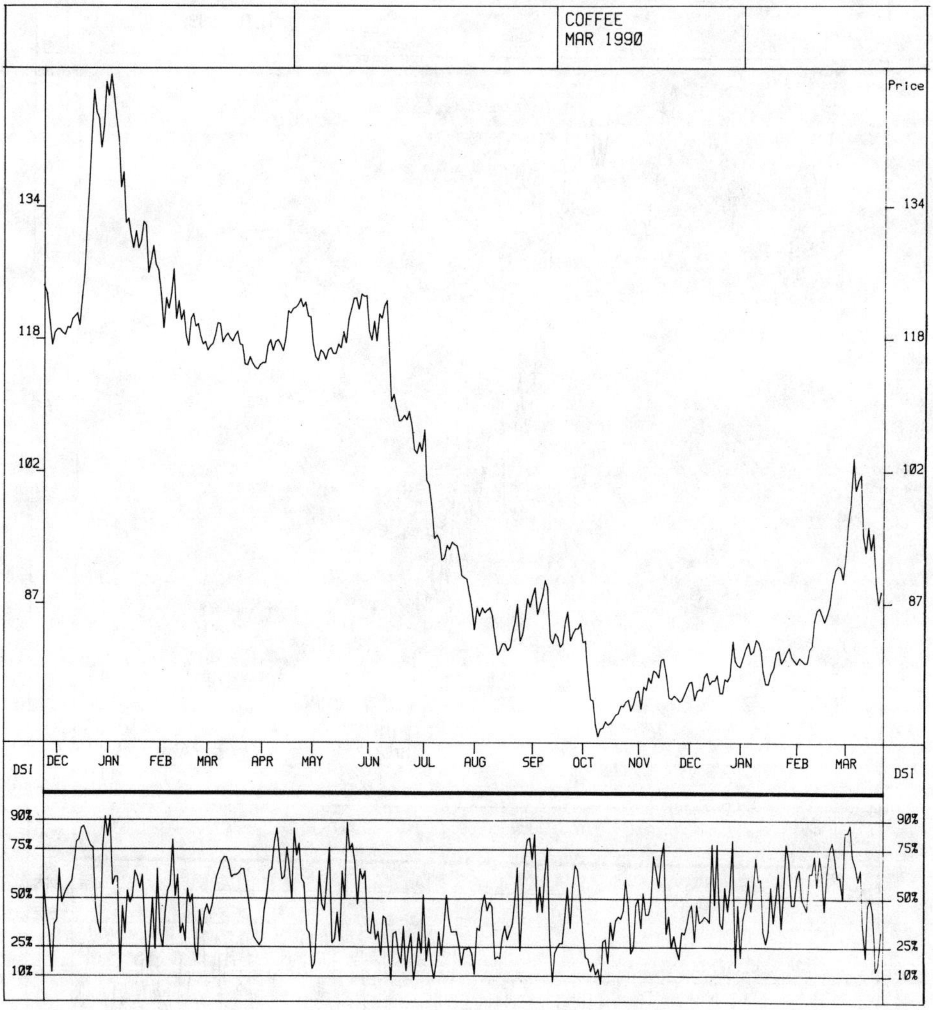

Cocoa—March 1990

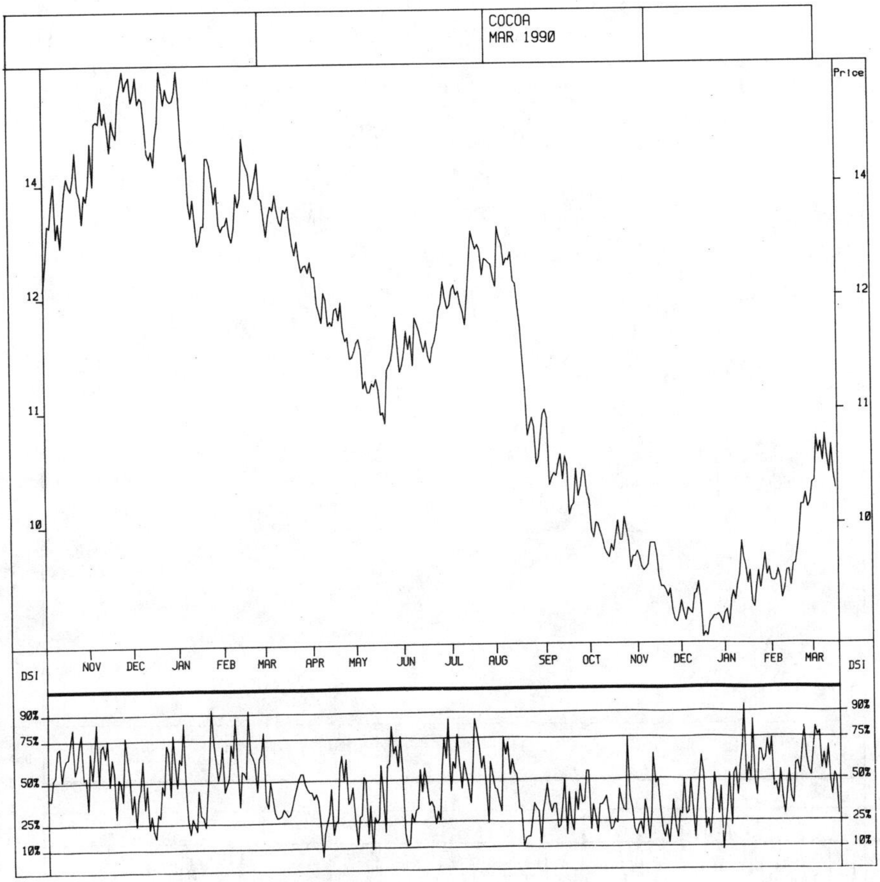

Copper—September 1989

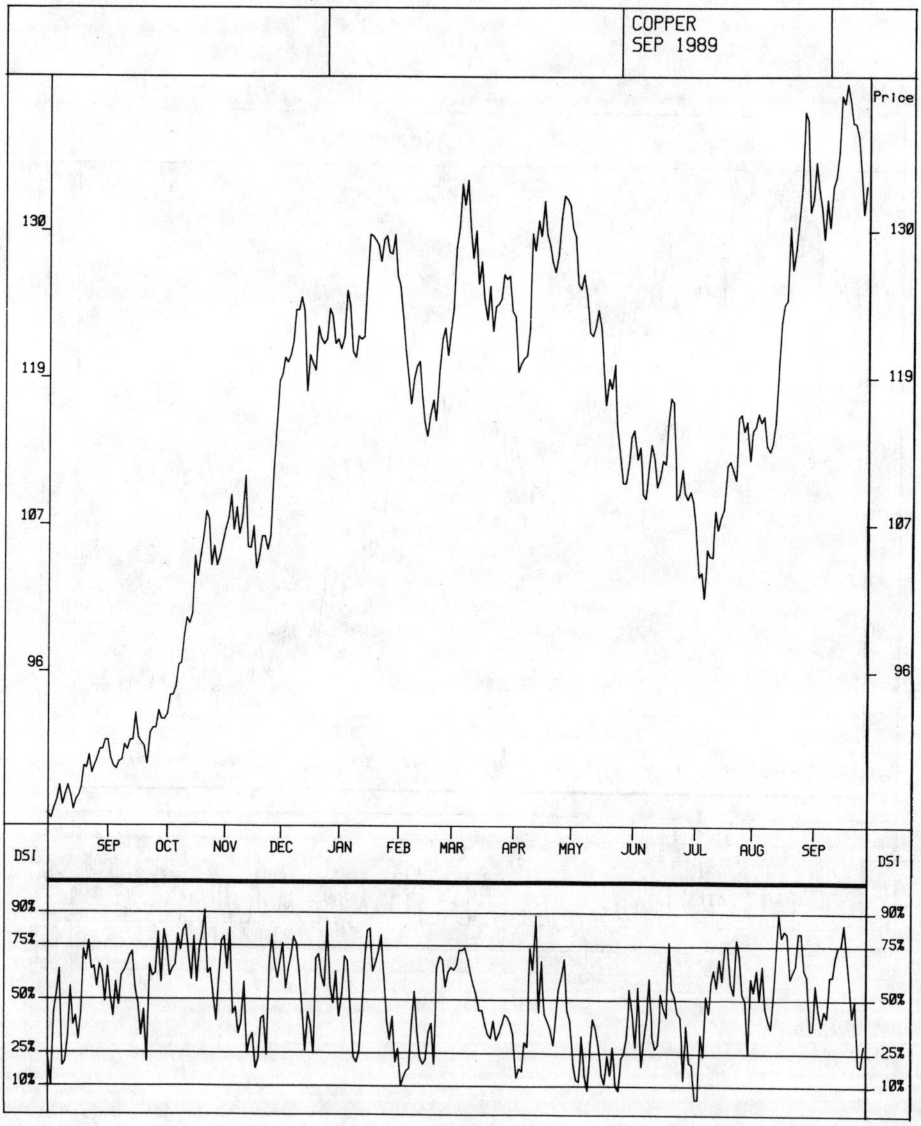

Gold—February 1989

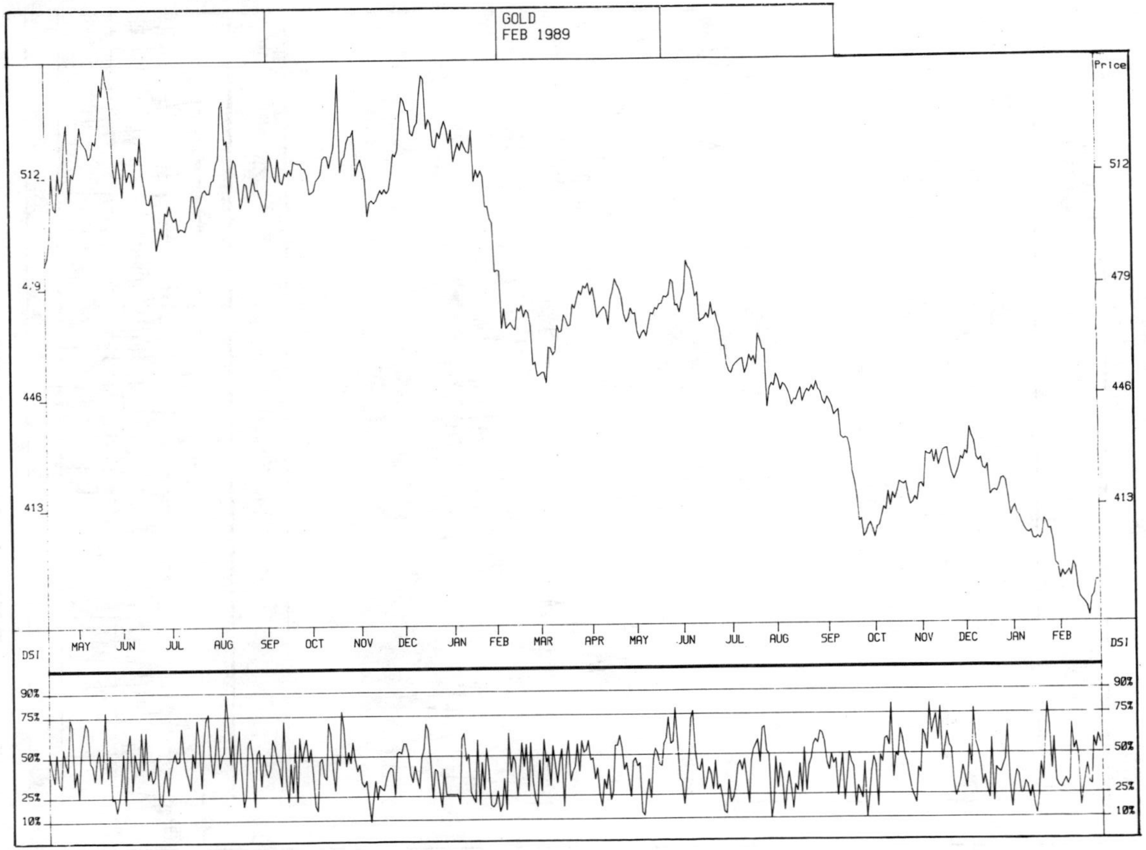

Live Cattle—June 1990

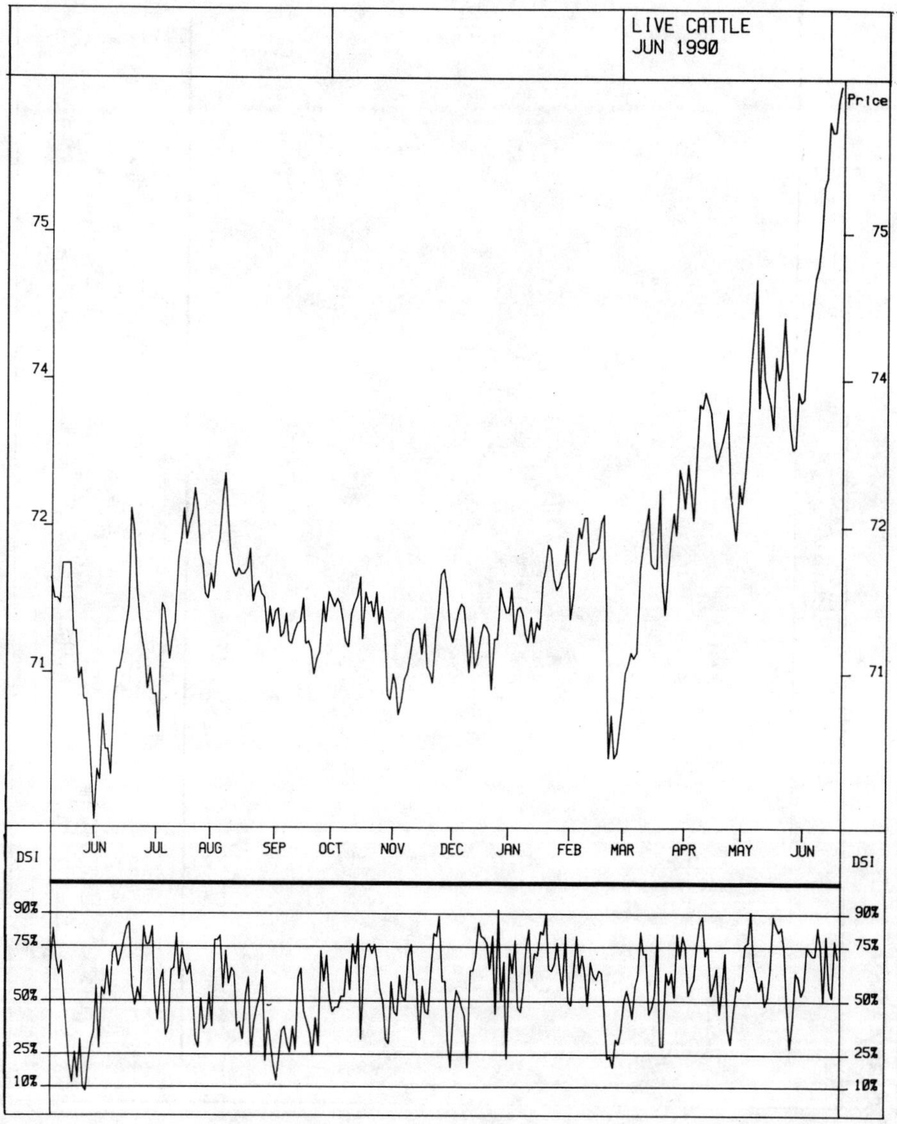

Platinum—July 1990

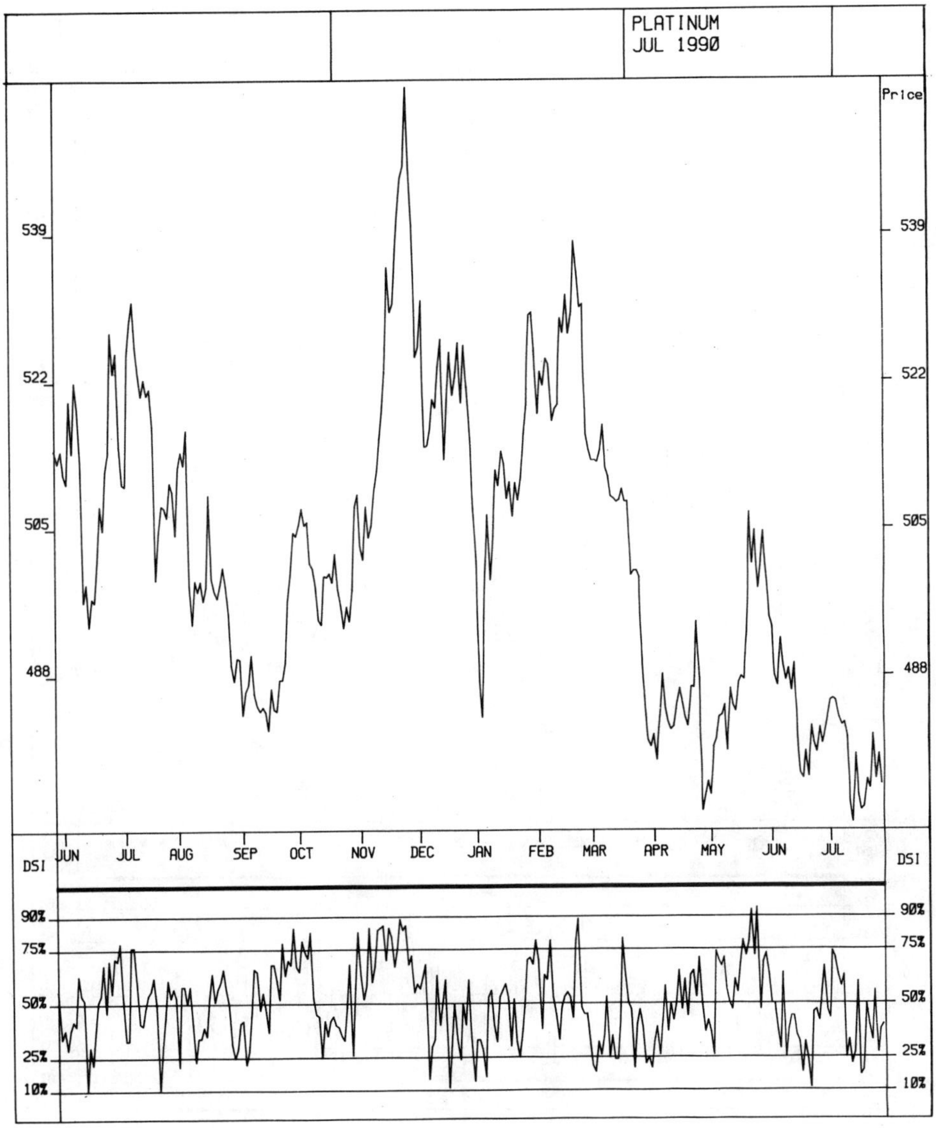

Japanese Yen—March 1990

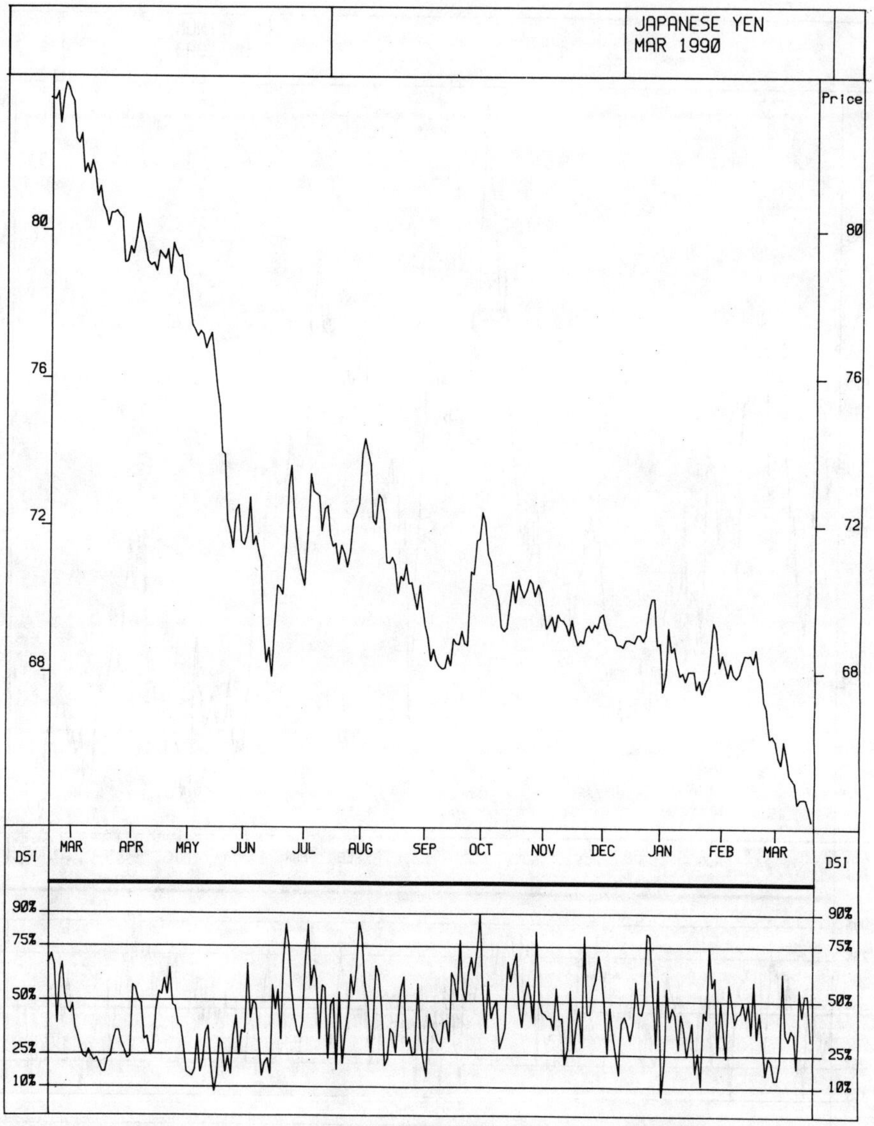

Lumber—May 1989

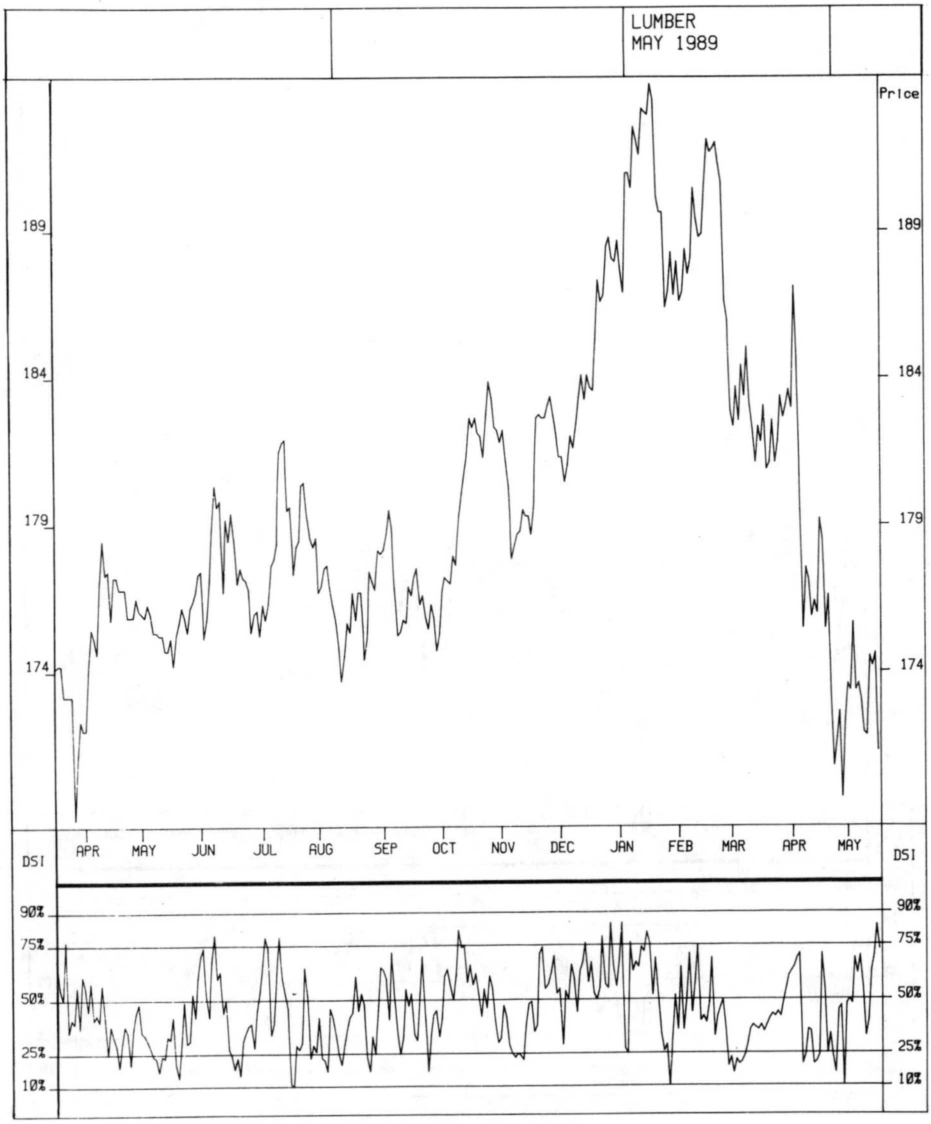

Live Cattle—June 1990

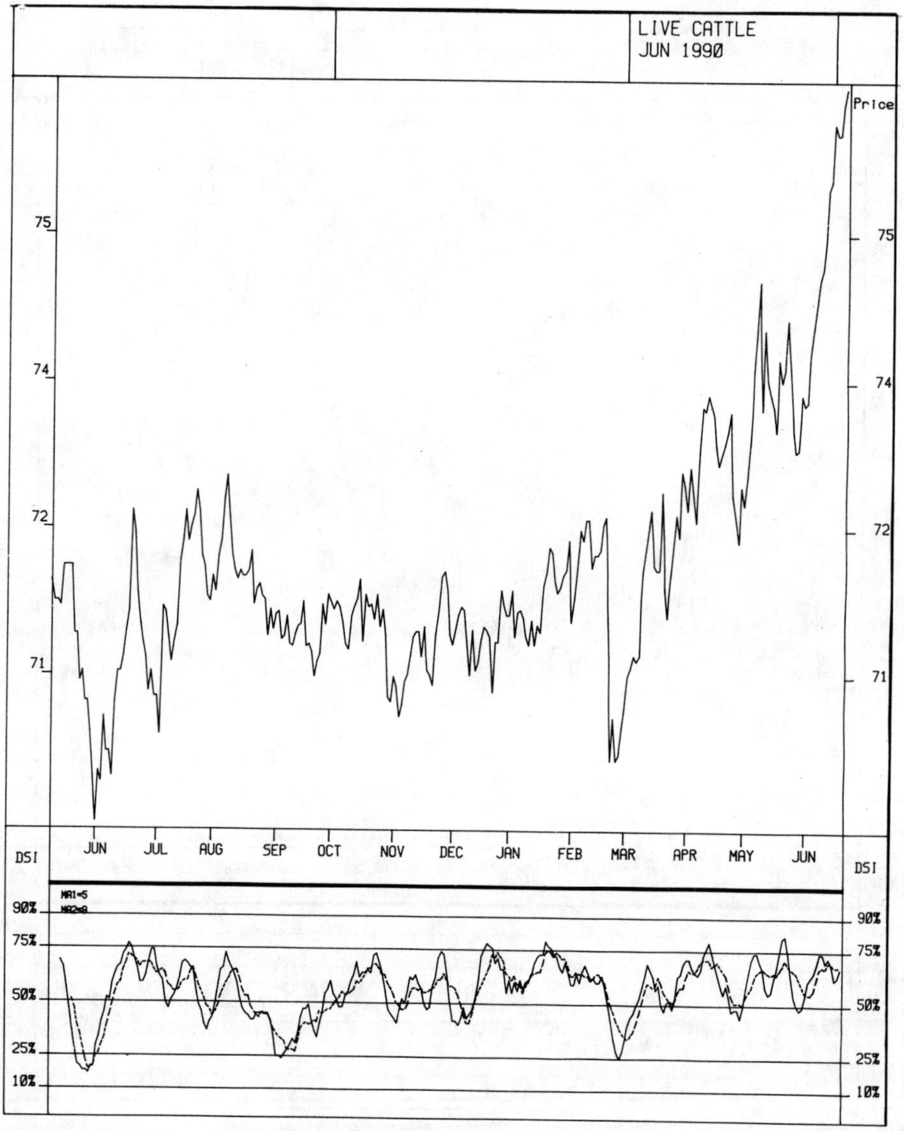

Live Cattle—June 1989

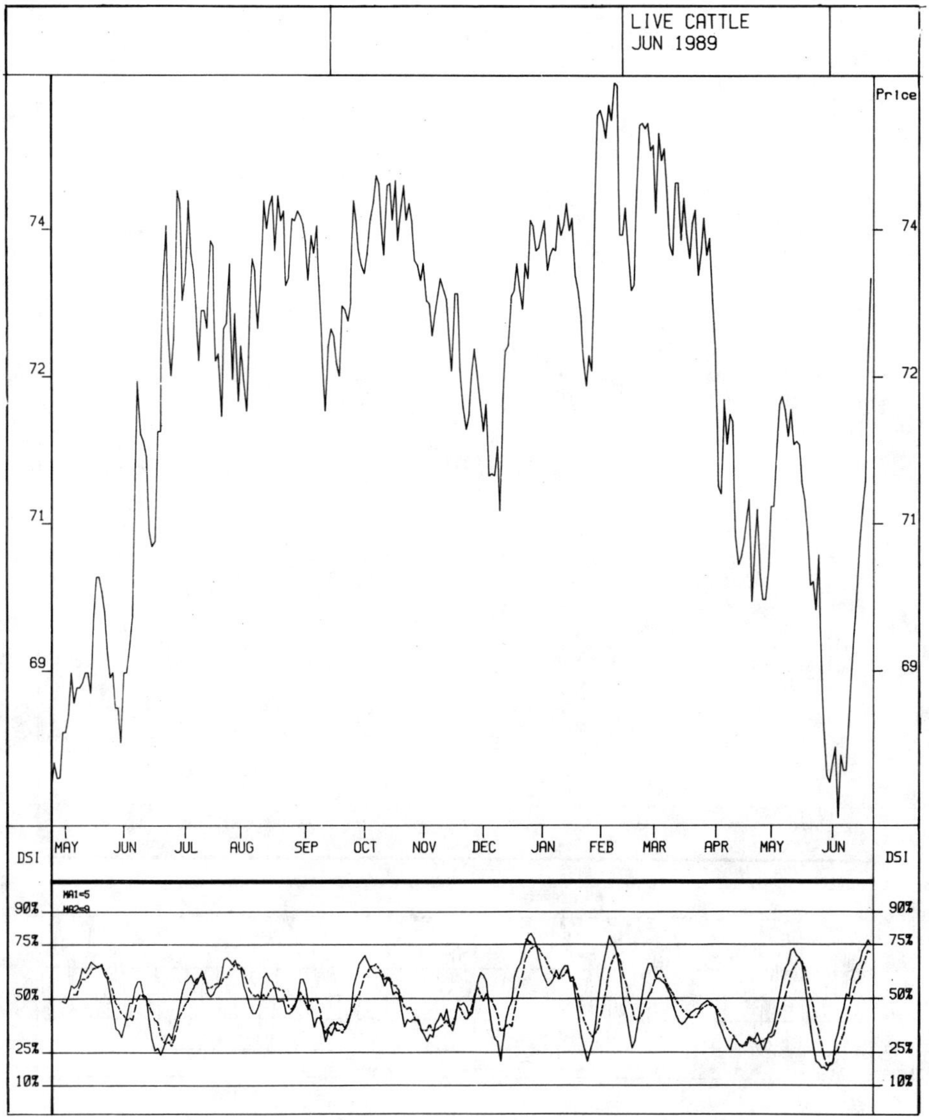

Soy Oil—September 1989

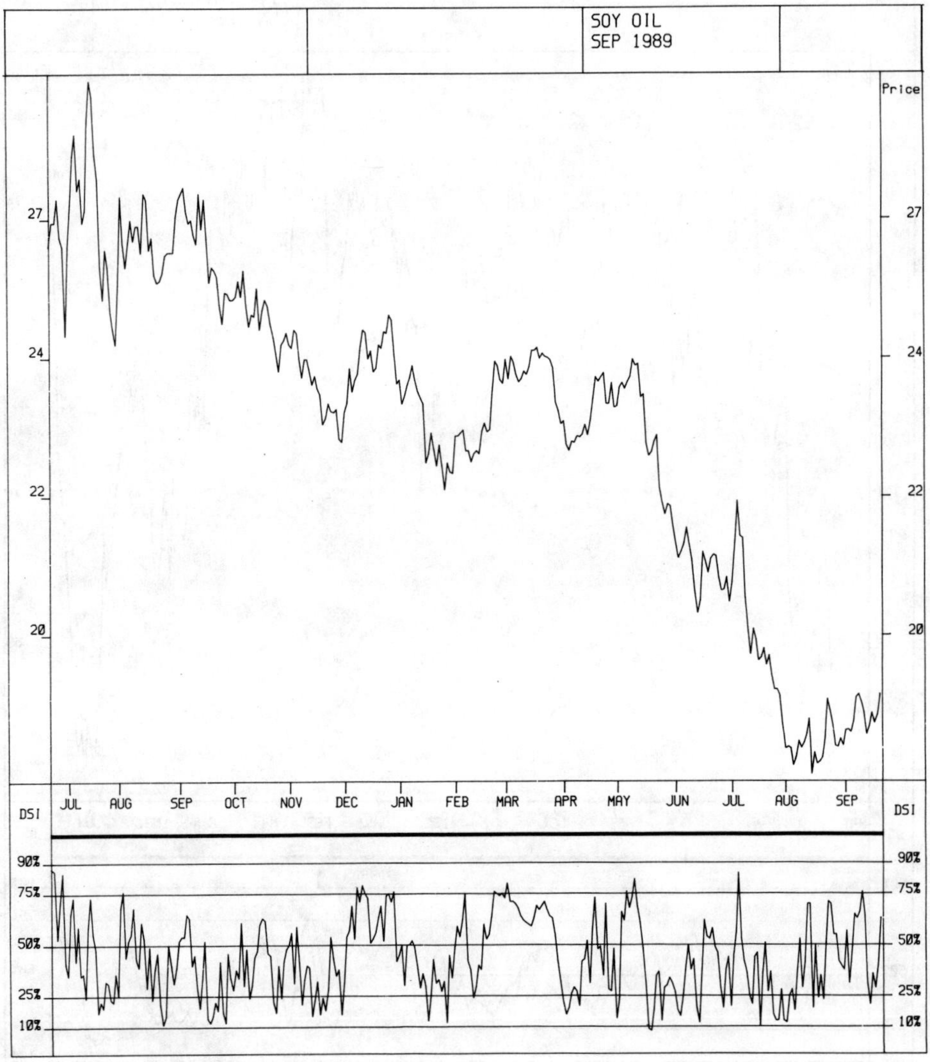

Wheat—December 1989

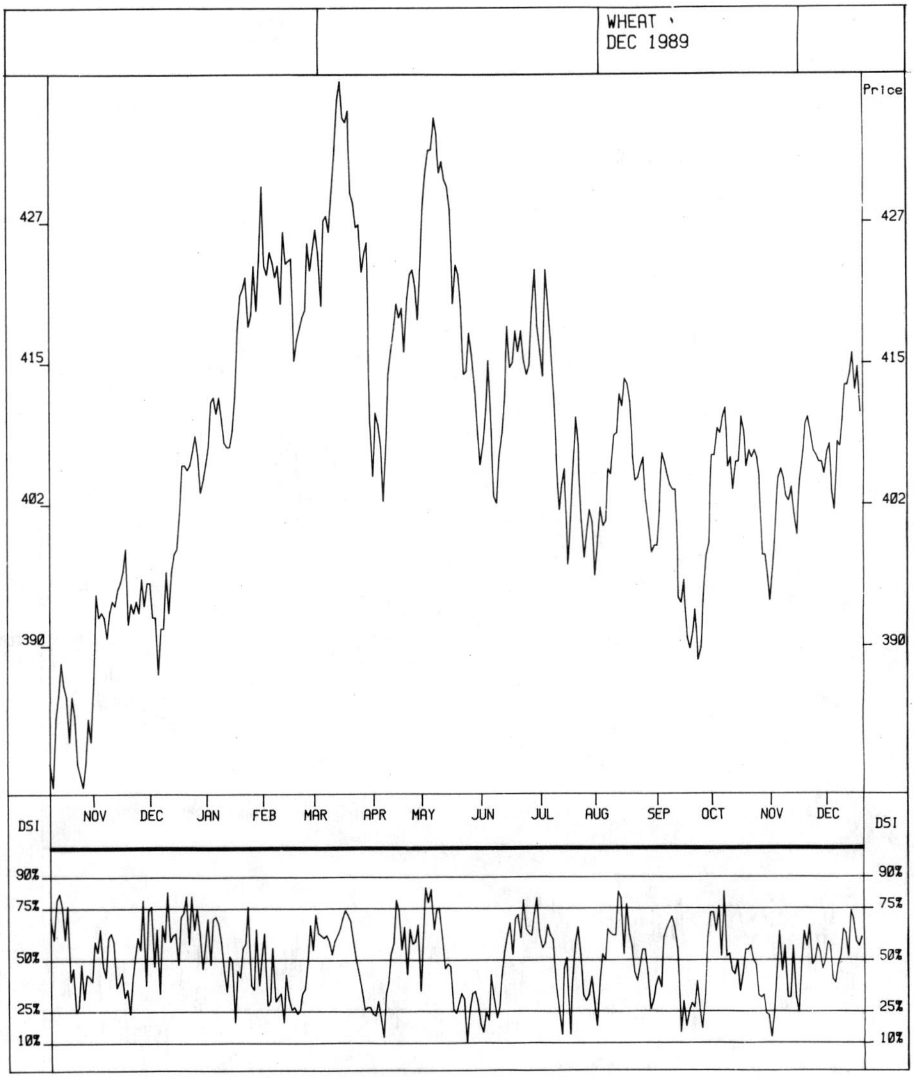

Wheat—March 1990

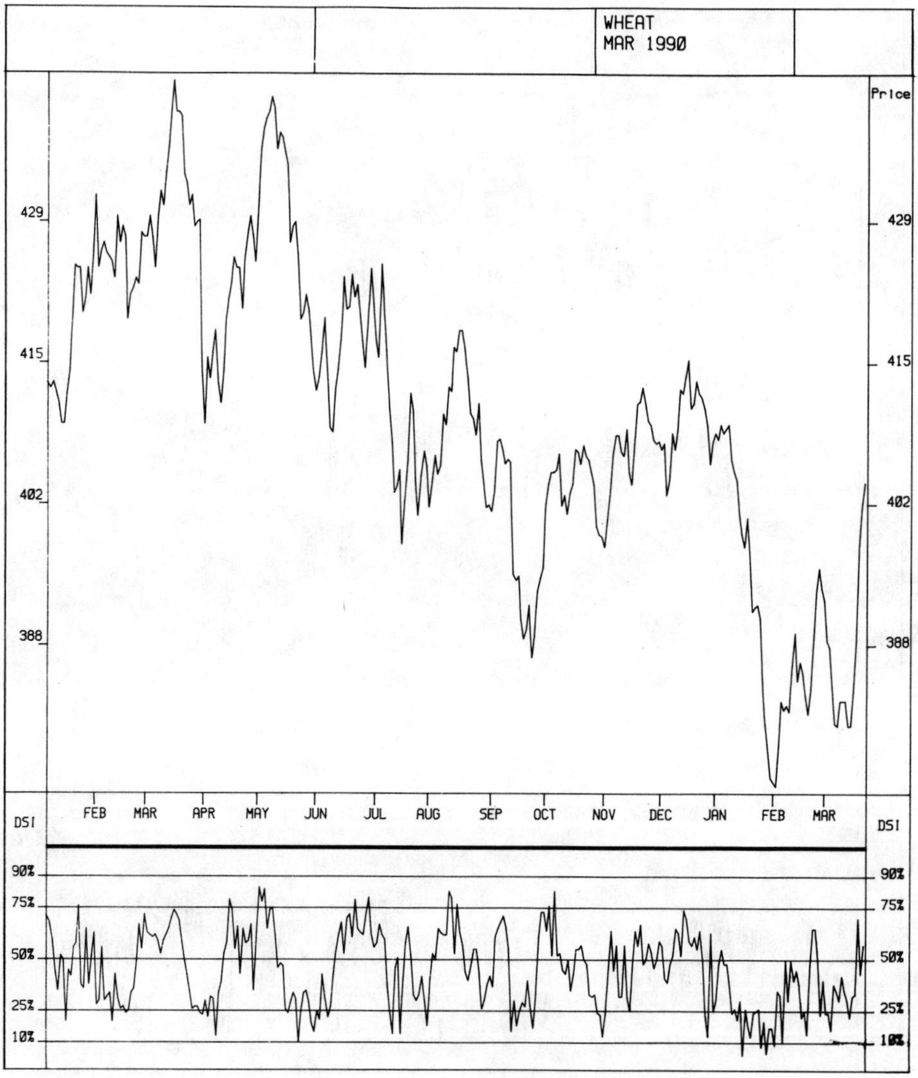

Index

Additional Titles by Jake Bernstein Available from Probus Publishing

Analysis & Forecasting of Long-Term Trends in the Cash and Futures Market

Short-Term Trading in Futures: A Manual of Systems, Strategies and Techniques

Timing Signals in the Futures Market: The Trader's Guide to Buy/Sell Indicators

Forthcoming Titles

New Facts on Futures: Insight and Strategies for Winning in the Futures Market. Anticipated Publication Date: August 1992.

Short-Term Futures Trading: Systems, Strategies, & Techniques for the Day-Trader. Anticipated Publication Date: November 1992.

About the Publisher

PROBUS PUBLISHING COMPANY

Probus Publishing Company fills the informational needs of today's business professional by publishing authoritative, quality books on timely and relevant topics, including:

- Investing
- Futures/Options Trading
- Banking
- Finance
- Marketing and Sales
- Manufacturing and Project Management
- Personal Finance, Real Estate, Insurance and Estate Planning
- Entrepreneurship
- Management

Probus books are available at quantity discounts when purchased for business, educational or sales promotional use. For more information, please call the Director, Corporate/Institutional Sales at 1-800-PROBUS-1, or write:

Director, Corporate/Institutional Sales
Probus Publishing Company
1925 N. Clybourn Avenue
Chicago, Illinois 60614
FAX (312) 868-6250